HABEAS CODFISH

HABEAS CODFISH

Reflections on Food and the Law

Barry M. Levenson

The University of Wisconsin Press

The University of Wisconsin Press
1930 Monroe Street
Madison, Wisconsin 53711

www.wisc.edu/wisconsinpress/

3 Henrietta Street
London WC2E 8LU, England

1   3   5   4   2

Printed in the United States of America

Library of Congress Cataloging-in-Publication Data
Levenson, Barry M.
Habeas codfish : reflections on food and
the law / Barry M. Levenson.
282 pp.   cm.
ISBN 0-299-17510-3 (cloth: alk. paper)
1. Food law and legislation—United States—Cases.
2. Law—Anecdotes.   3. Law—Humor.   I. Title.
KF3875.A7 L48   2001
340—dc21   2001002080

To Minnie and Jimmy

*Living proof that a parent's love
is the greatest nutrient
and most satisfying meal of all.*

Happy sixtieth anniversary!

CONTENTS

ILLUSTRATIONS

PREFACE

Habeas Codfish began as an act of desperation, a rescue from a boredom only lawyers can understand. In 1982, I was an attorney for the Wisconsin Public Service Commission, doing my best to find legal support for a state agency trying to regulate public utilities and virtually everything else that moved within the confines of the Badger State.

No matter how you slice it, public utility law is tedious, grim, and lifeless. I sat in the law library, researching some obscure and remote point of administrative procedure (designed, no doubt, to cloud some greater issue) when I realized two things: first, my brain was approaching a critical state of irreversible lethargy and, second, my stomach was crying for food.

I remedied the situation by furtively munching on a cookie and slamming shut the dusty volume of mind-numbing sophistry. I reached for another book and skimmed through its pages, almost without thought but believing some great and interesting notion would reveal itself. One did.

The book opened to an old case involving a traveler who objected to the requirement of a dinner jacket in the Fred Harvey Restaurant along the Santa Fe Railroad Line. The court took the suit as an occasion to salute the fine cuisine of the Fred Harvey Restaurants that

dotted the American landscape and to chastise the ungrateful bar-
barian who did not appreciate the nuances of fine dining. What a great
case! (For more on the "gourmet" Fred Harvey case, see chapter 14.)

Why did I not get cases like that one? Why did I have to toil in the
drudgery of imputed costs and the never-ending "blah blah blah" of
public utility law? Why could I not sink my teeth into some juicy food
dispute?

My career at the Public Service Commission was short lived. In 1983,
I landed a job at the Criminal Appeals Division of the Wisconsin Justice Department and wrote brief after brief in support of the state's
efforts to keep the bad guys in prison. A bright spot came when I was
assigned the usually mundane task of reviewing a draft of an attorney
general's opinion. The issue was whether a mobile cart vendor selling
hot dogs was subject to certain hygiene requirements. I took it as an
opportunity to review the entire case law of frankfurters and hot dogs
and to report my findings to the attorney general; I am sure he appreciated my efforts. I kept my eye out for any and all food cases, search-
ing the digests and periodicals for anything food related. (That was in
my spare time, of course, and *never* at the expense of the taxpayer.)

I collected cases, notes, references, news stories—anything to do
with food and the law. One day, I thought, it would make for a fine
book.

Food had always been, for me, far more than simple nourishment.
The dinner table at the Levenson home on Chandler Street in Worcester, Massachusetts, was never fancy but always filled with hearty and
pleasing foods. You know the fare: sirloin steaks, lemon meringue pie,
and fish on Friday (my mother always made fried haddock on Friday,
so I concluded that all Jewish people ate fish on Fridays).

I discovered haute cuisine in 1966 when Rabbi Jerry Davidson took
me to dinner on the way to a meeting in Connecticut. I did not recognize one thing on the menu so I readily took his suggestion: "Try the
coq au vin, I think you'll like it." He was right.

In 1969, I was an intern at the Council of Economic Advisers in Washington. My roommate Bill and I were to share the cooking responsibil-
ities but that plan came to an abrupt halt when Bill announced that he
would make Spam whenever it was his turn. I had to fend for myself.
Lucky for me, Irene Lurie, the staff "poverty economist," invited me to
dinner one night. She prepared Chicken Bordeaux from the *New York*

Times Cookbook. I could not believe that a mere mortal could make such a heavenly dish. She laughed at my praises and insisted that anyone could prepare that sort of food. It was, after all, just a recipe. I rushed to buy the book and began cooking with a vengeance.

Like so many young professionals and wanna-be yuppies, I became enchanted with gourmet food. The food foundation for *Habeas Codfish* was solidly in place and ready for an anxious young lawyer. But one more food event was necessary for the birth of this book.

In 1986, food took on a mystical quality for me. When my beloved Red Sox lost the World Series to the New York Mets, I was devastated. In the hours after the seventh game, I could not sleep. I went to an all-night supermarket and walked the aisles, realizing that it was not healthy for an adult male to be so depressed over a silly baseball game. I resolved to embrace some hobby that would take my mind off the angst of being a Red Sox fan. That night I began to collect mustards.

I tell you this because I am sure that this book will show a marked prejudice against ketchup and mayonnaise (what I call "the lesser condiments") and in favor of mustard. Although I continued to practice law with all of my skills and talents, I knew that my interest in food would some day overtake my legal career. I continued to gather cases and materials about food and the law because I found the interplay between the two subjects so fascinating. And I continued to collect jars of mustard because, well, for no sane reason at all. But I amassed about two hundred different jars of mustard by the end of 1987. It was good therapy for a Red Sox fan in mourning.

Mustard and the law came together in 1987 when I was about to argue my one and only case before the United States Supreme Court. As I left my room at the Hyatt, I noticed a small, unopened jar of Dickinson's Stone Ground Mustard on the discarded room service tray of the room across the hall. I checked my list (because I never left home without it) and discovered that it was a mustard I did not have. I had precious little time to dawdle because I was due at the Supreme Court in only a few minutes. But it was the greatest ethical dilemma of my professional life.

Was it theft to take an unopened, small (less than two ounces) jar of mustard from a discarded room-service tray? I had no time for extensive research on the issue so I did what I imagined every good lawyer would have done. I looked to my left, looked to my right, saw that no one was around, and deftly pocketed the mustard. I hurried to the Supreme Court and argued the case of *Griffin v. Wisconsin* with that little jar of Dickinson's Mustard in my left pants pocket. Food and the law had come together in supreme fashion. (I won the case, by a 5–4 vote. You can look it up: 483 U.S. 868.)

I soon began to appreciate the seriousness of the connection between our legal system and the foods we eat. For every "cute" case I would find (like the casual diner trying to get into the jacket-required dining room of the Fred Harvey House), there were a dozen grim and somber cases. Food was money, big money, and when millions of dollars were at stake, litigation reared its ugly head. People got sick from eating tainted food and sometimes died. The mass of food regulations seemed to be growing into an unmanageable morass of red tape.

So the question seemed to ask itself: how has our complex system of laws affected how we eat and what we eat? As I researched the issue and its many facets, it became apparent that this was no trivial pursuit. The complexities of food and the law amazed me; my collection of materials soon filled boxes.

What is our history of food and the law? It seems to have started with the simple and innocent premise that society needs to protect itself from unscrupulous food vendors, merchants who would adulterate our spices, meats, breads, and basic foodstuffs.

Simple laws became complex mazes of rules and regulations. Food safety became the banner under which massive bureaucracies flourished. But did this mean that our food supply was indeed safer?

No matter how pervasive our food laws became, people still got sick. The remedy of choice was the civil lawsuit. When a New Mexico woman spilled hot coffee on her lap and a jury awarded her a sizeable sum of money, the media seized the moment and everyone was talking about "tort reform" as if awarding damages for food injuries was suddenly a runaway train. But was it?

I discovered a wonderful body of case law defining the rights and remedies of restaurants harmed by negative reviews by media critics. When the beef industry sued Oprah Winfrey for having the audacity to publicly question the safety of our beef supply, another variant of that same body of law, but with more complex results, surfaced on the American scene. Free speech and food would have to be addressed.

Later, I discovered a spirited food fight between two pizza giants and, to my great delight, the arena for this battle was the courtroom.

So many other issues were out there. It was only a question of putting my cookbooks on the same shelf as my law books and observing the dynamics that had always been there.

What about food in prison? What about crimes committed with food? The law of intellectual property (patents, trademarks, and copyrights) was also an integral part of the food scene. Truth in labeling was a hot-button issue. What about the state laws allowing the government to enter into the realm of religion—the laws that seemed to permit kosher inspections to be the blessing of the state?

What about the labyrinth of laws passed to protect consumers from the "evils" of oleomargarine? I found out that Wisconsin was the last state to allow the sale of colored margarine—and this was in the 1960s—otherwise trying to guard its citizens from the terrible fraud being perpetrated on them by the cheap butter substitute.

It was time to bring food and the law between two covers.

I admit that when I first entertained the thought of a book about food and the law, it was light and almost silly. I imagine that many judges are relieved whenever food cases come into their courtrooms. After all, a case involving the history of chowder (a favorite among law school professors intent on deceiving first-year students that the next three years will be tolerable; I have reprinted it for you in chapter 6) is far more entertaining than most cases on the docket.

The novelty of food cases would certainly make for an amusing little book, but that is not the intended scope of *Habeas Codfish*. Although much of this book may strike the reader as odd or even whimsical, it is because much of what has happened over the years in the development of food law strikes us today as being odd and whimsical—it was probably never intended to amuse future generations.

Food and the law is serious business. Yet, because it relates to something so close to all of us, so approachable, so mundane, it need not be treated in a tedious and somber way. Like the foods we eat, I hope that *Habeas Codfish* nourishes and pleases the mind. That is why I have selected as a title such a playful and waggish phrase; we need take neither food nor law too seriously.

I have written *Habeas Codfish* for people curious about the foods we eat and the legal system that pervades our lives. Although I have a legal background (I think of myself as a "recovering lawyer"), I have not written *Habeas Codfish* as a reference for practicing lawyers. This is food for thought and thoughts about food.

In the widely growing area of food law, we assume that the government tries to protect us. If you learn but one thing from *Habeas Codfish,* learn this: let the eater beware. Our legal system can sometimes leave a funny taste in our mouths.

Habeas Codfish is not the complete and definitive work on food and the law. You may wonder why I have omitted certain topics, such as the federal milk price support programs and various tax and tariff issues. The lawyer in me would say to you, "Go write your own book!" The human being in me says, "I apologize; there is just so much that can go into this first attempt at looking at food and the law."

Although food and the law is international in its origins and in its current scope, much of *Habeas Codfish* deals with the development of this relationship in the United States. Food may be universal, but laws are particular to various jurisdictions. My training as a lawyer here in the United States dictates that I write about what I know best. Besides, what better country is there when it comes to extensive litigation?

Think about what went into that rare hamburger you just ordered, that hot cup of coffee you just took away from the drive-through window, and that gallon of "homemade" ice cream you just bought at the grocery. You are thinking about food and the law.

Many people have helped in the evolution and development of this book. I am grateful to the good people at Westlaw for allowing me access to the great Westlaw online database; if only I had had such a tool back in my law school days! Heartfelt thanks to my "law clerk" and friend Elizabeth Firer who not only researched and wrote but, more important, offered sensitive insights that have shaped this book for the better.

Thank you, Jane Dystal, for being such a patient and persevering agent. I am at a loss for words that express my deepest thanks to Steve Salemson, my editor at the University of Wisconsin Press. Some writers might cringe at discovering that their editor happens to live literally down the block, but for me it was a blessing. Special thanks to Mr.

Rawson, my ninth-grade creative writing teacher at Chandler Junior High School, wherever you are.

To my wife, Patti, who put up with me throughout the course of the book, thank you for giving me the time and space I needed, and, mostly, for believing in me. To my son, Matthew, thanks for being such an inspiration to me; I look forward to the publication of your first book.

Authors are supposed to humbly take responsibility for the errors, omissions, and shortcomings of their books. Lawyers, on the other hand, usually find someone else to blame and sue them for causing the aforesaid errors, omissions, and shortcomings. I no longer practice law so I gladly take the responsibility. However, I promise that as a recovering lawyer I will try to avoid the *aforesaids, to-wits,* and *notwithstandings*—the perversions of the English language (legalese) that have made the legal profession seem so arrogant.

Good eating and good reading! And do your very best to stay in the dining room and out of the courtroom.

HABEAS CODFISH

ASSAULT WITH
A BREADLY WEAPON

Laws are like sausages. It's better
not to see them being made.
—*Attributed to Otto von Bismarck*

The task of exploring the connection between food and the law is a daunting one, a veritable feast of history and ideas. Let us first whet our appetites with an assortment of appetizers (legal hors d'oeuvres, if you will).

We present these tasty morsels to you as we would to a jury in a courtroom. They are a smorgasbord of exhibits from all over the world. Savor them as we set the table for *Habeas Codfish*.

Exhibit A—Paris, France. Who can possibly dispute the culinary significance of France? There must be plenty of examples of French cuisine and the law. Take the celebrated case of Monsieur Boulanger, who, according to legend, sold his soup with mutton feet in a white sauce from his pushcart in 1765. The guild of *traiteurs* (cook-caterers) complained that Boulanger was infringing on their territory by selling such a dish and hauled him into court.

Depending on the source, Boulanger either won or lost. According to Giles MacDonogh[1] and Vernon Pizer,[2] Monsieur Boulanger won and his victory was hailed as the beginning of the modern restaurant. According to Rebecca L. Spang, the legend is that Boulanger lost, but it is simply that—legend; there is no historical record of the case in the judicial archives of France.[3] The Chinese appear to have had restaurants not unlike today's eateries as early as the thirteenth century,[4] but we will not try to resolve that dispute.

Exhibit B—Vienna, Austria. The sweetest lawsuit of all was undoubtedly the dispute between the Sacher Hotel and Demel's, Vienna's renowned sugar baker. Which establishment could rightfully declare its creation the authentic *"Sachertorte"*? The *Sachertorte*, created in 1832 by Franz Sacher to honor Prince Metternich, is a dense chocolate torte with apricot jam and rich chocolate icing. Franz's son Eduard opened the famous Sacher Hotel in 1876, but the recipe was later sold to Demel's. The courts of Austria struggled with this case for many years (six times from 1938 to 1993). Perhaps this is not the most far-reaching legal issue of all time, but it serves to remind us that some tortes are better than other torts.[5]

Exhibit C—Castile, Spain. King Alfonso of Castile despised garlic so much that he issued an edict forbidding any knight who had eaten garlic or onions within four weeks from coming to the royal court or from speaking to an official courtier.[6] This was as heavy-handed a food law as was ever passed. Alfonso knew he had the power but he knew nothing of the glories of Spanish food; one cannot make a credible paella without garlic. Then again, Shakespeare echoed those exact sentiments through the character Bottom in *A Midsummer Night's Dream*, who advised the actors: "...eat no onions nor garlic, for we are to utter sweet breath" (act 4, scene 2). Believe it or not, the city of Gary, Indiana, once had a law that prohibited anyone who had eaten garlic within four hours from attending a movie house or riding a public streetcar.[7]

Exhibit D—The Vatican. We stop here not because Catholics were once forbidden from eating meat on Fridays (repealed in 1966) but because in the year 732, Pope Gregory II ordered that Catholics should no longer eat horseflesh. Eating horse meat, reasoned the Pope, was what the Visigoths did and there was certainly no need to be like them.[8] We also commend Pope John XXII (1316–1334) who created for his nephew the official position of Chief Mustard Maker to the Pope, although that act is infused with irony. "Chief mustard maker to the pope" is a term given to a vain and not-so-capable dullard.[9] Perhaps we need to redefine the term and give it a kinder, gentler meaning.

Exhibit E—Prussia. It was 1744 and the peasants were starving. A simple solution was at hand—potatoes. Unfortunately, centuries of false tales and legends led the peasants to believe that potatoes were poisonous and evil. Frederick II, with the best interests of his subjects at heart, issued a decree that all in his kingdom would plant potatoes or suffer the extreme penalty of having their ears and noses cut off.[10] How ironic that a vice president of the United States (you remember Dan Quayle, don't you?) was unable to spell "*p-o-t-a-t-o-e-s.*"

Exhibit F—The U.S. Supreme Court, Washington, D.C. The final arbiter of law in this country, food and nonfood alike, is the Supreme Court. Perhaps our attention is drawn to this venue because two of its justices were named after the most popular American foods: Justices Felix *Frankfurter* and Warren *Burger.* More than a century ago, when faced with the ultimate legal question of whether a tomato is a fruit or a vegetable, the high court eschewed the science of botany and chose the common sense of the dinner table: in the eyes of the law, the tomato is a vegetable because we eat it as a vegetable! Justice Gray wrote:

> Botanically speaking, tomatoes are the fruit of a vine, just as are cucumbers, squashes, beans and peas. But in the common language of the people, whether sellers or consumers of provisions, all these are vegetables, which are grown in kitchen gardens, and which, whether eaten cooked or raw, are, like potatoes, carrots, parsnips, turnips, beets, cauliflower, cabbage, celery and lettuce, usually served at dinner in, with or after the soup, fish or meats which constitute the principal part of the repast, and not, like fruits generally, as dessert.[11]

Exhibit G—Ancient Syria. Gatis, Queen of Syria, adored fish so much that she ruled that all fish caught in her kingdom had to be brought directly to her. No one could eat fish without her permission. Perhaps she was the one who coined the phrase, "It's good to be the queen!"[12]

Exhibit H—West Lebanon, New Hampshire. The Denny's Restaurant in West Lebanon was the scene of a curious food crime that took place on 7 February 1995. A short-order cook by the name of Michael

Towne was charged with assault for spiking with Tabasco sauce the egg dishes ordered by a pair of state troopers.[13] There must be something about disgruntled New England short-order cooks and the police: Thomas Sears, another quickie chef, got four months in jail after blood tests proved that he was the one who spit on a state trooper's food at the KFC restaurant in Essex, Vermont.[14]

Exhibit I—Djakarta, Indonesia. Early in 2001, two officials of a Japanese seasoning manufacturer faced five years in prison for adulterating a flavor enhancer widely sold in Indonesia. What was the adulteration? The flavor enhancer contained enzymes that were based on pork fat.[15] That is a big no-no in the Muslim-dominated country of Indonesia. Sell anything with pork fat in various parts of the United States and you are a hero.

Exhibit J—Piedmont, Italy. In the eighteenth century, the government of Italy took stringent measures to make sure no one took its magnificent Piedmont rice out of the country. At least one person smuggled two bags out of Italy. That nefarious criminal was Thomas Jefferson.[16]

Exhibit K—Denison, Texas. Here we find food as hero, fighting crime as it nourishes humanity. In December 1996, a checkout clerk at a convenience store in this south Texas town stopped a would-be robber by pelting him with cans of Spam, the famous luncheon meat. Can food ever play a nobler role in the eyes of the law?[17]

Exhibit L—Hollywood, California. While we are on the subject of Spam, shouldn't Hollywood get some consideration here? The Hormel Foods Company, makers of Spam luncheon meat since 1937, went into federal court to try to stop Jim Henson Productions from releasing the movie *Muppet Treasure Island* because one of the characters, a scruffy little wild boar, was named Spa'am. (I am not making this up!)

Judge Kimba Wood had a lot of fun with the case but had no trouble telling Hormel that it had nothing to worry about, that it should be happy with the publicity, and that the court was not going to enjoin the release of the film.[18]

Exhibit M—Lansing Township, Michigan. There are times when the law just does not understand the importance of food. That was the case in Michigan where three women were convicted of joyriding and indecent exposure. Charlene Roper, Doshaline McCuin, and Sandra Lewis, wearing nothing but a coating of mustard, mayonnaise, and pickle relish (and high-heeled shoes) commandeered a United Parcel Service truck. Their defense was that they were engulfed by a wave of religious fervor. Surely no other city or town can boast of such a condimentally correct food crime.[19]

Exhibit N—Volusia County, Florida. While we are on the subject of condiments, we must pause along the east coast of Florida where the residents of Volusia County once learned a hard lesson about taking certain of the lesser condiments too seriously. One Vera Casey, celebrating the new (as in 1970) year at the Ivanhoe Bar on U.S. Highway 1, thought that an unruly patron, George Klikna, had spilled ketchup on her dress. Vera was so offended by Klikna's rude behavior that she demanded that her boyfriend, John Bryan, avenge her scorned dignity by taking him outside and doing something about it. Bryan agreed to defend his lover's honor and summoned Klikna outside—where he shot and killed him. Vera was charged with aiding and abetting first-degree murder and subsequently convicted of third degree murder. On appeal, her conviction was reversed on the theory that the evidence showed only that she wished her boyfriend to beat up the ketchup-spilling Klikna but not to kill him. Oh, how ketchup can do bad things to people![20]

Exhibit O—Prescott, Arkansas. There is no way that Prescott, Arkansas, would catch our attention were it not for this tiny lawsuit from 1939. Louella Dempsey slipped on a banana peel at the Kroger Grocery in Prescott (it happens in real life, not just in cartoons). She sued and got a whopping $400 from Kroger. Kroger took the case all the way to the Arkansas Supreme Court where it won; lawyers must have been cheap in 1939. The case is still good law because the mere fact of a banana peel on a floor does not automatically constitute negligence. It depends on how long it was there and the grocer's reasonable opportunity to clean it up.[21]

I suppose that Hibbing, Minnesota, might argue that its banana peel case warrants consideration because it was more serious; the poor woman died after slipping on a banana peel in the local Red Owl Store. The Minnesota Supreme Court let stand the trial court's decision to throw out the jury's award of $8,500 because there was no evidence to show exactly how the peel got there or that the floor was not otherwise clean.[22] Slipping on a banana peel does not mean big bucks for the "slipper" if the "slippee" has a good law firm representing it.

"In my courtroom, putting mayo on a corned beef sandwich is a felony. Twenty Years!"

(Cartoon by Dennis Schmidt)

Exhibit P—The Bronx, New York. Here's another reason why they call New York "The Big Apple." In February 2000, seven Department of Agriculture produce inspectors based at the Hunts Point Terminal Market in the Bronx pleaded guilty to accepting bribes from wholesalers in exchange for lowering grades for fruits and vegetables. Who got hurt here? The farmers. When farmers make deals with wholesalers and distributors, the farmers warrant that the produce will be of a certain quality. If an inspector grades the produce lower than the grade originally agreed upon, the farmers get less money.

The Big Apple was a very good apple but the farmers were told it wasn't so great. I guess you could say those corrupt inspectors were rotten to the core. And if food puns ever become a federal crime, I'll be the first to plead guilty and ask the court for mercy.

Exhibit Q—Concord, California. Don't you just love California cuisine? For a fleeting moment the Golden State symbolized consumer frustration with the food industry. Mayrdawna Davis's mouth was watering for the $2.49 breakfast advertised on television by the International House of Pancakes. What a breakfast it was! Two eggs, two pancakes, sausage and bacon! The end of the ad stated that the offer was "available at participating stores." The International House of Pancakes in Concord did not participate and Ms. Davis was deeply disappointed. More than that, she claimed that she suffered both hunger and humiliation. She sued for $2 billion. She lost.[23]

Exhibit R—Sacramento, California. The legal decisions that affect us at the dinner table are not necessarily big headline-grabbing cases. In 1941, the California Supreme Court struggled with a mundane issue that has enormous implications for millions of Americans: is a sandwich a meal?

The plaintiff, a catering company, sold sandwiches (hot dogs and hamburgers), wrapped in paper napkins, for customers to take with them as they were wandering through the Golden Gate International Exposition. Sometimes they purchased drinks, too. The state tried to collect sales tax on the burgers and dogs. The issue was whether the take-away sandwiches were "meals" within the meaning of the law. The court ruled:

> The generally accepted concept of a meal is that it not only consists of a larger quantity of food than that which ordinarily comprises a

single sandwich, but that it usually consists of a diversified selection of foods which would not be susceptible of consumption in the absence of at least some articles of tableware and which could not conveniently be consumed while one was standing or walking about. A "hot dog" or hamburger sandwich is the type of food frequently offered for sale to and desired by persons who wish to eat something while walking about. It is not the type of food generally ordered by a person who patronizes a hotel, restaurant or other public eating establishment with the intention of securing a "meal." Nor do we agree with defendant's contention that, in any event, where a beverage is consumed with a sandwich it necessarily amounts to a "meal." The questions whether the sandwiches sold by plaintiff constituted "meals"—where consumed with or without a beverage—and whether, within the import of the statute, plaintiff "served" meals, were primarily for the trial court. It may not be said that one has "served" a meal who merely prepares a sandwich for consumption, wraps it in a paper napkin and hands it to a purchaser without offering any facilities for its consumption on the premises, and with the intention that it be consumed elsewhere.[24]

The state tried one last effort: it argued that the hot dogs and hamburgers were served with "tableware," proving that the patrons were indeed served "meals." What tableware? The paper napkins that wrapped them! The court was not persuaded.

This was a time when civilized people would not even think of a sandwich as a meal. Today, for better or for worse, millions of Americans do consider sandwiches to be meals. Does this tell us something about how much bigger our sandwiches are or rather how much lower our standards of dining have become? And what would McDonald's say to all the little children who order Happy Meals by the millions? "Enjoy your happy sandwich but please do not think of it as a real meal."

As theologians may argue over how many angels may dance on the head of a pin, lawyers at their best debate over what is a meal. So let us analyze this weighty question further. Just because the California Supreme Court ruled that a sandwich is too meager to be a meal, we need not give up on this point. Perhaps we can find another court in another jurisdiction that will decide the issue differently. Perhaps New York, where sandwiches can be enormous (have you known anyone who has even come close to finishing the Carnegie Deli's famous "Carnegie Haul," a triple-decker pastrami, tongue, and salami sandwich?), will have a contrary approach.

Exhibit S—Yonkers, New York. The issue was not a sandwich but a piece of herring. Waldbaums Supermarket sold herring by the piece rather than by weight. The City of Yonkers required that all "meat, poultry, and fish" be sold by weight and not by the piece except where the product is a "ready-to-eat meal sold as a unit for consumption elsewhere than on the premises where sold."[25] Is a single piece of herring a meal?

If Waldbaums were in California, it would have been in trouble. Luckily, the courts in New York look at meals in a different light. Quoting an older New York case, the court was satisfied that "there is no particular kind or quantity of food which the law demands for a meal . . . it all depending upon the person to be served and the condition of his appetite."[26]

Judge Robert Cacace reviewed all the cases and found a quote from one that settled the issue. "[I]t has been authoritatively held . . . that a sandwich, or a bowl of soup, or a plate of food which at a time satisfies the appetite or desire of the person taking it constitutes a meal."[27] So, if your appetite is satisfied by a piece of herring, it's a meal, at least in New York.

But wait! What if your appetite is satisfied by a container of potato salad, or some cold cuts, or some baked beans? Aren't these foods the ones the law intended to be sold by net weight and not by the piece, no matter how happy you are to make a meal of these items? The judge was troubled by the application of his reasoning to these items so he did what few judges have done: he found a sensible approach. Herring had been sold by the piece for more than one hundred years to citizens of New York, especially the Jewish population who have long feasted on pieces of herring. It was *tradition!* So, ruled the court, we will grant an exception for pieces of herring because it is the right thing to do.

This is how the law sometimes works. Legal reasoning, when it is fluid and dynamic, can be surprisingly elegant and soothing. The English considered a similar issue with analysis and judgment equally compelling. We need to move our appetite back across the ocean.

Exhibit T—London, England. I could write a whole book on whether a sandwich or a single piece of fish is a meal but that may be more than what the public can bear. We will conclude our investigation into what constitutes a meal with this 1956 case that came before the Queen's Bench Division and was decided by Lords Goddard, Cassels, and Donovan.[28] A certain shopkeeper sold a smoked kipper at his shop on a Sunday, allegedly in violation of the Shops Act. But if the kipper were deemed a "meal" or "refreshment," the shopkeeper would be innocent. The learned judges waxed eloquent on the virtues of the smoked, albeit raw, kipper. First, we have the wisdom of Lord Goddard:

> Why cannot a kipper be a meal or refreshment? For the life of me I cannot see why, except that some people do not eat raw kippers; but some people do. A kipper is partly cooked, at any rate it is smoked, and think of the absurdity when one can sell smoked salmon. One can sell smoked trout, smoked eel, and then there are other preparations of herring and things of that sort. Yet it is said that one cannot sell a smoked herring, namely, a kipper. In my opinion, it is impossible to say that a kipper cannot be a meal or a refreshment. A person comes home unexpectedly and sends out for a meal, and is brought back a kipper, and what better meal can one have if one likes kippers, and most people do.[29]

Lord Cassels agreed because in his estimation one can eat kippers without cooking them. Lord Donovan also agreed with the judgment that raw kippers (okay, *smoked herring*) can be meals or refreshments, even though he was not a big fan of them:

> The question . . . is whether a kipper comes within the words "meal or refreshment," and I think instinctively most people would apply a subjective test to that problem, for example, many people having breakfast at home or in an hotel and finding a raw kipper served would be rather surprised if they were told "That is your meal; that is your refreshment"; but then there is ground for believing that people do eat raw kippers, which merely shows that in the matter of food there really is no accounting for taste.[30]

These cases, these little gems, are what the law is all about. As silly as some of them may seem, there is a legitimate and sober reason for taking our first course in England before we begin our more extensive investigation. It is the "Assize of Bread," the earliest and most long-standing English food law. If there is a Magna Carta or Holy Grail in the field of food law, this is it.

In the early years of the thirteenth century, probably around 1210, King John issued an edict fixing the price of bread. Under Henry III in the year 1266, this edict became the famous "Assize of Bread."[31] This law addressed a serious problem in medieval England: bakers were ripping off the public. Not only were the loyal subjects of the crown victims of short weights, they were sometimes given bread made from ingredients that had no place in an honest loaf of bread. Certain bakers adulterated their products with ingredients (tiny stones, dirt, and other undigestibles) that were harmful to human health. The Assize of Bread regulated both the price and quality of the most basic of all foodstuffs. A common practice of unscrupulous bakers was to give the shopper who ordered a dozen rolls only eleven, hence giving rise to the term "baker's dozen."[32]

Breaches of the English bread laws were common in medieval times, so much so that a fourteenth-century law, the Statute of York, barred anyone involved in enforcing the Assize from being a baker during the term of his office. The bakers could not be trusted.[33]

Bakers found guilty of adulterating loaves of bread were placed in the pillory with the offending bread burned in front of their noses. Although the law changed over the centuries, some form of the Assize of Bread remained on the books until the early days of the nineteenth century (1815).[34] The free hand of capitalism could not be trusted when it came to the basic staff of life.

Even after England finally repealed its bread laws, Parliament paid close attention to the more general problem of food adulteration in all parts of the marketplace. In 1820, scandal broke out all over England when chemist Frederick Accum published a book on the widespread practice of spice adulteration.[35] Accum's book, *A Treatise on Adulteration of Food and Culinary Poisons, exhibiting the fraudulent sophistications of bread, beer, wine, spiritous liquors, tea, coffee, cream, confectionery, vinegar, mustard, pepper, cheese, olive oil, pickles, and other articles employed in domestic economy and Methods for Detecting them,* shocked the British establishment with its long-winded title and startling revelations.

During the 1850s, more reports on food adulteration surfaced in England, exposing practices such as the whitening of bread with alum and the dilution of coffee with chicory. In addition, arsenic, copper, lead, and mercury were all found to be added to various foods. Parliament responded with the first British Adulteration of Foods Law in 1860, more than forty years before the United States enacted its Pure Food and Drug Law of 1906.[36]

These are of the most primal sort of food laws, designed to protect the public from the harm that the producers of food do, either intentionally or through carelessness. The debate over sandwiches as meals, the iron hand of a monarch with a distaste for garlic, and the occasional use of food as a weapon are interesting and certainly do involve food and the law, but they do not reach to the core of human behavior. Although the central focus of *Habeas Codfish* is food and law in the United States, England also reminds us of our common law heritage.

We seek four qualities in our food. The least significant, although sometimes it may seem of paramount importance to many of us (especially when someone else is paying the bill) is taste. Don't get me wrong; I adore the sweet taste of lobster, the salty elegance of caviar, and the glorious flavors that so many other foods have to offer. But if I had to do without flavor, I could get by. I would sooner give up my appreciation of food than lose my ability to drink in a Beethoven symphony or feast my eyes upon a Monet waterscape. Taste is great, but it is "extra."

The second quality of food that we desire is nutrition. We ingest food because without it we would die. Food is fuel. Some foods offer more nutrition than other foods but we expect that our diet will somehow sustain our presence on the planet. We have learned that nutrition is anything but simple. What is good for us today may turn out to be harmful tomorrow. Food as a bundle of vitamins, minerals, calories, fats, acids, carbohydrates, and chemical compounds may strike us as cold and unromantic but it is the truth.

The third quality of food that we want is honesty. If we pay for Beluga caviar only to receive the roe of paddlefish, we may be equally nourished and perhaps even equally satisfied by its taste but learning of the switch will certainly leave a bitter taste in our mouths. If the menu indicates a stroganoff of tenderloin but the dish contains a less-expensive cut of meat, no matter how flavorful the finished product, we are dissatisfied.

The final attribute of food is a rock-bottom minimum requirement: it must not harm us. Tasting good is a plus but flavor is not essential to survival. Adequate nutrition is important but there are many avenues to good nutrition. Honesty is important but dishonest food, if it is otherwise tasty and nutritious, is hardly the end of the world. But when food causes us direct and dramatic harm, that is a different story.

Food can harm us in so many ways. A piece of glass in a jar of jam, a pearl in an oyster, a bone in what we believed was a boneless fish fillet, a hamburger tainted by some unseen bacteria, a poisonous mushroom—they can maim and they can kill. These are some of the instruments that can bring about the tragic and unforseen consequences of an innocent and ordinary act, the act of eating food.

When our expectations of life's fortunes are not met, we turn to our cultural and societal institutions. We vent our disappointment in the arts by writing songs, poems, and novels (and enjoying those created by others). We may paint a mournful picture that captures our lowly spirits. We turn to religion and the solace of spiritualism. We turn to the healing arts, physical and emotional, to mend our broken bones and hearts. And we turn to the law.

Food laws address all four attributes of what we eat. The primal food laws consider safety, the basic premise of all food. But how do food laws accomplish the task of ensuring safety? A loaf of bread does not know if it has been adulterated and cannot be dissuaded from harming its consumer by threat of a penalty. A sirloin roast cannot form what the law calls "criminal intent." A cup of coffee cannot be "negligent."

Primal food laws are directed at the preparers of the foods we eat. These laws reveal a monstrous side of humanity. In the absence of primal food laws, certain individuals will elevate their desire for money over the health and safety of the community.

Consider this most horrible hypothetical scenario: a man threatens to destroy the human race by poisoning the world's food supply. We would not hesitate to brand him with the strongest terms of condemnation. He would be a villain of the highest order because he threatens the survival of the species. On a smaller scale, does that not describe the butcher who knowingly sells bad meat?

Is there another species on the planet that would knowingly harm the food supply of its own kind? It is a sad commentary on our own selves that we need laws to protect our food supply from our own inherent greed.

This book will examine our resort to legal institutions as we try to somehow guarantee that food is safe, nutritious, honest, and delicious. It should be obvious already that laws that cover food safety are probably more significant than those that try to address food "taste."

Food is, of course, more than packets of nutrients. It can appeal to our sense of taste, sight, touch, smell, and even sound (remember Snap, Crackle, and Pop?). It is part of culture, the fabric of human existence. It is important to recognize the primal food laws, protecting us from harm, but we need not limit ourselves to those basic laws. The law is the glue of societal living and it is inevitable that food and law will come together, sometimes in harmony, sometimes in dissonance.

2

BIG BEEF SUPREME

If it tastes good, it's trying to kill you.
—*Roy Qualley,* 637 Best Things Anybody Ever Said

One man's meat is another man's poison.
—*Oswald Dykes*

Memories of the foods of our youth can haunt us through our years. The great and unforgettable hamburger of my childhood was the "Big Beef" sandwich at the Friendly Ice Cream shop at Tatnuck Square in Worcester, Massachusetts. It came on buttered toast and I always ordered it rare, with a slice of raw onion.

You could get a Big Beef at any one of the dozens of Friendly Ice Cream shops that blanketed the American Northeast in the early 1960s. For some reason, though, the Big Beef at Tatnuck Square was special. Maybe it was because I would ride my bike to the hardware store in hopes that my dad would find time to take a break and have lunch with his son. As busy as he was, he always found the time.

My father, who had once worked as a butcher, instructed me on the finer points of hamburger appreciation. He taught me that a burger cooked medium or beyond was a sin. So it was that I discovered the pleasures of a good burger, quickly seared on the outside but with a fine red interior. Juicy, delicious, and entirely satisfying, even at the handsome price of forty-five cents each.

In 1970, I moved away from the northeast and my beloved Big Beef sandwiches. They remained in my mind the standard against which all burgers would be judged and against which nearly all would fall pitifully short. Twenty-seven years later I returned to New England and to Friendly's, bent on a mission. I would share with my son what my father had given me, that first taste of the ultimate hamburger.

The Big Beef was still on the menu. I ordered two, one for me and one for Matthew. "On buttered toast, with a slice of raw onion, and cooked rare."

"I'm sorry sir, all of our hamburgers are cooked medium well."

"But I want it rare. That's the only way to eat a good hamburger. Can't you prepare ours the way we want?"

"We cook all of our hamburgers medium well done, without any trace of pink. It's for your own protection, sir."

My protection? Friendly's was not protecting me back in 1960, and I am glad of it. No, back then they were serving me a great burger. I tried to negotiate the matter, offering to settle for a medium-rare burger. The server would not budge from the corporate position of medium well or none at all.

Matthew and I settled for the Big Beef on toast, medium well. It was one of the most underwhelming experiences of my culinary life. Friendly's was ostensibly protecting us from the dangers of food-borne bacteria, like salmonella and *Escherichia coli,* which survive in a rare hamburger. Or maybe the real truth was that Friendly's was protecting its own corporate rump roast from the dangers of a lawsuit. I was disappointed, but my disappointment pales when you look at what happened to Brianna Kriefall.

In the summer of 2000, three-year-old Brianna Kriefall of South Milwaukee, Wisconsin, died—an apparent victim of food poisoning. Technically speaking, she died of hemolytic uremic syndrome, more commonly known as HUS, a complication of *E. coli* 0157:H7. The cause of this particularly virulent strain of the bacterium *E. coli* was traced to a fast-food restaurant, more specifically to the watermelon cut and served to customers at a local Sizzler. Apparently, the melon had been cut on the same surface on which raw chicken had been handled.

Little Brianna's death did not make national headlines. Although she was as cute a three-year-old as you would ever want to meet, her tragic death did not receive national attention because at least nine thousand other Americans were expected to die from food poisoning in the year 2000. To "round up the usual suspects" in cases of food-related deaths or illnesses means to look for evidence of *E. coli,* salmonella, botulin, *Listeria,* and other microscopic culprits. Unlike the Jeffrey Dahmers and John Wayne Gaceys of the world, these microbial serial killers have no faces and are not likely to appear on the wanted posters in your local post office.

With all the food laws on the books, ranging in scope from local restaurant codes to the weighty rules and regulations of the Food and Drug Administration (FDA), you would think it should be next to impossible for food poisoning to be an issue in our daily lives. In addition, the food industry has developed amazing new methods and technologies to virtually guarantee a safe food supply—at least that is what we have been led to believe. Moreover, we know so much more about safe food handling that there seems to be no excuse for anyone getting sick from food. Yet, by many accounts, food poisoning is as serious a problem now as it ever was.

Food poisoning has been a grim fact of life since the dawn of culinary civilization. In the year 857, thousands in the Rhine Valley died after eating tainted bread.[1] The same fate befell the citizens of Limoges in 943.[2] In 1534, Pope Clement VII died from eating poisonous mushrooms.[3] In 1971, a prominent New York banker died from botulism after eating canned vichyssoise soup; the incident ultimately bankrupted the Bon Vivant company after 108 years of business.[4] In 1981, twenty thousand Spaniards became seriously ill after using adulterated olive oil.[5] In 1993, an outbreak of *E. coli* in Washington State caused about three hundred cases of serious illness and one death; the problem was traced to undercooked hamburgers at a Jack in the Box fast-food restaurant.[6]

So how can we protect ourselves from the ravages of food poisoning? We turn first to science and then to the law. How easy it would be if Congress could legislate the matter away with a simple enactment: "No one shall get sick from food." Because food pays no attention to the law, we do the next best thing: we devise laws that regulate what people do with and to our food.

Efforts to enact federal legislation governing the safety of the American food supply began in the middle of the nineteenth century but were met with stiff opposition from powerful business interests.

"How can anyone be against food safety?" you may ask. A very good question indeed, although I think you know the answer.

During the Spanish-American War, newspapers blamed the meat industry for shipping "embalmed" meat products that caused severe illness among the ranks of American soldiers. (The meat left out in the hot Cuban sun may have been the real cause of most of the illnesses.) Cries for legislative action to regulate the meat industry began to rumble through the halls of Congress but nothing happened. Then came the "report" of the horrible event that finally prompted decisive action.

Reports to Congress can make for some very good reading. In the late 1990s, the report of Special Prosecutor Ken Starr was filled with lurid details of President Clinton's sexual escapades with intern Monica Lewinsky and led to the president's impeachment by the House of Representatives. As shocking as the Starr report was in its excruciating detail, it is a child's G-rated bedtime story when compared with this bit of graphic prose, written nearly a century before, about the American meat industry:

> For it was the custom, as they found, whenever meat was so spoiled that it could not be used for anything else, either to can it or else to chop it up into sausages. With what had been told them by [X], who had worked in the pickle rooms, they could now study the whole of the spoiled-meat industry on the inside, and read a new and grim meaning into that old Packingtown jest—that they use everything of the pig except the squeal.
>
> [X] had told them how the meat that was taken out of pickle would often be found sour, and how they would rub it up with soda to take away the smell, and sell it to be eaten on free-lunch counters; also of all the miracles of chemistry which they performed, giving to any sort of meat, fresh or salted, whole or chopped, any colour and any flavour, any odour they chose. In the pickling of hams they had an ingenious apparatus by which they saved time and increased the capacity of the plant—a machine consisting of a hollow needle attached to a pump; by plunging this needle into the meat and working with his foot, a man could fill a ham with pickle in a few seconds. And yet, in spite of this, there would be hams found spoiled, some of them with an odour so bad that a man could hardly bear to be in the room with them. To pump into these the packers had a second and much stronger pickle which destroyed the odour—a process known

to the workers as "giving them thirty per cent." Also, after the hams had been smoked, there would be found some that had gone to the bad. Formerly these had been sold as "Number Three Grade," but later on some ingenious person had hit upon a new device, and now they would extract the bone, about which the bad part generally lay, and insert in the hole a white-hot iron. After this invention there was no longer Number One, Two, and Three Grade—there was only Number One Grade. The packers were always originating such schemes—they had what they called "boneless hams," which were all the odds and ends of pork stuffed into casings; and "California hams," which were the shoulders, with big knuckle-joints, and nearly all the meat cut out; and fancy "skinned hams," which were made of the oldest hogs, whose skins were so heavy and coarse that no one would buy them—that is, until they had been cooked and chopped fine and labelled "head cheese!"

It was only when the whole ham was spoiled that it came into the department of [Y]. Cut up by the two-thousand-revolutions-a-minute flyers, and mixed with half a ton of other meat, no odour that ever was in a ham could make any difference. There was never the least attention paid to what was cut up for sausages; there would come all the way back from Europe old sausage that had been rejected, and that was mouldy and white—it would be dosed with borax and glycerine, and dumped into the hoppers, and made over again for home consumption. There would be meat that had tumbled out on the floor, in the dirt and sawdust, where the workers had tramped and spit uncounted billions of consumption germs. There would be meat stored in great piles in rooms; and the water from leaky roofs would drip over it, and thousands of rats would race about on it. It was too dark in these storage places to see well, but a man could run his hand over these piles of meat and sweep off handfuls of the dried dung of rats. These rats were nuisances, and the packers would put poisoned bread out for them; they would die, and then rats, bread, and meat would go into the hoppers together. This is no fairy story and no joke; the meat would be shovelled into carts, and the man who did the shoveling would not trouble to lift out a rat even when he saw one—there were things that went into the sausage in comparison with which a poisoned rat was tidbit. There was no place for the men to wash their hands before they ate their dinner, and so they made a practice of washing them in the water that was to be ladled into the sausage. There were the butt ends of smoked meat, and the scraps of corned beef, and all the odds and ends of the waste of the plants, that would be dumped into old barrels in the cellar and left there. Under the system of rigid economy which the packers enforced, there were some jobs that it only paid to do once in a long time, and among these was the cleaning out of the waste barrels. Every spring they did it; and in the barrels would be dirt and rust, and old nails and stale water—and cartload after cartload of it would be taken up and dumped into the hoppers with fresh meat, and send out to the public's breakfast; Some of it they would make into "smoked" sausage—but as the smoking took time, and was therefore expensive, they would call upon their chemistry department, and preserve it with borax and colour it with gelatine to make it brown. All of their sausage came out of the same bowl, but when they came to wrap it they would stamp some of it "special," and for this they would charge two cents more a pound.[7]

Grim reading, indeed! Yet, this was no congressional study, no task force white paper, and no investigative report ever delivered to the Congress. It is fiction, powerful fiction, that is credited with President Theodore Roosevelt signing the 1905 Meat Inspection Act and the 1906 Pure Food Law. It is, of course, an excerpt from Upton Sinclair's socialist novel *The Jungle.* How ironic (and so very American) that a piece of fiction did what years of reports and truth gathering had failed to accomplish.

Upton Sinclair's novel is generally credited with moving the Congress to pass and President Theodore Roosevelt to sign the first all-encompassing federal food safety laws, the Federal Meat Inspection Act and the Federal Pure Food Law. The truth is subtler. Although publication of *The Jungle* created a sense of public outrage and probably motivated the federal government to take final legislative action, the development of food-safety laws cannot be traced to one event, be it born of fact or fiction. Furthermore, *The Jungle* is not about the meat packing industry; it is about immigrant life in Chicago where the meat packing industry happened to be the largest employer. Actually, the above excerpt is the most damning part of the novel. The rest is pretty tame and boring. (William Prosser, the preeminent legal scholar in the area of tort law went back and reread *The Jungle* and remarked how he could not "refrain from expressing his opinion as to how bad a piece of literature it is."[8])

Food safety laws came neither quickly nor easily to the United States. While our English cousins passed laws to regulate all aspects of the food industry during the nineteenth century, American lawmakers hesitated to thrust the heavy hand of government into the business of food manufacturing.

Massachusetts is the first state credited with any serious food law. On 8 March 1785, the Bay State enacted this tidy piece of legislation:

> Whereas some evilly disposed persons, from motives of avarice and filthy lucre, have been induced to sell diseased, corrupted, contagious or unwholesome provisions, to the great nuisance of public health and peace:
>
> Be it therefore enacted by the Senate and House of Representatives in General Court assembled, and by the authority of the same, That if any person shall sell any such diseased, corrupted, contagious or unwholesome provisions, whether for meat or drink, knowing the same, without making it known to the buyer, and being thereof convicted before the Justices of the General Sessions of the Peace, in the county where such offence shall be committed, or the Justices of the Supreme Judicial Court, he shall be punished by fine, imprisonment, standing in the pillory, and binding to the good behavior, or one or more of the punishments, to be inflicted according to the degree and aggravation of the offence.

Human nature, then, in the form of "avarice and filthy lucre," was to blame for the necessity of these laws. Although legislators today almost never condemn the food industry with such colorful terms of censure (the lobbyists would not stand for such language), is there any doubt that some things have not changed?

Little happened on the legislative front in any of the states in the decades following the Massachusetts law. A few states gradually perceived the need to protect their citizens from certain abuses of food purveyors. In 1881, the states of New York, New Jersey, Michigan, and Illinois passed a series of early pure food laws but the emergence of a national economy made it clear that state laws would be limited in their effectiveness.[9]

Peter Collier, chief chemist for the United States Department of Agriculture's Bureau of Chemistry (later to become the FDA), first began to investigate adulteration of food products in 1879. For the next twenty-seven years, more than one hundred attempts were made to pass a federal food and drug law. In 1889, a Pure Food Law was introduced in the U.S. Congress but it was met with scorn and ridicule.

Dr. Harvey Washington Wiley, a state chemist from Indiana, is the man credited with finally getting a federal Food and Drug Act passed in 1906. Wiley, in turn, credited the nonvoting women's clubs and associations throughout the country for engaging in an extensive public information campaign that turned up the heat on congressional representatives. Wiley (who also wrote a regular column for *Good Housekeeping*) became famous for his "Poison Squad," a group of a dozen Bureau of Chemistry volunteers who ingested foods containing various amounts of additives and preservatives in order to determine what was safe.

The culmination of Wiley's efforts was passage of the 1905 Meat Inspection Act, and the 1906 Food and Drug Act, both to be administered by the United States Department of Agriculture (USDA). (Meat inspection remains to this day under the aegis of the USDA but the FDA is now under the Department of Health and Human Services.) Not that anyone is keeping score, but we should credit the goal to the hard-working Wiley with an assist from the fan favorite, Sinclair.

The balance of this chapter is about meat and we will ignore the 1906 Pure Food and Drug Act for now for one simple and pragmatic reason: it does precious little to regulate the meat industry.

The United States is a nation of meat eaters. We consume tremendous amounts of pork, chicken, and above all, beef. It is perhaps the greatest act of faith that we do so, not with fear or trembling, but with confidence and delight. What makes us so sure that our meat is safe?

Whenever we buy a chuck roast at the supermarket, we probably think the meat has been inspected by some government official. Technically speaking, it has been "inspected." But considering the massive amounts of beef, pork, and chicken (not to mention the other meats— like lamb, duck, and turkey) we prepare at home or consume at restaurants, does anyone seriously think that the inspection is careful and rigorous?

The law requires that meat sold in interstate commerce be inspected. That is the job of the Food Safety Inspection Service (FSIS), under the direction of the Secretary of Agriculture. What kind of inspection does an FSIS meat inspector do? For years, since the enactment of the federal laws requiring inspection, these inspections have been *organoleptic.* This means that the inspector uses his or her senses of sight, smell, and touch to discover signs of disease in the live animal or in the recently slaughtered carcass. The FSIS employs about 7,400 meat inspectors. These government workers inspect about 6 billion poultry animals and 120 million meat animals (beef, lamb, and pork) each year. You do the math: how rigorous can these inspections be? How "scientific" can they be? And if you don't want to do the math, I'll do it for you. Assume that the average inspector works forty-eight weeks a year, forty hours a week. Having worked for the government, I know that there are training conferences, administrative duties, and plenty of nonproductive hours in the average workweek. Let's assume that each inspector actually puts in the equivalent of forty full weeks of inspecting every year. (I know I'm being very generous because I am not factoring in paperwork obligations, coffee breaks, retirement parties, and time for extended lunch hours). That means that each inspector would have to inspect 507 birds plus 10 big animal carcasses every hour. That's about seven seconds per bird and a whopping six minutes per large carcass.

In response to the public's demands and expectations, the United States government, during the early 1990s, came up with a new approach to food safety in general and meat safety in particular. You may have heard of the term or have seen it on a label in your supermarket. Then again, maybe you haven't heard of HACCP; I stationed myself near a frozen seafood counter at a large supermarket in Madison, Wisconsin, in September 2000. I found packages of frozen fish with a label that read: "Prepared under HACCP Controls." I asked the first twenty-three people who walked by if they knew what HACCP meant. No one did, although three thought that it "meant something good."

"HACCP"—pronounced "hassup" by those in the industry—stands for "Hazard Analysis Critical Control Point."[10] Some critics of HACCP say it stands for "Have A Cup of Coffee and Pray." You decide if HACCP is a good idea.[11]

HACCP is supposed to be based on science. The theory is that processors and manufacturers can identify those points in their production process that are most likely to be at risk for introducing pathogens or unwanted bacteria into the product. The manufacturers, having identified all the key points in their processing operations, come up with a detailed program that solves the problems before they even happen. The government then evaluates the effectiveness of the program by sampling the finished product. After all, the proof should be "in the pudding," should it not? Not according to the U.S. District Court for the Northern District of Texas.[12]

In June 1998, Supreme Beef, a meat processor, implemented a HACCP pathogen control plan. Later that year the FSIS started to test the company's finished product for salmonella. The test results showed an alarming 47 percent of product contaminated with salmonella. The FSIS issued the company a "Noncompliance Report" that warned Supreme that it had to take immediate action to meet the government's performance standards.

Supreme Beef asked for and received more time so it could evaluate its laboratory data and current HACCP program. The FSIS again tested the finished product in April 1999 and although the level of salmonella contamination had improved (now only 20.8 percent), it still was unacceptable. Supreme Beef claimed its own test results showed a much lower level of contamination but agreed to institute new procedures (like installing a 180-degree water source on all boning and trimming lines) in an effort to improve the test results.

The third set of tests began on 27 August 1999. After a few weeks of testing, it was obvious that Supreme Beef would again fail to meet the government's 7.5 percent standard. The FSIS got tough and gave Supreme Beef until October nineteenth to show that its HACCP controls were adequate or to show that it had achieved "regulatory compliance." The company promised to meet the 7.5 percent performance standard but did not explain what it would change to do so. The FSIS got tougher and announced that it would soon withdraw its inspectors from the plant.

Withdrawal of FSIS inspection would be a death sentence for Supreme Beef because federal law prohibits the sale or transport in interstate commerce of any meat that has not been labeled "inspected and passed."[13] Unable to satisfy the FSIS inspectors and unable to pass the performance standard of no more than 7.5 percent salmonella in its finished product, Supreme Beef did what every right-thinking beef processor with a high concentration of salmonella in its meat would do: it went to court to stop the government from withdrawing its inspectors.

This must have been an easy case to decide, you are thinking. After all, if the proof is in the pudding, did not the continuing high concentrations of salmonella require the court to let the FSIS withdraw its inspections and not let the tainted Supreme Beef meat enter the stream of interstate commerce?

Supreme Beef did not contest the salmonella-level test results but argued, in essence, "So what?" Supreme Beef argued that the government cannot use the salmonella tests to evaluate the sanitation conditions of a plant. The government's position was simple: the failure of Supreme Beef to pass the salmonella tests meant that the product it was trying to sell in interstate commerce was "adulterated." Because the law prohibits the FSIS from labeling as "inspected and passed" any meat that is, in fact, "adulterated," withdrawal of inspection was perfectly reasonable.

But what was Supreme Beef to do? It had developed as good a HACCP pathogen reduction program as it could but, for some unknown reason, the end product still contained unacceptable levels of salmonella. "It's not our fault," they claimed. "Besides, the government can't point to any unsanitary conditions in our plant."

At the hearing in the case, FSIS administrator Thomas J. Billy took the stand:

Q. So this plant could be spotless, most sanitary plant in the world, and if it fails the Salmonella performance standards, then it's automatically deemed to be insanitary [that is the term used by the USDA], correct?

A. Yes.[14]

The court granted Supreme Beef's motion for an injunction and threw out the government's performance standard as a measure of sanitary conditions. The problem with the government's theory, according to the court, was not that it made no sense but rather that it was not authorized by Congress. I wonder: how would a witness from Supreme Beef have answered this question: So, if every box of beef coming out of your plant tested positive for salmonella, the government would have to let you keep shipping it unless they could show some unsanitary condition that was the likely cause of the salmonella?

Because the salmonella tests used by the FSIS did not necessarily measure the actual conditions of the plant, the government had no basis for finding the conditions of the plant unsanitary and therefore wrongfully concluded that Supreme Beef's product was "adulterated." It may have had high levels of salmonella but it was not "adulterated."[15] If this strikes you as nonsensical, you are not alone. The government announced its intention to appeal.

Why did Supreme Beef's finished product continue to test so badly for salmonella levels? No one knows for certain, but the most likely explanation, according to the government's own witness, was that the carcasses that came to the plant were already contaminated with salmonella. A kind of "garbage in, garbage out" explanation. If that were the case, argued the government, Supreme Beef had a duty to institute controls that measure the pathogen levels of incoming product. The court agreed that these controls might be a good idea but a lack of these controls could not justify the government's action.

Would you care to dine on burgers processed in the Supreme Beef plant? I must confess that I would have hesitated if the server at the Friendly Ice Cream shop had given in to my request for a rare Big Beef by adding, "You don't mind if it's the latest shipment from Supreme Beef?"

The problem for the Food Safety and Inspection Service was that Congress never authorized withdrawal of its inspectors on the basis of salmonella test results, only on the basis of finding some actual unsanitary conditions. Of course, the government argued and would argue on appeal that the laws currently on the books did not bar the use of performance-based standards in concluding that a plant was producing adulterated meat and that, as a matter of logic, had unsanitary conditions.

The court of appeals may or may not agree with the FSIS but the government always has another avenue of relief. It can ask Congress to change the law and specifically authorize the use of salmonella tests as a measure of a plant's sanitary conditions. The government can always try to change the rules. Sometimes you can "beat city hall" but city hall has a way of getting even.

In a real economic way, the USDA got in the last word. In addition to inspecting the nation's meat supply, the USDA purchases meat. In fact, the USDA buys about 70 percent of the ground beef used in schools. In response to the court's decision in the Supreme Beef case, the government required all ground beef to be completely free of salmonella. Because Supreme Beef did not meet the "zero-tolerance" standard, the government canceled its substantial contract with Supreme Beef.[16]

According to some studies, this knee-jerk reaction by the USDA resulted in a sharp decrease in salmonella contamination in the ground beef served in our schools. The food industry began to lobby for a relaxation in the new standards, arguing that they were too difficult to meet and that proper cooking of the meat would make the zero-tolerance standard unnecessary.

It should come as no surprise to anyone that the law of food safety is the ever-changing result of the ongoing battle between food industry interests and consumer advocates. The Department of Agriculture is supposed to promote the interests of the food industry while protecting the safety of food consumers. The end result is not always obvious, instead depending on compromise and sometimes on litigation.

Inspection and oversight of our food supply is a daunting task. We believe that our meat is "inspected" but have to wonder how so much meat can be "inspected" by so few "inspectors." Are you still in awe of those gifted inspectors who need only seven seconds per bird and ten minutes per steer? The government is aware of the awesome numbers that threaten to make meat inspection a joke (if it is not already) and tried to do something about it.

In an effort to use its limited resources more efficiently, the FSIS came up with a program that allowed employees of meat processing plants to conduct inspections of animal carcasses under the direction, supervision, and observations of a federal FSIS inspector. The government believed that by watching others do the inspections, it was carrying out its sworn and sacred duty to inspect our nation's meat supply. One might cynically conclude that it's like the boy in charge of watching the henhouse paying the fox to watch the hens.

Naturally, there was a lawsuit, brought by a group of federal meat and poultry inspectors, their union, and the Community Nutrition Institute. They brought the suit to enjoin the Secretary of Agriculture from "authorizing anything other than the carcass-by-carcass post-mortem inspection by a federal government inspector."

The court, in language dripping with sarcasm ("One might as well say that umpires are pitchers because they carefully watch others throw baseballs.") declared that the federal inspectors were not inspecting meat by watching employees of the meat packers inspect their own meat. The system would have to hobble along, understaffed and overwhelmed.[17]

Do not think that the problem of limited inspection resources is confined to meat or that somehow vegetarians are exempt from dangers of contamination. Case in point: the salad bar. In a blistering exposé of Manhattan establishments offering help-yourself salad bars, the *New York Times* reported that these popular eateries showed alarming evidence of high amounts of bacteria, yeasts, and molds. State and local inspections were woefully inadequate to clean up the problem. Let the eater beware.[18]

The government has embarked on new initiatives to improve the state of food safety. Perhaps the most important, and one that is virtually impossible to criticize, is consumer and industry education. Still, food safety is a matter of science and its application to daily living. The law can do only so much. It can regulate human behavior but is powerless to affect the conduct of the microbial villains that can wreak havoc on us.

Food safety is entrusted to a century-old system of laws that rely heavily on physical inspection. Even in 1906, this was hardly a revolutionary concept; the Greeks invented the health inspector around 500 B.C.[19] Entering the twenty-first century, we can only wonder how long the system can survive.

There is another way in which the law can encourage food producers to make food safer, although it is an aspect of the law that has come under fire. It is the civil lawsuit for damages, the process by which processors of unsafe food are held accountable by the courts, albeit after the damage has been done. Civil suits for money damages are the topic of chapters 5 and 6 but they should not be dismissed as irrelevant to the long-term goal of promoting food safety. It is not the after-the-fact expensive lawsuit that encourages food producers to make food safer but rather the fear of future expensive lawsuits that may make a difference.

Food is a risk. The Japanese tora fugu (blowfish) is a delicacy that can be deadly unless prepared by expert trained chefs. The FDA prohibited restaurants in the United States from serving it. In 1984, a New York restaurant staged a tora fugu demonstration and ultimately got the FDA to relax its rule; soon, tora fugu could be prepared but only under close supervision and only after chefs were carefully trained in its preparation. Is it worth it? Never having dined on tora fugu, I withhold judgment.

My venture into the world of meat safety has put me in a pickle. I love the taste of hamburgers cooked bloody-red rare but I understand that such a dish is, relatively speaking, risky business. My stomach and my brain are in conflict. The food industry recognizes this risk and sometimes makes the decision for us. For example, on the menu of Damon's, a national restaurant chain, I found the following: "For your safety, we cook all of our burgers medium well to well done." Try ordering a rare quarter pounder at your local McDonald's. Does this mean you cannot get a rare hamburger anymore?

It's not hard to get a rare hamburger, if you look in the right places. I walk down the street to the Main Street Pub, a Mount Horeb tavern, where I have no difficulty ordering burgers bloody rare. I asked the owner about the possibility of someone getting sick and suing her. "If you want your hamburger rare, I'll make it for you rare," says Laurie. "And no one's gonna bother suing me because I don't have any money." In Wisconsin, taverns without a lot of money are usually a good bet for rare hamburgers.

The other place I go for rare hamburgers is the Wilson Street Grill, an upscale restaurant in downtown Madison, Wisconsin. Owner Nancy Christie also appreciates the elegance of a rare hamburger and buys her meat from a nearby farm. She has total confidence in the ground beef she uses. She admits that there still is a risk but understands that life is all about risk. Her rare burgers are exquisite and have made me forget about the Big Beef of my youth. Stomach and head will just have to learn to live with the conflict. And the law be damned.

3

NUTRITION FACTS, NUTRITION FICTIONS

Thou Shalt Not Commit Adulteration!

The mere suggestion that consumers
have a right to know what they eat is always
enough to give food lobbyists the jitters.
—*Ruth deForest Lamb,* American Chamber of Horrors

Never eat anything whose listed ingredients
cover more than one-third of the package.
—*Joseph Leonard,* San Francisco Chronicle

I went to the grocery store and bought a package of goodies to satisfy my cravings. It now sits before me, in all of its packaged splendor. The package protects my tummy's desire from wind, dust, and rain, but it does so much more. I am most fortunate because federal law requires the manufacturer to list all of the ingredients and a wealth of nutritional information. In a type size that would make the small print on an insurance contract seem like a billboard in comparison, I read the following listing of ingredients:

Ingredients: Sugar, Enriched Wheat Flour (Flour, Ferrous Sulfate [Iron], "B" Vitamins [Niacin, Thiamine Mononitrate (B1), Riboflavin (B2), Folic Acid]), Water, Vegetable and/or Animal Shortening (Contains One or More of Partially Hydrogenated Soybean, Cottonseed, or Canola Oil, Beef Fat), Corn Syrup, High Fructose Corn Syrup, Cocoa Processed with Alkalai, Contains 2% or less of: Whey, Modified Corn

Starch, Leavening (Baking Soda, Sodium Acid Pyrophosphate, Mono-
calcium Phosphate, Sodium Phosphate), Salt, Corn Syrup Solids, Cal-
cium Carbonate, Cornstarch, Calcium Sulfate, Dextrose, Soy Lecithin,
Polysorbate 60, Mono and Diglycerides, Cellulose Gum, Calcium
Caseinate, Wheat Gluten, Agar, Gelatin, Sodium Stearoyl Lactylate,
Locust Bean Gum, Chocolate Liquor, natural and Artificial Flavors,
Caramel Color, Potassium Sorbate and Sorbic Acid (To Retain Fresh-
ness).

As for the legally mandated Nutrition Facts, in substantially larger
print size, I find that each serving (there were three servings in the
package that I bought) contains 100 calories, 50 of which came from
fat. I also learn that each serving contains the following (the percentage figures in parentheses are the percentage "Daily Value" based on
a 2,000 calorie diet):

Total Fat: 6 grams (9%)
Saturated Fat: 2.5 grams (13%)
Cholesterol: 5 milligrams (2%)
Sodium: 290 milligrams (12%)
Total Carbohydrates: 30 grams (10%)
Dietary Fiber: 1 gram (4%)
Sugars: 17 grams
Protein: 2 grams

As for various vitamins and minerals, I discover from the label that
each serving contains 0 percent of my recommended intake of vitamin A, 0 percent of vitamin C, 10 percent of calcium, and 6 percent
of iron.

I also ascertain the name of the manufacturer, along with its city,
state, and zip code. There is no mailing address or telephone number.
A union label assures me that I am supporting the rank and file of
America.

What did I buy? What toothsome treat did I procure? What scrump-
tious morsels do I have before me? On what delectable victuals did I
disburse the princely sum of ninety-nine cents? I realize the suspense
is eating you alive, as it should in a book of this magnitude, so I have
placed the answer at the end of this chapter.

Food labeling is a relatively recent phenomenon in the human experience of eating. The cave dwellers certainly had no experience with food labels; they ate what they gathered or hunted. The ancient Israelites received manna from heaven, presumably unlabeled and unbranded. As food became part of the marketplace and part of the industrialized world, labels found their way onto food products. Early labels identified the maker of the product but it was only a matter of time before society and the law demanded more of what goes on the outside of every food product.

The industrial revolution meant that we could no longer count on food coming from the farm down the road. The growth of cities, even before widespread industrialization as we understand it, made it necessary to bring foods from faraway places. That meant the rise of a new industry: commercial food processing. It also meant the use of chemical preservatives and other additives to make our food look better and last longer. These added ingredients were not necessarily healthy or desirable but unless they were listed on a "label," no one would know.[1]

Food labeling became a matter of federal law with the passage of the Pure Food Law of 1906. It would have been entirely appropriate if the new food law had been called "The Food Labeling Law" because accurate and honest labeling, more than food safety, was at the core of the radical new legislation.

Upton Sinclair may have stirred up the populace with his horrific account of the meat packers in *The Jungle,* but no one provoked any similar sense of outrage with stories of misleading labels. Yet labeling became the central concern of the new federal food bureaucracy that has become the Food and Drug Administration.

I do not mean to denigrate the importance of honest labeling in the food industry. To the contrary, labels that mislead or misrepresent what is inside the package should not be tolerated. But a food product that is mislabeled or misbranded may be entirely safe and totally healthy. The Pure Food and Drug Act of 1906 worked on a basic assumption: if people are given accurate information about the foods they are eating, they will make safe and healthy choices.

The early federal food watchdogs took their jobs seriously. They went after every food imaginable, from Coca-Cola[2] to the fruit-flavored spreads we put on our morning toast. I am careful to call these foods "spreads" and not "jams" because that was the very issue in the case that went up to the Eighth Circuit Court of Appeals in 1931 with the strange name of *United States v. Ten Cases, More or Less, of Bred Spred.*[3] The case symbolizes the valiant efforts of the early food crusaders in Washington.

"Bred Spred" was a strawberry-flavored jelled substance made of 17 parts strawberries, 55 parts sugar, 11.5 parts water, .25 part pectin, and .04 part tartaric acid. No one disputed the fact that Bred Spred was a food that possessed some nutritional value. The government seized several cases of Bred Spred that had been shipped in interstate commerce and asked the court to condemn the product as adulterated and misbranded. The trial court dismissed the government's claim and it went to the Eighth Circuit on appeal.

The court began by summarizing the purpose of the Food and Drug Act:

> . . . the primary purpose of Congress was to prevent injury to the public health by the sale and transportation in interstate commerce of misbranded and adulterated foods. The legislation, as against misbranding, intended to make it possible that the consumer should know that an article purchased was what it purported to be; that it might be bought for what it really was, and not upon misrepresentations as to character and quality. As against adulteration, the statute was intended to protect the public health from possible injury by adding to articles of food consumption poisonous and deleterious substances which might render such articles injurious to the health of consumers.[4]

What was wrong with Bred Spred? According to the government, its damning flaw was that it was *not* jam. More specifically, it was a jam imposter. Jam, as everyone then knew, was about 50 percent fruit and 50 percent sugar. At worst, it was no less than 45 percent fruit. Because Bred Spred contained so little fruit, it was damaged or inferior in a way that would deceive the consumer.

To prove adulteration, the government had to prove that Bred Spred was a "damaged or inferior food product" because one or more of its ingredients was damaged or inferior. The government also had to show that it was made in such a way that its inferiority was concealed. The problem, according to the court, was one of comparison: inferior to what?

Bread Spred was made from natural and wholesome ingredients, albeit not as much fruit as might be found in traditional jam. But Bred Spred never claimed to be jam. It was not "inferior" to jam, it was just different. Judgment for the low-price "Spred."

Was Bred Spred an imitation jam? It was used as a substitute for jam because it cost less than jam. Does the fact that it did not call itself "jam" really matter? The problem for the government was the law as written gave it no power to go after clever imitations. We are probably sympathetic to the government's actions in going after Bred Spred because we believe, rightly or wrongly, that more fruit is better than less.

The Bred Spred case was a frustrating loss for the FDA. It underscored the limitations of the 1906 Act and emphasized the need for an expanded jurisdiction. That came about in 1938 with the passage of the federal Food, Drug, and Cosmetic Act. The most important change in the law was a requirement that food "standards of identity" be established for hundreds of food items. No longer would custom and the marketplace be allowed to decide what is or is not "jam" or "peanut butter" or even "ketchup." The government would decide the minimum standards for these foods. To give greater bite to the law, section 403 of the new law defined a food to be "misbranded" if it was found to be an imitation of another food unless the label prominently proclaimed that it was an imitation.

What a difference a new law can make! In a case virtually identical to the Bred Spred case, a federal court upheld the condemnation of Leader Brand Fruit Spreds because, although plainly labeled as fruit spreads, they resembled jams and preserves in a way that would likely deceive the consumer. Although the ingredients of these spreads were without question "wholesome, nutritious, and palatable," the product they were in amounted to an economic fraud on the public. The court even took note of the earlier Bred Spred case but had not trouble in seeing that Congress had effectively overruled it.[5]

Consider then another case brought under the new law, *United States v. 651 Cases, More or Less, of Chocolate Chil-Zert.*[6] The government seized a whole bunch of Rich's Chocolate Chil-Zert on the grounds that it was an imitation ice cream and misbranded because it did not state on the label that it was an "imitation." Chil-Zert contained the usual ingredients of chocolate ice cream in roughly the same proportions except that soy fat and soy protein were substituted for milk fat and milk protein. What was on the label? Immediately below the words "Rich's Chocolate Chil-Zert" were the words, in prominent letters, "Not an Ice Cream." The label further disclosed that the product contained no milk or milk fat.

Was there anything deceptive or misleading about Chil-Zert? Not at all. Yet the government persisted in its claim that because it was made to imitate chocolate ice cream, Chil-Zert was required to admit on the label that it was an "imitation" or else suffer the fate of being branded as "misbranded."

What standards were there to apply? As Rich's so deftly pointed out, there were no official standards for chocolate ice cream. The government had published standards for dozens of foods but, for reasons we may never know or even care to know, did not bother to define ice cream. Furthermore, even the word "imitation" had never been defined by Congress. The court recognized that there was no all-inclusive test of "imitation" but decided the matter anyway in a masterful flourish of logic.

The court began with the premise that imitation connotes inferiority, in the sense that it is cheapened by the substitution of lower-cost ingredients. (I've always believed the old saying that imitation is the sincerest form of flattery, but that never entered into the court's thinking.) Chil-Zert, as the court found, was identical with ice cream in its method of manufacture, packaging, and sale. It was similar in taste, appearance, color, texture, body, and melting qualities. The court used a variant of the duck theory of jurisprudence: if it looks like a duck, walks like a duck, and talks like a duck it is either (a) a duck or (b) an imitation duck.

Then came the clincher: the only significant difference between the two products was the substitution in Chil-Zert of a "cheaper" ingredient, vegetable oil, for milk fat. The learned judge concluded: "It is, therefore, something less than the genuine article chocolate ice cream. It is inescapable that the ordinary understanding of English speech would denominate it as an imitation of ice cream."[7]

How does this case differ from the Bred Spred case? The obvious difference is that the government had the ammunition—specific congressional enactments—that allowed it to go after Chil-Zert where it could not go after Bred Spred. Yet, Chil-Zert was totally honest and up front about what it was and what it was not by the prominent wording on the label "Not An Ice Cream." No such similar disclaimer appeared on the Bred Spred label. Our sympathies (mine anyway) go with Chil-Zert because substituting vegetable oil for milk fat meant a potentially healthier product. Besides, there it was, in black and white, or whatever colors they chose: "Not An Ice Cream." It did not matter; Chil-Zert lost.

I love to take the court's reasoning in Chil-Zert one step further. If, as the court held, the substitution of a "cheaper" ingredient (vegetable oil) for the more expensive ingredient (milk fat), makes for an imitation, what would a court do if for some bizarre reason, due to wild fluctuations in the marketplace, vegetable oil became more expensive than milk fat? Would that not mean that chocolate ice cream had become an imitation of Chil-Zert?

When I reviewed the Chil-Zert case for this book, I noticed that the judge who decided the matter was Judge Brennan. I gasped. How could the future Justice William Brennan, the great and compassionate liberal Supreme Court jurist, charged by his critics as being a left-wing activist, have been such a strict and literal constructionist? Then I learned that it was Judge Stephen Brennan, not William Brennan. It was obviously an imitation Brennan, a misbranded Brennan, who decided that if the statute requires the word "imitation," nothing else would do.

The words and images on a food label do matter. The government pays careful attention to the tens of thousands of food labels in our grocery stores. Sometimes it's the FDA, sometimes the USDA, and sometimes the FTC (Federal Trade Commission). The FTC jumped into the food/law arena in 1938 when congressional action (the Wheeler Lea Act) gave the FTC jurisdiction over false and misleading advertising even if it did not result in unfair competition.

The early days of the FTC saw the agency enjoin Standard Brands from claiming that its Fleischman's Yeast is "rich in hormone-like substances," helps prevent colds, and cures constipation. It went after Quaker Oats for claiming that its product contained "the magical yeast vitamin" that curbed nervousness, prevented constipation, and stimulated children's appetites.[8]

Having recently left the subject of ice cream, I must report that at least three brands of commercially available ice cream claim to be "homemade." I found cartons of Breyers, Edy's, and Wells' Blue Bunny, all describing their ice cream products as homemade. You and I know they are not homemade. Take, for example, Edy's Home Made Double Chocolate Chunk. Grandma never put carrageenan, butter oil, high fructose corn syrup, guar gum, dextrose, corn starch, and carob bean gum in the ice cream she churned in her kitchen. So how can they get off calling their products "homemade?" Aren't these ice creams mis-branded, mislabeled, misleading and utterly fraudulent? Where are the regulators and zealous bureaucrats when we need them most?

I raised the issue about "homemade" commercial ice cream with the Wisconsin Department of Agriculture, but my letter was ignored. They must have concluded that only a crackpot would send such a letter. Also, I wrote directly to the three ice cream companies. Only one, Wells' Dairy, replied with any kind of real response to my concerns:

Dear Mr. Levenson:

Thank you for your letter dated May 2 expressing your concern with the use of "homemade" on a recently purchased package of Wells' Blue Bunny Super Premium Ice Cream Bars. We appreciated hearing from you.

We at Wells' Dairy, Inc. are committed to providing premium quality products to meet the needs and desires of our customers. Therefore, we have developed an expensive product line which included a variety of fluid milks, juices, dips, sour creams, cottage cheeses, cultured yogurts, ice creams, sherbets, frozen yogurts, and numerous novelties.

We do our best to portray the package's contents by using descriptive words, phrases and photographs. Our intent is to describe the product as thoroughly as possible to help our customers choose those products which they feel are best suited for them. We use the term "homemade" in reference to the flavor of ice cream. It is not used to mislead our customers into believing the ice cream is actu-ally made in someone's home.

Mr. Levenson, we appreciate you taking the time to share your comments with us. I hope you will use the enclosed coupon to enjoy a half gallon of Wells' Blue Bunny ice cream.[9]

At least an executive vice president took the time to write. Thanks for the coupon. But seriously, Mr. Wells, if it is not intended to mislead customers into believing the product is "actually made in someone's home," why are you calling it "homemade?"

I suppose if you are dumb enough to believe for half a minute that a commercially available ice cream is really homemade, you deserve to be misled. One day an ice cream maker will have the courage to proclaim on the label of its product: "Factory produced in our enormous industrial facility in very large quantities." That would be an honest label and I would buy some. I suspect it would taste just like some big company's "homemade" ice cream.

I do not mean to be obsessed with ice cream labeling but I must report another questionable claim that I found on a package of Kemps brand vanilla ice cream. The product purported to be Kemps "Old Fashioned All Natural Vanilla Ice Cream." I have no problem with "old fashioned" as a descriptor; nobody is dumb enough to believe that the term "old fashioned" means anything in today's world. But should I be able to expect something in a product that claims to be "all natural?" Foolish consumer that I am, I believed that the product would not contain substances such as "mono and diglycerides" and "calcium sulfate." (I won't quibble about the locust bean gum and carrageenan.) Sure enough, the "all natural vanilla ice cream" contained a healthy dose of both mono and diglycerides and calcium sulfate. What gives? I called the company and was first told that the phrase "all natural" doesn't really mean anything. I pressed the point and then got a more ingenious explanation: the term "all natural" in "old fashioned all natural vanilla ice cream" modifies the term "vanilla," not "ice cream." So the vanilla is natural (whoopee!) but the ice cream isn't.

A food label is an advertisement attached so intimately to the food itself that we think of it as part of the food. The government thinks that way, too, because the label is generally within the jurisdiction of the FDA (or the USDA when it comes to meat) but off-product advertising is generally the province of the Federal Trade Commission. We have ignored the FTC to this point, but here's a case that will make you yearn for one of mom's great grilled-cheese sandwiches.

The FTC found that Kraft was misleading the public when it claimed in its advertising campaign that Kraft Singles are made with five ounces of milk each and are "concentrated with calcium."

Kraft Singles are, of course, "Kraft Singles American Pasteurized Process [that is the correct technical term] Cheese Food" We know and

"Our calcium disodium EDTA and artificial flavors are all organic and natural. That's Grandma's story and she's sticking to it—until the FDA says otherwise!"

(Cartoon by Dennis Schmidt)

love them, don't we? Millions of grilled cheese sandwiches are made using these handy slices.

The problem, as the court pointed out, is that the market for individually wrapped process cheese slices is both competitive and confusing. Remember: this is process cheese, meaning that it is not exactly the cheese that was made on the farm. The reason for the confusion is that there are three types of products on the market.

First, there is process cheese slices, which must contain at least 51 percent natural cheese according to federal regulation.[10]

Then there are "imitation cheese slices," which contain little or no real cheese. What do they have? If you really want to know and have the stomach for it, they contain mostly water, vegetable oil, flavoring agents, and fortifying agents. Tastier living through chemistry. It is possible for these imitation cheese slices to be as healthy as regular process cheese slices in some nutrient categories simply by virtue of the addition of particular nutrients. Nevertheless, these have to be labeled "imitation."

The third category almost defies logic and intuition. Some imitation slices can be nutritionally superior to both the standard imitation cheese slices and process cheese slices on a particular nutritional score by virtue of large additions of that particular nutrient. These are called "substitute slices." We'll call both the "imitation" and "substitute" slices "imitation slices" because that is what the court did. And it makes sense for the purposes of what the court had to decide.

So which is the best source of calcium: process cheese or imitation cheese? Which is the better source of calcium: a slice of process cheese made from five ounces of milk or a slice of imitation cheese made from who-knows-what? Here's a tidbit of information you may not know—roughly 30 percent of the calcium contained in the milk from which the process cheese slice is made is lost during processing. And here's the real kicker: the vast majority of imitation slices sold in the United States when Kraft launched its ad campaign contained roughly the same amount of calcium as did the Kraft slices.

When it came to calcium content, mother nature was fooled, or at least she was adequately compensated. Kraft revised its ad campaign to disclose (not very prominently) that each Kraft Single has 70 percent of the calcium of five ounces of milk. It didn't matter; the FTC ordered Kraft to cease and desist because reasonable consumers would get the impression that Kraft Singles (being made from five ounces of milk) have more calcium than imitation slices (made from little or no milk).

Kraft raised some serious claims in the court of appeal, claims that affect all food-related nutrition claims today. First, should the FTC be required to rely on some extrinsic evidence of consumer deception before it enjoins an advertising campaign? This requirement, argued Kraft, should apply especially in cases of "implied" nutritional claims as was before the court here (as opposed to "express" nutritional claims). Kraft attacked the ability of the FTC to fairly and fully evaluate these claims. The court was not buying, although it seemed to recognize that as a policy matter, Kraft was not entirely unpersuasive.

The second issue that Kraft raised cut even deeper. It argued that the FTC's approach chilled commercial speech in violation of the First Amendment. Once again the court, while recognizing a certain strength to some of Kraft's logic, refused to protect misleading advertising.

Next, Kraft defended its advertising campaign with great passion and zeal. The ads were literally true, argued Kraft, because the Kraft Singles were made from five ounces of milk and do have a high concentration of calcium. That did not move the court because in the field of advertising, especially food advertising, "even literally true statements can have misleading implications."

Kraft's final arguments were laughable: consumers don't really care about the milk equivalency and calcium superiority claims. Oh yes they do, and that's why Kraft ran the ads in the first place. And they were indeed successful, as a Kraft internal memo revealed.[11]

As food companies spend millions on advertising (what I call "off-product labeling"), the FTC has been active. In 1977, the FTC obtained a consent order against ITT Continental for claiming that its Fresh Horizons bread contained five times as much fiber as whole-wheat bread. The claim was literally true but the extra fiber came via the addition of wood pulp. Yes, we were chewing trees as we ate our tuna salad sandwiches.[12]

You say you like ketchup? Do you know what ketchup is? You may think it to be a thick, moderately spicy tomato-based condiment. Not according to the federal government. Ketchup (or catsup) has a "standard of identity," meaning that in order to be called "tomato ketchup" (which many right-thinking humanoids consider a tool of desecration on an otherwise perfectly good steak or hamburger) it must conform to strict federal standards. Here is how the government, in the all-knowing and all-correct Code of Federal Regulations, defines ketchup:

21 C.F. R. SEC. 155.194 CATSUP

(a) Identity—(1) Definition. Catsup, ketchup, or catchup is the food prepared from one or any combination of two or more of the following optional tomato ingredients:

(i) Tomato concentrate as defined in sec. 155.191(a)(1), except that lemon juice, concentrated lemon juice, or safe and suitable organic acids may be used in quantities no greater than necessary to adjust the pH, and in compliance with sec. 155.191(b).

(ii) The liquid derived from mature tomatoes of the red or reddish varieties *Lycopersicum esculentum* P. Mill.

(iii) The liquid obtained from the residue from preparing such tomatoes for canning, consisting of peelings and cores with or without such tomatoes or pieces thereof.

(iv) The liquid obtained from the residue from partial extraction of juice from such tomatoes.

Such liquid is strained so as to exclude skins, seeds, and other coarse or hard substances in accordance with current good manufacturing practice. Prior to straining, food-grade hydrochloric acid may be added to the tomato material in an amount to obtain a pH no lower than 2.0. Such acid is then neutralized with food-grade sodium hydroxide so that the treated tomato material is restored to a pH of 4.2 +/- 0.2. The final composition of the food may be adjusted by concentration and/or by the addition of water. The food may contain salt (sodium chloride formed during acid neutralization shall be considered added salt) and is seasoned with ingredients as specified in paragraph (a)(2) of this section. The food is preserved by heat sterilization (canning), refrigeration, or freezing. When sealed in a container to be held at ambient temperatures, it is so processed by heat, before or after sealing, as to prevent spoilage.

(2) Ingredients. One or any combination of two or more of the following safe and suitable ingredients in each of the following categories is added to the tomato ingredients specified in paragraph (a)(1) of this section:

(i) Vinegars.

(ii) Nutritive carbohydrate sweeteners. Such sweeteners if defined in Part 168 of this chapter shall be as defined therein.

(iii) Spices, flavoring, onions, or garlic.

(3) Labeling. (i) The name of the food is "Catsup," "Ketchup," or "Catchup."

(ii) The following shall be included as part of the name or in close proximity to the name of the food:

(a) The statement "Made from" or "Made in part from," as the case may be, "residual tomato material from canning" if the optional tomato ingredient specified in paragraph (a)(1)(iii) of this section or tomato concentrate containing the ingredient specified in sec. 155.191(a)(1)(ii) is present.

(b) The statement "Made from" or "Made in part from," as the case may be, "residual tomato material from partial extraction of juice" if the optional tomato ingredient specified in paragraph (a)(1)(iv) of this section or tomato concentrate containing the ingredient specified in sec. 155.191(a)(1)(iii) is present.

(iii) Label declaration. Each of the ingredients used in the food shall be declared on the label as required by the applicable sections of parts 101 and 130 of this chapter; except that the name "tomato concentrate" may be used in lieu of the names "tomato puree," "tomato pulp," or "tomato paste" and when tomato concentrates are used, the labeling requirements of sec. 155.191(a)(3)(ii)(a) and (a)(3)(ii)(b) do not apply.

(b) Quality. (1) The standard of quality for catsup is as follows: The consistency of the finished food is such that its flow is not more than 14 centimeters in 30 seconds at 20 degrees C when tested in a Bostwick Consistometer in the following manner: Check temperature of mixture and adjust to 20 +/-1 degrees C. The trough must also be at a temperature close to 20 degrees C. Adjust end-to-end level of Bostwick Consistometer by means of the spirit level placed in trough of instrument. Side-to-side level may be adjusted by means of the built-in spirit level. Transfer sample to the dry sample chamber of the Bostwick Consistometer. Fill the chamber slightly more than level full, avoiding air bubbles as far as possible. Pass a straight edge across top of chamber starting from the gate end to remove excess product. Release gate of instrument by gradual pressure on lever, holding the instrument down at the same time to prevent its movement as the gate is released. Immediately start the stop watch or interval timer, and after 30 seconds read the maximum distance of flow to the nearest 0.1 centimeter. Clean and dry the instrument and repeat the reading on another portion of sample. Do not wash instrument with hot water if it is to be used immediately for the next determination, as this may result in an increase in temperature of the sample. For highest accuracy, the instrument should be maintained at a temperature of 20 +/- 1 [degrees] C. If readings vary more than 0.2 centimeter, repeat a third time or until satisfactory agreement is obtained. Report the average of two or more readings, excluding any that appear to be abnormal.

(2) Determine compliance as specified in sec. 155.3(b).

(3) If the quality of catsup falls below the standard prescribed in paragraphs (b) (1) and (2) of this section, the label shall bear the general statement of substandard quality specified in sec. 130.14(a) of this chapter, in the manner and form therein specified, but in lieu of such general statement of substandard quality when the quality of the catsup falls below the standard, the label may bear the alternative statement, "Below Standard in Quality—Low Consistency."

(c) Fill of container. (1) The standard of fill of container for catsup, as determined by the general method for fill of container prescribed in sec. 130.12(b) of this chapter, is not less than 90 percent of the total capacity except:

(i) When the food is frozen, or

(ii) When the food is packaged in individual serving-size packages containing 56.7 grams (2 ounces) or less.

(2) Determine compliance as specified in sec. 155.3(b).

(3) If the catsup falls below the standard of fill prescribed in paragraphs (c) (1) and (2) of this section, the label shall bear the general statement of substandard fill as specified in sec. 130.14(b) of this chapter, in the manner and form therein specified.[13]

That is one tasty ketchup. (I know you are dying to know: there are no federal regulations that define mustard.) Note that the definition of ketchup does not even mention various chemical preservatives, such as sodium benzoate, a commonly used preservative. What if a ketchup maker wants to preserve the company's cherished product by adding sodium benzoate? The law does not expressly prohibit the addition of sodium benzoate but it does not expressly allow it. Perhaps the safest and most honest route is to not only list it as an ingredient but to label the product not as simply "ketchup" but rather as "tomato catsup with preservative."

You can't ask any more of a manufacturer than that, complete up-front honesty on the label. The problem for the Libby Company back in 1945 was that the government claimed that their large cans of "tomato catsup with preservative" was a "misbranded food" and tried to condemn the product.

Libby was astounded. Here was an honestly labeled product, a "catsup" that seemed to be no different from other "catsups" with one tiny exception: one-tenth of one percent of benzoate of soda added as a preservative. Libby argued that its product was safe, truthfully labeled, not deceptively packaged, and accurately descriptive of what was inside. There was no claim that the ketchup was harmful because sodium benzoate was indeed permitted in many other foods.

Judge Simons, writing for the Second Circuit Court of Appeals, gave us the lowdown on the world of ketchup. There is "fancy" ketchup and there is "standard" ketchup, he explained. "Fancy" ketchup (talk about your oxymorons!) is packed in bottles for table use and costs more because it contains more sugar. That is not a misprint; sugar was expensive in 1945 and adding it to ketchup drove up the cost nearly 25 percent. "Standard" ketchup was used primarily in restaurants and hotels for cooking and the preparation of sauces although it was used as table ketchup in low-priced restaurants.

What was the harm in Libby's product? Libby added a tiny amount of a commonly used preservative to ketchup and clearly labeled the item. No matter, ruled the court, the ketchup may not have been "adulterated" but it was still "misbranded." "If producers of food products may, by adding to the common name of any such product mere words of qualification or description, escape the regulation of the Administrator, then the fixing of a standard for commonly known foods becomes utterly futile as an instrument for the protection of the consuming public."[14] The standards of identity of the 1938 law were set in stone.

As a last-gasp effort, Libby appealed to common sense. By not permitting manufacturers the ability to add certain wholesome ingredients, the court would be stifling creativity and development in the food industry. The court acknowledged that argument but directed Libby to Congress for relief: "The argument that an affirmance of the decision below will prevent the development of new foods and 'lay a dead hand on progress' is one that may more appropriately be addressed to the Administrator or to Congress than to the courts."[15]

As biased as I am against ketchup, the Libby decision makes no sense. Fortunately, the government no longer takes such a narrow view of the federal regulations. Manufacturers can now offer "flavored" ketchups and other variations on standardized foods so long as they are honest about what is going into the jar and the basic product remains as defined by the Code of Federal Regulations. What the Libby case shows is the zeal with which the federal government tried to enforce the new food laws. The feds were focused on fighting any semblance of economic adulteration.

What about health claims? Manufacturers have always been tempted to emphasize the health benefits of their products but the law recognizes that health claims can sometimes go too far. That was the issue when the government went after Manischewitz Diet Thins.[16] The FDA claimed that the use of the word "diet" on the packages of these wispy matzo crackers would lead the purchaser to believe that the crackers were lower in calories than "regular" matzo crackers. Indeed, they were not lower in calories.

Manischewitz countered that the term "diet" has more applications than "weight control." The crackers in question were made from enriched flour (wow!), thus they had more vitamin content than regular matzos, which were made with non-enriched flour. The caloric content of both crackers was the same.

Manischewitz also claimed that the FDA had previously approved the label in question years before. The FDA denied ever having approved the label. Furthermore, the allegedly approved label was on a package of "Diet Thins" that were thinner than the regular matzo crackers; at least they were lower in calories, although not on an ounce-for-ounce basis.

The court ruled that consumers would undoubtedly be led to believe that the "diet thin" matzos were lower in calories that the regular ones. It was not necessary to prove actual deception. The law requires a manufacturer to gear its message not to the "reasonable consumer" but to "the ignorant, the unthinking and the credulous" buyer. "Even a technically accurate description of a food or drug's content may violate [the law] if the description is misleading in other respects."[17]

"Purchasers of diet products are often pathetically eager to obtain a more slender figure," wrote the court. The government, including the courts, is looking out for us and is not above insulting us in the process. What about those who are "pathetically eager" to eat junk food?

Standards of identity remain a significant part of federal food law, defining several hundred common foods. For example, you may think you know what peanut butter is. "Ground up peanuts with a little oil," you might say. Here's how the United States government defines peanut butter:

21 C.F.R. SEC. 164.150 PEANUT BUTTER

(a) Peanut butter is the food prepared by grinding one of the shelled and roasted peanut ingredients provided for by paragraph (b) of this section, to which may be added safe and suitable seasoning and stabilizing ingredients provided for by paragraph (c) of this section, but such seasoning and stabilizing ingredients do not in the aggregate exceed 10 percent of the weight of the finished food. To the ground peanuts, cut or chopped, shelled, and roasted peanuts may be added. During processing, the oil content of the peanut ingredient may be adjusted by the addition or subtraction of peanut oil. The fat content of the finished food shall not exceed 55 percent when determined as prescribed in "Official Methods of Analysis of the Association of Official Analytical Chemists," 13th Ed. (1980), section 27.006(a) under "Crude Fat—Official First Action, Direct Method," in paragraph (a), which is incorporated by reference. Copies may be obtained from the Association of Official Analytical Chemists International, 481 North Frederick Ave., suite 500, Gaithersburg, MD 20877-2504, or may be examined at the Office of the Federal Register, 800 North Capitol Street, NW, suite 700, Washington, DC.

(b) The peanut ingredients referred to in paragraph (a) of this section are:

(1) Blanched peanuts, in which the germ may or may not be included.

(2) Unblanched peanuts, including the skins and germ.

(c) The seasoning and stabilizing ingredients referred to in paragraph (a) of this section are suitable substances which are not food additives as defined in section 201(s) of the Federal Food, Drug, and Cosmetic Act (the act), or if they are food additives as so defined, they are used in conformity with regulations established pursuant to section 409 of the act. Seasoning and stabilizing ingredients that perform a useful function are regarded as suitable, except that artificial flavorings, artificial sweeteners, chemical preservatives, and color additives are not suitable ingredients in peanut butter. Oil products used as optional stabilizing ingredients shall be hydrogenated vegetable oils. For the purposes of this section, hydrogenated vegetable oil shall be considered to include partially hydrogenated vegetable oil.

(d) If peanut butter is prepared from unblanched peanuts as specified in paragraph (b)(2) of this section, the name shall show that fact by some such statement as "prepared from unblanched peanuts (skins left on)." Such statement shall appear prominently and conspicuously and shall be in type of the same style and not less than half of the point size of that used for the words "peanut butter." This statement shall immediately precede or follow the words "peanut butter," without intervening written, printed, or graphic matter.

(e) Label declaration. Each of the ingredients used in the food shall be declared on the label as required by the applicable sections of parts 101 and 130 of this chapter.[18]

It should be now obvious that in the world of food the power to define is the power to control. These "laws" that define hundreds of food items are not laws debated by our legislators on the floor of the House of Representatives and the Senate. They are "administrative rules," established by government agencies under authority granted by Congress. Yet, these administrative rules have the same force and effect as any direct congressional enactment. The process of making these rules is an area of law about which most people have not a clue. It is called "administrative law" and those who want to affect the law of food must know it as well as the more publicized and glamorous fields of tort law, criminal law, constitutional law, and other laws traditionally found in courtrooms. Administrative law is where food law happens.

That does not mean that the field of administrative law and the process by which rules are made never get to the courthouse. It means that by the time the matter does get to the courthouse, the rules have been made, the engine has already been put in motion, and the proverbial train may have already left the station. Citizens and citizen groups can affect the rule-making procedure but only if they know the "rules" for doing so. Once the rules are made by the FDA or USDA or FTC, it is not easy to undo them. In baseball, the "tie goes to the runner." In law, courts generally defer to the judgment of government agencies—especially when the courts believe these agencies have a particular kind of expertise.

New acts and amendments to the 1938 law gave the government even more power over food. The 1950s brought the Pesticides Amendment, which outlined procedures for determining acceptable levels of pesticide residues on raw agricultural products. The Food Additives Amendment finally required producers of food additives to establish the safety of their products. The famous "Delaney Clause" prohibited adding to food any substance that had been found to cause cancer in laboratory animals or in humans, in any concentration.

In 1959, shortly before Thanksgiving, the FDA used the Delaney Clause to issue a warning not to buy cranberries grown in two states because they had been contaminated (allegedly) with aminothiazole, a weed killer, which had been associated with thyroid cancer in rats. Almost the entire United States cranberry crop was wasted and the government had to bail out cranberry growers with emergency loans. It was later discovered that a human being would have to eat fifteen thousand pounds of cranberries for many days in order to suffer any ill effects of the pesticide residue.[19] The Delaney Clause, intended to be a "zero-tolerance" standard, was weakened as the years passed.

The government remained active in policing the supermarket aisles. In 1991, the FDA seized two thousand cases of Citrus Hill Fresh Choice orange juice because it wasn't fresh-squeezed orange juice.[20] (Maybe there is hope that someone will go after those makers of "homemade" ice cream.) How many times have you been scammed by a restaurant claiming to serve "fresh" orange juice when it wasn't?

Food labeling took a dramatic turn in the 1990s, from passive protectionism to active consumerism. It would no longer be enough for food labels to be honest, they now had to be informative. Nutritional labeling would have been unthinkable to those who championed the original 1906 act; after all, it had nothing to do with misbranding or adulteration. Labeling a product to disclose the nutritional value of its contents was as radically proactive a concept as has ever taken place in food regulation. Did the government have the power to require manufacturers to put such information on product labels?

The precursor to nutrition labeling was the Fair Packaging and Labeling Act of 1966. The purpose was again to prevent deceptive and unfair business practices by requiring honest and informative labeling. Now the law defined the elements of a label. The table was set for radical legislation.

We are all familiar with the Nutrition Facts statements that now appear on almost all of our package foods but they are a relatively recent phenomenon. The Nutrition Labeling and Education Act (NLEA) became law in 1990. It clarified and strengthened the FDA's legal authority to require nutritional labeling. If the FDA had required nutritional labeling in the absence of the NLEA, it might have prevailed but the litigation expense would have been enormous as the food industry would have challenged its authority to do so. The NLEA removed any doubts as to what Congress wanted. Now it was time to not only require the nutritional content of familiar foods to be carefully and precisely listed, but terms such as "light" or "lite" would take on specific meanings.

Passage of the NLEA did not mean that litigation was averted, only that a different kind of lawsuit would be filed. The litigation that has sprouted from the NLEA has been both spirited and creative as consumer groups have tried to expand food labeling contents while manufacturers have tried to narrow its coverage or, at the very least, to maintain the status quo.

An example of early NLEA litigation was a suit filed by a consumer group to challenge the final regulations concerning nutritional labeling of raw fish and produce. The NLEA established voluntary guidelines under which retail stores would provide consumers with nutritional information regarding raw produce and fish. If the FDA would find that retail stores in general are not in "substantial compliance" with the guidelines, then the FDA would have to establish mandatory food labeling regulations. The Center for Science in the Public Interest challenged the FDA's definition of "substantial compliance" as being so low as to be meaningless. The challenge "failed"[21] in a technical sense, but the case was typical of the galvanizing efforts of food activists who see the courtroom as but one battleground for a greater struggle.

Another attempt to expand nutrition labeling came in the case of *Public Citizen et al. v. Shalala*[22] in which two public interest groups challenged the decision of the FDA to exempt restaurant menus from the NLEA requirements governing both nutrient content claims and health claims. The plaintiffs here convinced the court that the government was not playing by the rules in exempting restaurant menus from the nutrient content and health claim provisions of the NLEA.

The issue is now information. Consumers want more information about the foods they eat. Or do they? While it may seem self-evident that too much information can never hurt you, manufacturers sometimes see it otherwise. For example, do hot dog eaters really want to know about tiny bone fragments in their hot dogs?

Consider the lowly hot dog. As the Kansas Supreme Court described it, "[T]he term 'hot dog' is used to describe some form of meat often found in the center of sandwiches which are designed to be edible, even if of doubtful digestibility."[23] Then again we have the contrary view of the North Carolina Supreme Court, opining that "[t]o a great many people it is a palatable and appetizing article of food."[24] A more recent case tells us more about hot dogs than we care to know.

The issue was labeling requirements for hot dogs, promulgated by the secretary of agriculture and challenged by consumer groups on the grounds that the new labels permit the sale of misbranded and adulterated food.[25] The opinion of the U.S. Court of Appeals was penned by Judge Antonin Scalia, only a few years before he ascended to the U.S. Supreme Court. It is vintage Scalia, beginning with his puckish introduction:

> This case, involving legal requirements for the content and labeling of meat products such as frankfurters, affords a rare opportunity to explore simultaneously both parts of Bismarck's aphorism that "No man should see how laws or sausages are made."

Judge Scalia has treated the world to a short course on the industrial process known as hot dog manufacturing. In the old days, butchers would cut the meat from the carcass by hand and then grind it up with spices, etc., into the sausage known as hot dogs and frankfurters. Hand deboning wastes a lot of meat. In the 1960s, the Japanese developed a mechanical deboning process that relies on sieves to separate bone pieces from meat. The United States then developed the technology for domestic meat processing. After removing most of the meat by hand, the rest of the carcass is crushed into a fine paste and a fine sieve is used to recapture most of the bone. Most, but not all.

The resulting product is known as "mechanically separated beef" or "mechanically separated pork." Whatever the meat, it is "mechanically separated" something. The USDA wanted to let the beef industry use this economical process without requiring any special labeling. This meant that consumers would have no way of knowing that their hot dogs might contain up to 3 percent bone particles. Would you know the difference? Not according to the taste panel commissioned by the government to eat a lot of hot dogs, with and without bone particles. "There's no difference," the panel proclaimed. Another panel of experts found that the bone particles presented no health or safety concerns.

The players gathered to fight it out. Industry groups wanted nothing about bone particles on the labels while consumer groups wanted full disclosure. The USDA, displaying the wisdom of Solomon about to split the child in half (first by hand then by mechanical means), came up with a solution. The new regulations modified the label requirements to change the term "mechanically processed" to "mechanically separated." The new rules also replaced "powdered bone content" with a more generic calcium content.

The consumer groups wanted full disclosure and the industry groups wanted to mask the presence of bone particles as much as possible. The industry groups persuaded the USDA to see it their way and the court could find no legal reason for overturning the government's choice of rules for labeling.

The consumer groups tried valiantly to convince the court that frankfurters made with mechanically separated meat are either misbranded or adulterated. The court was not buying. The normal composition of hot dogs includes a significant proportion of ingredients other than meat; so what's the big deal if some of these other ingredients happen to be bone particles?

Judge Scalia did not avoid the important issue: do consumers have the right to know everything about what is in the foods they eat? Not necessarily, he ruled. That is up to the government—in this case, the secretary of agriculture—who is empowered to "decide what consumers *should* want to be prominently informed of."[26] Is this not paternalism? Absolutely, wrote Judge Scalia. Therefore, there was no law to require the prominent labeling of frankfurters with information about bone particles, just as there was no law that required a label to list "esophagus" in the statement of ingredients. (Hot dogs can contain ground esophagus.) Judge Scalia continued:

The fastidious reader will be comforted to know, however, that snouts and ears cannot be included unless the product contains the phrase "with variety meats" or "with by-products."[27] Not so, of course, with liver sausage (liverwurst) where one takes his chances.[28]

Tube steak, anyone?

I hope the bone particles in the hot dog case strike a familiar chord with you. It should. The case is not important because it allows bone chips in hot dogs without prominent labeling. It is important because it demonstrates the raw political nature of food labeling. If the secretary of agriculture had decided to require prominent labeling and full disclosure of bone particles in hot dogs, Judge Scalia would have upheld his right to do so. But that is not what the secretary chose to do because the industry lobbyists were more, shall we say, "persuasive" than the consumer groups. It is not about the law; it is about power. Power will dictate what the law is. The courts will enforce the results of the power struggle. In the meantime, we have lots to read on our food labels. We read and we read and we read. How much do we understand?

By the way, what did I eat at the beginning of this chapter? I ate a Hostess Cupcake. Are you jealous or what?

FOOD FIGHT

A Tale of Two Pizzas

Better Ingredients, Better Pizza!
—*Papa John's advertising claim*

In 1979, I went to Italy in search of the perfect pizza. I met Vincenzo, who sold watches out of the back of his car. But he knew where to get the best pizza, or so he claimed. We drove to what seemed to me a desolate area, far from civilization. When Vincenzo's car screeched to a stop in front of a dimly lit rustic wooden building, I wondered: was this all a ruse? Was I being kidnapped, and would I ever see my loved ones again? Vincenzo spoke no English and my Italian was limited to *non sparate!* (don't shoot!) and *dov'è il gabinetto?* (where is the bathroom?). I prayed that this would be the scene of wonderful pizza and not the bloody murder of a naive American. I smiled and nervously asked, "Pizza? Pizza?"

"Si, pizza!"

It was extraordinary pizza, crafted by a big burly man who sang opera as he tended to his dough. The crust was dotted with blackened ash from the carefully selected wood that fired the oven that night. The fresh tomatoes (not sauce) created a welcome bed for the richest mozzarella I had ever tasted. The melted cheese had formed its own sensual crust, and the gentle douse of olive oil and fresh herbs created a passionate expression of the soul of Italy.

So much for my great pizza memory. The subject of this chapter is a lawsuit between two giant American pizza corporations, Pizza Hut and Papa John's, that arose because one thought the other didn't play fair in its advertising campaign.

Lest you forget, pizza is big business in the United States. Pizza chains dot the American landscape like an outbreak of the measles. Frozen pizzas are in every supermarket and every convenience store, without exception (I beg you: prove me wrong). It is, by some estimates, a $32 billion-a-year industry and Americans devour 350 slices every second.[1]

By the end of 1999, the biggest pizza chain in the United States was Pizza Hut, claiming more than seven thousand outlets, and a 22 percent share of the total market.[2] That's a lot of pizza but not as much, as a percentage of market share, as it once was. Although the Domino's chain was second in market share, the great pizza war of the late 1990s was between the front-runner Pizza Hut and an upstart fifth-place company called Papa John's. It got so nasty that it ended up in court.

The Pizza Hut/Papa John's skirmish landed on the steps of the federal courthouse when Pizza Hut found itself on the receiving end of a no-holds-barred Papa John's ad campaign. It was a not-so-gentle reminder that even advertising has its limits.

There were several aspects to Papa John's advertising campaign that Pizza Hut found objectionable. First, there was the matter of the sauce. Although tomato sauce is not a necessary ingredient to pizza— the authoritative Italian cook Marcella Hazan calls for ripe plum tomatoes or, if they are not available, canned Italian tomatoes that have been drained and scalded with a little olive oil and salt[3]—the major pizza chains all use tomato sauce.

According to Judge William Sanderson, Papa John's has always gotten its sauce from one supplier, Stanislaus Products. Stanislaus used what the court called the "fresh pack" method to process vine-ripened California tomatoes into the pizza sauce for Papa John's. The tomatoes are cooked, seasoned with oil and spices, and then canned. The cans go out to the many Papa John's pizzerias where they are ultimately opened and, with minimal additional doctoring, get spread on the pizzas. That's how Papa John's makes pizza sauce.

Pizza Hut does it differently. From the evidence presented, the court described the Pizza Hut method as "multi step processing." First, vine-ripened tomatoes are reduced to what is called "remanufactured tomato paste" or "sauce on demand." This tomato paste is, as you would expect, quite viscous and thick because a lot of water has been removed. No seasoning goes on at this stage; it is stored in bulk form for the next step.

Various third-party vendors, such as Hunt-Wesson, take the tomato paste base and process it further, according to Pizza Hut's exact specifications, by adding water, oil, and spices to create a "tomato sauce concentrate." It is then packed and shipped to Pizza Hut distribution centers for delivery to the individual Pizza Hut restaurants. Before going on the pizzas, the "tomato sauce concentrate" is thinned out with water to come up with the desired consistency for the pizza sauce.

Are these methods different? Decidedly so. Do they yield different sauces? That depends on who is tasting. Pizza Hut presented evidence of scientific tasting results and the jury found (and the judge accepted their finding) that the end result was the same. If you think that this must have been a fun case for a juror, tasting different pizzas, think again. No juror ever tasted a single slice of pizza. Here is what Judge Sanderson found:

> At the time they are placed on uncooked pizzas, the consistency and water content of the tomato sauces used by the parties in their pizza products are essentially identical. Although different processing methods are used by each from the time the fresh tomatoes are cooked until the tomato sauce is applied to a pizza, there is no discernable measurable difference between the tomato sauces used by Papa John's and Pizza Hut.[4]

The problem for Papa John's was that it had developed an ad campaign that denigrated the Pizza Hut method of making sauce. Ads, both print and television, showed water being unceremoniously added to globs of tomato paste with the announcer saying that was how the big pizza chains make their sauce; one ad showed an unappetizing glob of tomato paste being doused with water from a faucet. In juxtaposition, the ads showed Papa John's pizza sauce in a kettle.

Unfair? You bet, at least in the court's eyes. Papa John's would have to stop its commercials vilifying Pizza Hut's sauce. What was the legal basis for the court's power? After all, do not the principles of free speech allow restaurants to suggest to consumers which sauce is better? Besides, there appears to have been at least a factual basis for Papa John's claims. Pizza Hut takes fresh tomatoes and makes them into a paste that is later reconstituted with water. Where is the harm?

The legal basis of Pizza Hut's complaint was the same statute that protects trademarks and trade names, the Lanham Act:

> Any person who ... in commercial advertising or promotion, misrepresents the nature, characteristics, quality, or geographic origin of his or another person's goods, services, or commercial activities, shall be liable in a civil action by any person who believes that he or she is likely to be damaged by such act.[5]

Judge Sanderson explained:

> Without any scientific support or properly conducted taste preference test, by the written and/or oral negative connotations conveyed that pizza made from tomato paste concentrate is inferior to the "fresh pack" method used by Papa John's, its sauce advertisements convey an impression which is misleading and which is likely to mislead a substantial number of ordinarily prudent consumers into believing that Papa John's tomato sauce is superior to that of Pizza Hut's and of other major pizza chains. Papa John's sauce commercials are also false to the extent that they portray congealed tomato paste—in a can or free-standing—as the ultimate ingredient of other pizza chains' tomato sauce....
>
> The Lanham Act does not prohibit a seller from fairly and truthfully expounding upon the characteristics and properties of its own products in its promotional advertising. However, when a seller chooses to engage in advertising that compares its products to products of its competitors, it is unlawful to make false comparisons and to engage in advertising that misleads ordinarily prudent consumers into believing unfounded claims of superiority.[6]

Can't a pizza maker claim that its sauce is better than the competition's? When the obvious reference to "the competition" is a particular competitor (as it was here, sometimes explicitly but sometimes implicitly), the law, according to the district court, requires more than the pizza maker's personal belief that its sauce is "better."

We all know that sauce is only part of the story. (Some pizza purists would argue that it does not even belong on a pizza, but we will assume here that sauce is appropriate.) For many, the real test of a great pizza is the dough. What did Papa John's claim about its dough and what did Pizza Hut do about it?

Just as pizza sauce is made in different ways, so is pizza dough—four different ways, according to the evidence. The Papa John's method is the "cold" or "slow fermentation" method. This is pretty basic, a variant of the way you or I might make pizza dough from scratch. Flour, yeast, and filtered water are combined and kneaded to make dough in individual pizza-size balls. After a first rising, the balls of dough are refrigerated; this stops the "proofing" so that the dough can last up to 6.5 days before having to be thrown away. The Papa John's dough is never frozen.

Pizza Hut uses three methods. The most common method is the frozen dough method. The pizza crusts are made using flour, yeast, and water and then frozen, to be defrosted and baked by the Pizza Hut restaurant for delivery to the consumer. Another Pizza Hut method is the "par-baking" method; crusts are partially baked and finished off when the pizza is prepared for the customer. The last method is the dry premix method; Pizza Hut prepares a dry mix of flour and yeast that is combined with water to make a dough at the restaurant. The dry mix does not last indefinitely because the yeast can die before it is used.

Papa John's ran advertisements that touted the fact that its dough was made with filtered water while "the biggest chain" used "whatever comes out of the tap." Another series of ads boasted of how its pizza dough was never frozen.

Pizza Hut was now on the defensive. It ran ads that claimed that Papa John's dough was trucked in from afar and could be as much as six days old. The ads further claimed that Pizza Hut dough was made fresh daily. Of course, the evidence showed that most of Pizza Hut's dough was of the frozen variety.

As to the "fresh versus frozen" issue, what would you rather eat, pizza made from "fresh" dough (even though it could be as much as six days old) or "frozen" dough? The evidence showed that most consumers believe that pizza crust made from "fresh" dough is better than pizza crust prepared from "frozen" dough. Similarly, most people would probably prefer pizza dough made with "pure filtered water" over dough made from ordinary tap water.

The problem was that the taste tests showed that both companies' pizza crusts were "qualitatively indistinguishable." A pox on both of their houses, ruled the court.

There is nothing quite like a taste test to convince consumers that a particular product is terrific. There is also nothing quite like a taste test to confuse consumers about the worth of a particular product. That was the third facet of the case that the jury considered. Papa John's ran ads claiming that in "independent taste tests," Papa John's "won, won big time."

The court found that these test results were misleading. Chalk up one for Pizza Hut. Pizza Hut also complained about Papa John's using a man named Frank Carney in its ads. Frank Carney was a cofounder of Pizza Hut but had since jumped ship to Papa John's (he apparently owns several Papa John's franchises). The court refused to bar Papa John from continuing to use Frank Carney in its ads but required Papa John to inform consumers in these ads that Mr. Carney had not been connected with Pizza Hut since 1980.

Perhaps the best ad campaign run by Papa John's was its catchy slogan, "better ingredients, better pizza." Who can argue with the logic of such a slogan? Besides, it was just a slogan and, at worst, "puffery," argued the lawyers for Papa John's. The problem is that, given the prior context of the misleading ad campaigns relative to the sauce and the dough, the court felt it had no choice but to enjoin Papa John's from using the slogan anymore.

The long and the short of the case was that Papa John's had to stop its "better ingredients, better pizza" campaign and was ordered to pay Pizza Hut $467,619.75. Pizza Hut had to stop some of its ads, too, and Papa John's was required to modify some of its other existing ads (like the Frank Carney ads).

Both sides put their respective spins on the outcome of the case on their web sites. According to Papa John's, the court's ruling was "unprecedented" and would "significantly change advertising" in the United States. A Papa John's spokesman hinted that it might use the court's decision to go after Pizza Hut's new slogan, "best pizzas under one roof."

Pizza Hut's web site basked in the glow of the court's decision with its spokesperson hailing it as "a landmark victory for consumers." If the jury's findings and the court's decision represented a landmark victory for consumers, then consumers got the short end of the pepperoni. No matter, because the "landmark victory" was short lived. On 19 September 2000, the Fifth Circuit Court of Appeals reversed the lower court's decision. In a phrase, Papa John's won, "big time."[7]

The appeals court took a commonsense look at Papa John's ad campaign and ruled that it was "puffery," and therefore could not form the basis for liability under the Lanham Act. Puffery means "exaggerated advertising, blustering and boasting upon which no reasonable buyer would rely." Another way of looking at "puffing" is to consider it as "a seller's privilege to lie his head off, so long as he says nothing specific, on the theory that no reasonable man would believe him, or that no reasonable man would be influenced by such talk."[8]

The slogan "better ingredients, better pizza" is typical puffery, held the appellate court. "What makes one food ingredient 'better' than another comparable ingredient, without further description, is wholly a matter of individual taste or preference not subject to scientific quantification."[9] When it comes to flavor, it's all a matter of taste.

But were not the sauce ads and dough ads misleading? If they were, did not the "better ingredients, better pizza" slogan take on new meaning with a quasi-scientific orientation? Maybe so, held the appeals court, but it did not matter because there was no evidence that consumers were influenced by the possibly misleading slogan. In short, the court of appeals ruled that Pizza Hut failed to prove that America's pizza eaters were so stupid as to be taken in by the Papa John's slogan.

The end result was a waste of judicial resources. Curiously, in the weeks following the court of appeals decision, no mention of it appeared on the Pizza Hut web site (where the district court's decision had been hailed only months before).

Comparative advertising lawsuits, in all aspects of consumer goods but especially in the area of food, are troubling because the public interest is rarely considered. Take a look at who participated in the

Pizza Hut lawsuit. Besides a hoard of lawyers representing Pizza Hut and Papa John's, there were lawyers representing the tomato sauce suppliers: Paradise Tomato Kitchens, Stanislaus Food Products, Morning Star Packing Company, and Hunt Wesson. The district court's decision lists twenty-four lawyers as representing the litigants and interested parties—enough for a full-blown full-contact football game and a wrestling match as the halftime show. Add to that roster of brilliant legal minds the names of those appellate specialists who briefed and argued the case and you have more than enough legal fees to buy pizza for many small-to-medium cities for a lifetime.

Who represented the public interest? No consumer groups, no food magazines, no culinary schools were involved in the case. The Pizza Hut/Papa John's fight was a fight between two giant (okay, one was more gigantic than the other) pizza industrialists and the outcome of the suit did nothing to protect the real pizza aficionado.

Sometimes the public interest tries to get heard in food advertising lawsuits. Therefore, we interrupt this chapter all about pizza to consider the baby-food case of Pamela Jean Tylka against Gerber Products.[10] In 1996, Pamela Jean Tylka, Toni Cainkar, H. Joshua Chaet, Cheryl Keller, Barbara Berg, and Jeanette De Leon filed a lawsuit on behalf of themselves and "other similarly situated consumers" against the Gerber Company, the giant baby-food maker. The plaintiffs filed suit in federal court alleging fraudulent advertising.

That lawsuit had a history that helps explain why the plaintiffs had to bring a civil suit instead of relying on the federal government to protect them. In 1995, the Center for Science in the Public Interest (CSPI) asked the FDA to take action against Gerber because Gerber was using various starches and sugars in its baby foods. The FDA refused to take action. CSPI then asked the FTC to go after Gerber but the FTC also declined to pursue the matter. That left everything to a group of citizen plaintiffs who would try to argue that Gerber's ad campaign had worked a massive fraud upon the American public.

The gist of the plaintiffs' claims was that Gerber had been misleading the public by claiming that its baby-food products are nutritionally equal or superior to competing brands, when many of the Gerber products are diluted with modified starch, sugar, and water. Of the 180 Gerber baby-food products, 61 contain added sugar, 42 contain modified food starch, and 32 have a combination of both.

The plaintiffs pointed to a number of phrases in various Gerber advertising campaigns to make their point, including these: "optimum nutrition," "nutritionally, you can't buy a better baby food than Gerber," and "pure and natural is the way we make our food." There were many more like these. The plaintiffs went after Gerber with a vengeance, claiming $2.41 million in damages to Illinois consumers and more than $45 million in damages to consumers nationwide.

Gerber did not dispute its use of added sugar and modified food starch in many of its products but argued that its advertising campaign was simple puffery, not unlike the "better ingredients, better pizza" campaign of Papa John's. But the Papa John's campaign was about taste, admittedly a totally subjective concept. The plaintiffs here were talking about "nutrition," a more precise and scientific concept. Not so fast, held the district court:

> Nutrition is a nebulous concept, although quantifiable in some respects. With respect to the use of the term in Gerber's advertisements, it cannot be said that the term reasonably misleads consumers.... Statements such as "optimum nutrition" or "nutritionally, you can't buy a better food than Gerber," or "the most wholesome nutritious safe foods you can buy anywhere in the world," add little to the daily informational barrage to which consumers are exposed. These statements fall within the supermarket sales pitch; they address such a large market that they bespeak caution, and should put the reasonable consumer on alert that the comments are meaningless sales patter.[11]

Legally speaking, then, the multi-million-dollar ad campaigns of Pizza Hut, Papa John's, Gerber, and countless other food manufacturers and purveyors are "meaningless sales patter." Why are they spending so much money on meaningless sales patter? They may be "meaningless" but they induce people to buy. That means that the best food advertising campaigns are both effective (in the marketplace) and meaningless (in the courtroom).

So much for the baby-food interruption. Let's return to pizza.

We conducted our own taste test. We tried plain cheese pizzas from both Pizza Hut and Papa John's. (We had them delivered and called the orders in so the deliveries would come at the same time, wondering if the two delivery vehicles would engage in further hostilities. Sadly, they did not.) We matched both of the pizzas against a pizza we made at home, from Italian tomatoes and the best mozzarella we could find. We baked the pizza on unglazed quarry tiles, to simulate as best we could the oven that Vincenzo showed me in 1979.

The results? In the words of the famous Papa John's ad, the home-made pizza "won, won big time." In the words of one taster, it was "pizza to die for." The delivered pizzas were, in her words, "pizza to die from."

There is a legitimate need to root out deceptive advertising in the marketplace. Deceptive advertising should mean advertising that truly does deceive the public. Effective advertising, powerful and hard-hitting, should stay in the arena of public consideration. Really, now—was there ever anything deceptive about the slogan "better ingredients, better pizza?" Consumers will make up their own minds as to which is the better pizza, regardless of the hype that the ad agencies try to create. But when courts are called upon to referee backyard brawls between neighborhood brats—make that *rich* neighborhood brats—can we count on any more than lip service to the public interest? The Gerber case is certainly more troubling; we have different expectations when it comes to nutrition claims than when we hear flavor claims. It only goes to show that the maxim caveat emptor—let the buyer beware—is still the rule of the grocery store.

I wonder: what would the pizza court have done—what would the litigants have done—if the Culinary Institute of America had asked to be recognized as a party to the lawsuit?

The courts will have to wrestle with the application of the Lanham Act, enacted to protect the public from confusion, to charges of unfair comparative advertising brought by companies that cannot stand the heat but would rather go to court than exit their kitchens. In the meantime, I can't wait to see books on the bestseller list vying for the number-one spot with a campaign like "better adverbs, better novels!"

As a final reward for getting through this chapter, here is how you make the world's *best* pizza (anyone want to sue me for making that claim?):

Pizza "2Die4"

The Dough
1 1/2 cups bread flour (hard wheat flour)
1 teaspoon kosher salt

1/2 package dry yeast
1/2 cup warm water (about 100 degrees)
1 tablespoon olive oil

1. Dissolve the yeast in the warm water and add the olive oil.
2. In a food processor bowl, add the flour and salt and begin mixing. Slowly add the yeast/olive oil combo. Process until the dough begins to take shape as a ball; you may need to add a small amount of flour or water if you weren't too careful measuring.
3. Remove the dough from the bowl and finish kneading the dough by hand for five minutes. If you do not have a food processor, you can do the dough by hand; form the flour into a mound and add the salt and water/yeast/olive oil mixture and work it into dough.
4. Lightly oil an earthenware bowl. Add the dough and cover with a wet towel. Let it rest for 3–4 hours.
5. Do not freeze the dough. Do not partially bake it. Do not attempt to make it into a dry premix concoction for later use. Do not send it off to a distant distribution center.

The Pizza
1 pound fresh ripe plum tomatoes or 11/2 cups chopped canned Italian tomatoes
1 tablespoon olive oil
1 teaspoon kosher salt
6 ounces whole milk mozzarella
2 tablespoons olive oil
1 teaspoon oregano
chopped fresh basil
1 tablespoon freshly grated parmesan cheese

1. About one hour before you plan to make the pizza, grate the mozzarella into a bowl and add two tablespoons of olive oil. Let rest for one hour.
2. Also one hour before baking the pizza, chop the tomatoes and discard as many of the seeds as you can without going crazy. Place the chopped tomatoes in a strainer to let excess water drain, about five minutes. Put a sauté pan on the

stove on medium heat. Add the tomatoes and one table-spoon olive oil. Cook, stirring frequently, for about five min-utes. Remove from the pan and put the tomatoes back in the strainer to drain some more. Let cool.

3. Line the oven with either a pizza stone or unglazed quarry tiles. One-half hour before baking the pizza, heat the oven to 475 degrees.

4. On a lightly floured surface, roll out the dough with a rolling pin. Be careful not to poke any holes in the dough. It should measure about eleven inches in diameter.

5. On a wooden paddle (or stiff piece of cardboard), spread about two tablespoons of cornmeal. Place the dough on the cornmeal-dusted paddle.

6. Working quickly, spread the tomatoes on the dough, then the mozzarella cheese. Sprinkle with oregano, basil, and parmesan.

7. Slide the pizza onto the hot stone or quarry tiles. Bake about fifteen minutes, or until it is golden brown and bubbly. (You can also make this on a grill, fired by real wood. Use the pizza stone or quarry tiles.) Serve immediately. Do *not* put into a cardboard box.

That is pizza.

JAVA JURISPRUDENCE

The morning cup of coffee has an exhilaration about it
which the cheering influence of the afternoon
or evening cup of tea cannot be expected to reproduce.
—*Oliver Wendell Holmes Sr.*

Can a cup of hot coffee ever be so hot that it's "illegal?"

Stella Liebeck never wanted to be a plaintiff. On 27 February 1992, she wanted only a cup of hot coffee. When she ordered her "McBreakfast" at an Alburquerque McDonald's drive-through, she had no place to put the coffee in her grandson's Ford Probe so she put it between her knees. She began to work the lid off so she could add cream and sugar when the scalding coffee spilled into her lap.

Stella screamed in agony. Her grandson rushed her to a hospital where she was treated for second- and third-degree burns to her thighs and surrounding tissue. She later underwent painful skin grafts. She also sued McDonald's, claiming that the giant fast-food chain was negligent in serving its coffee "too hot."

It was not the first time someone had sued McDonald's over its hot coffee. But this one gained national notoriety when the jury awarded Stella Liebeck $160,000 for both medical expenses and "pain and suffering" and then tacked on another $2.7 million in punitive damages.

The famous "McDonald's hot coffee case" created a stir. Congressional conservatives, pushing for so-called tort reform, seized upon the case as an example of runaway jury verdicts that cried out for massive changes to the entire legal system. Late-night comedians feasted on the case; after all, here was a woman who put a cup of hot coffee— between her legs! Coffee lovers worried that they might never again get a cup of good *hot* coffee.

Before scrutinizing the case of *Liebeck v. McDonald's,* before we come to judgment on whether it was indeed a case of the jury system gone wild, it is necessary to step back and consider what this kind of lawsuit means to our food supply. It is also essential to reflect on the conditions and history that made that jury award possible.

All the New Mexico food safety laws in effect at the time Stella Liebeck ordered her coffee did not prevent the horrible burns that brought her such pain and suffering. There was no indication that McDonald's had broken any law, violated any code, or breached any regulation. Unlike the old English magistrate who ordered the spice adulterator to the pillory where the tainted spices would be burned before his nose, no judge gave thought (or had the power) to sentence Ronald McDonald to any such fate. The only justice that could prevail would come in the form of a civil action: Stella would seek to recover money from McDonald's to compensate her for her injuries.

These civil lawsuits address the rock-bottom requirement of our food supply: food must do no harm. When it hurts us, we sue. If food does not nourish us as we expect or if it does not taste good, it is hard to conceive of a civil suit for monetary damages. Can you imagine: "Ladies and gentlemen of the jury, you should compensate my client to the tune of one million dollars because the beef Wellington that the defendant served him did not measure up to his high culinary standards and had more fat and cholesterol than is healthy for an adult of his size." We have not yet reached that point in litigation excess. Not yet.

People are injured by food in nearly every way imaginable. They break teeth on unexpected hard objects, they bite into glass or sharp artifacts, they choke on pieces of food, they swallow tiny things that were never meant to be swallowed, they react to myriad toxins, they get food poisoning from any number of causes. They may undergo severe emotional distress upon eating certain foods. They may even die.

Lawsuits to recover damages for bad food or drink are nothing new in Anglo-American jurisprudence. As early as 1431, a plaintiff successfully recovered damages for personal injury caused by bad wine. The defendant innkeeper tried to argue that the innkeeper never really claimed (warranted) that it was good wine. The English court dismissed the unruly innkeeper with a principle that would last for centuries:

> For if I came into a tavern to eat and the taverner gives and sells me beer or food which is corrupt, by which I am put to great suffering, I shall clearly have an action against the taverner on the case even though he makes no warranty to me.[1]

Unfortunately, we know not what damages the poor man recovered but we do know that the courts would be open to his plea and to others similarly harmed.

Our elected officials have passed various laws to regulate what and how various civil actions injured plaintiffs may bring. However, the law of civil liability in food injury cases is a complex tapestry of the many cases that have been decided over the last two hundred years. This is the essence of our "common law" tradition. The appellate courts of the states and, to a lesser degree, the federal government, have wrestled with issues of law and policy and have developed a patchwork quilt of jurisprudence that defines in broad (but not always consistent) terms the civil law of food injuries.

How does one begin to comprehend this body of law? In law school, students learn by what is known as "the case method." By reading the appellate decisions of the various courts, certain themes and principles appear and develop into a body of law. This approach to the law is almost impressionistic, as one learns the essence of the law through a discovery process that is not always logical or linear but rather reflects the struggles of an emerging awareness of conflict resolution within a certain context. Here, that context is food.

When it comes to the law, every era has its sense of outrage. The McDonald's hot coffee case made headlines because the public (or was it the media?) saw the jury's decision as excessive. However, at the beginning of the century, a different kind of outrage permeated the legal system. It was the doctrine of "privity" and it worked a terrible hardship on families injured by badly prepared food.

Tongue in Cheek: No Laughing Matter

In December 1901, in Miller County, Arkansas, the Lucien B. Nelson family bought a canned tongue from A. J. Offenhauser, a dealer in family groceries. Offenhauser did not can the tongue himself; he bought it by the case from the Armour Packing Company and resold it to his customers.

The Nelson family opened the canned tongue ("Select Cooked Tongue" as the label described it) and feasted on it for dinner. Lucien became gravely ill after eating the tongue and, in the words of his complaint, "was very sick nigh unto death." Fortunately, he endured the pain and eventually recovered. He sued the Armour Packing Company for a whopping $1,800, alleging that the tongue was negligently prepared.

Nelson never got to present his case to a jury. The trial judge threw it out because Nelson had no contractual relationship with the Armour Packing Company. The Arkansas Supreme Court agreed and Lucien Nelson, cast upon death's door by a badly prepared lunch tongue, was without a remedy. The court's "reasoning" reflected the doctrine of privity in all of its oppressive glory:

> In the sale of provisions by one dealer to another, in the course of general commercial transactions, the maxim "caveat emptor" applies, and there is no implied warranty or representation of quality or fitness; but, when articles of human food are sold to the consumer for immediate use, there is an implied warranty or representation that they are sound and fit for food. . . .
>
> Unlike covenants as to the title of land, a warranty upon the sale of personal property does not run with the property. There is no privity of contract between the vendor in one sale and the vendees of the same property in subsequent sales. Each vendee can resort, as a general rule, only to his immediate vendor. In this case, there was no privity of contract between appellant and appellee, and no warranty passed with the property from appellee to appellant through his vendor.[2]

Because Mr. Nelson had no direct formal dealings (i.e., no "contractual relationship,") with the people at Armour Packing Company, he could not sue them. The "privity doctrine" means that the manufacturer is not liable to the ultimate consumer for damages resulting from the defects and impurities of the manufactured article. It is an old orthodox legal doctrine that meant that sellers of goods warranted the fitness of their products only to the direct purchaser. It meant that any warranty as to the fitness of the product ran from the seller to the initial buyer and no one else. It made sense, or at least did no harm, when consumers bought products directly from the manufacturer. As the food industry grew and changed, privity seemed arbitrary and unjust—and it worked great hardships on many innocent people. Where was the outrage, the hue and cry, of the media?

Of Privity and Pies

Nearly thirty years later, William Lynch discovered for himself the stinging hardship of the doctrine of privity. He purchased a pie from a Mrs. Lowe, proprietor of a grocery store in Cottage Park, Virginia. Mrs. Lowe did not bake the pie herself; she was the "middle woman," having bought it wholesale from the Connecticut Pie Company.

Bill Lynch took the pie home and cut off a slice. He took a bite and found something hard, so hard that it broke one of his teeth. The hard object was a nail. He sued the Connecticut Pie Company, alleging that he had a right to rely on an implied promise (or warranty) that the pie was fit for human consumption. The presence of the nail was a breach of that warranty. At trial, the judge instructed the jury that Lynch was indeed entitled to rely on that warranty. The jury found in Lynch's favor. So far so good for the injured pie eater.

The Connecticut Pie Company appealed to the District of Columbia Court of Appeals and won because "a manufacturer of food is not liable to third persons under an implied warranty, because there is no privity of contract between them." If Lynch had argued negligence, he might have prevailed. But he chose a strategy and theory grounded in contract. "Since there was no contractual relation between the parties, the pie company was entitled to a directed verdict."[3]

Injured eaters could not rely on an implied promise that the food they were buying was wholesome, at least when they were not buying the food directly from the manufacturer. Injured consumers could conceivably allege negligence and, according to the language in the Connecticut Pie Company decision, might prevail on that theory but only if negligence could be proven. That was a more difficult burden because consumers had little information about the manufacturing processes and would find it onerous to present a persuasive case of negligence. But not always. Sometimes, the facts were so outrageous that the negligence seemed to cry out for itself.

Something to Chew On

Technically speaking, this is not even a food case because what our poor plaintiff ingested was not really food. It was chewing tobacco. Nevertheless, this 1918 Mississippi case, although hardly a milestone in American jurisprudence, is instructive, albeit one that is "hard to swallow."

When Mr. Pillars opened a package of his favorite Brown Mule Chewing Tobacco, he had no idea what lay ahead for him. The first "plug" was fine (as chewing tobacco plugs go). When he bit into the second plug, he sensed that something was not right. He began to feel ill. Bright fellow that he was, he took another chew. He grew sicker. With the next chew, he bit into something hard. Upon closer inspection, he discovered a human toe, with skin and nail intact. (We warned you this would not be pretty.)

The doctor diagnosed Mr. Pillars as suffering from "ptomaine" poisoning (no pun intended) and he eventually sued both the manufacturer (Reynolds Tobacco Company) and the distributor (Corr-Williams Tobacco Company). For reasons we may never know, he did not sue the retail store in Jackson, Mississippi, where he bought the tobacco.

The trial judge dismissed the case without giving Mr. Pillars a chance to present his evidence. Because Mr. Pillars had no contractual relationship with either the manufacturer or the distributor (his relationship was with the unsued retailer), he had no recourse. This was the doctrine of "privity" rearing its ugly head and the R.J. Reynolds Tobacco Company was more than happy to use it to full advantage in the trial court.

Luckily for Mr. Pillars, the Mississippi Supreme Court was "enlightened" and allowed him to sue the Reynolds Tobacco Company as long as he could show negligence. In the finest example of judicial understatement, the Mississippi high court suggested that negligence was likely:

> We can imagine no reason why, with ordinary care, human toes could not be left out of chewing tobacco, and if toes are found in chewing tobacco, it seems to us that somebody has been very careless.[4]

Very careless, indeed! Still, if the circumstances of the case had not been so grotesque, negligence would not have been so obvious and Reynolds Tobacco would have probably escaped liability by hiding behind the hoary doctrine of privity. The Mississippi high court did not overturn the privity doctrine; it found a way around it in a case that screamed for justice.

We are all familiar with the concept of negligence. It is the basis for many civil actions. We see it all too often in the context of automobile accident cases because the claim is that the defendant was careless, lax, inattentive, or *negligent*. These are also called tort actions; a tort is a "civil wrong" (not to be confused with a *torte*, which is a culinary delight). In negligence cases, if the defendant is at fault, the defendant loses. If it was not the defendant's fault, the plaintiff loses. Assessing liability on the basis of fault requires the jury to find that the defendant did something wrong or breached some duty owed to the plaintiff.

An alternative theory of liability is based on the general notion of a contract. Part of any contract is the warranty or promise. An "implied warranty of fitness" means that a consumer can rely on a manufacturer promising that its food product is safe and fit for human consumption. Even though the manufacturer has never made this promise in writing or in any other explicit fashion, the law implies such a promise with every purchase of food or drink. The doctrine of implied warranty does not require any showing of negligence. The problem was that many courts refused to extend any warranty, implied or otherwise, to anyone except the party that purchased the item directly from the manufacturer. That was the hardship that privity caused.

When the plaintiff pleads negligence, the defendant wins if it can convince the jury that its manufacturing process is reasonable and free of negligence. It doesn't matter how serious the plaintiff's injuries may have been. The outcome of the case depends on proving carelessness on the part of the defendant. Because that can be difficult for plaintiffs to prove—after all, plaintiffs rarely have complete knowledge of or access to the defendant's operations—the courts have come up with doctrines that make it easier to prove negligence.

Life Is Like a Box of Defective Chocolates

In 1938, George Bagre won a box of chocolates in a bingo game. A few days later he treated himself to one of the candies and—crack!—he bit into something very hard. It was so hard that it ruined one of his teeth, requiring a trip to the dentist and an extraction. What was the offending object? It was a silver filling. Whose was it? Because George never had a filling in his life, we know it wasn't George's. George sued the Daggett Chocolate Company for negligence.

The company put on a great case. Its lawyers elicited evidence of how Daggett used the most modern machinery, provided for repeated inspections, and utilized a host of precautions to ensure that foreign objects could not possibly find their way into the chocolates. Nevertheless, the jury found negligence.

On appeal, the Connecticut Supreme Court let the verdict stand. It was a classic case of the doctrine of *res ipsa loquitor,* Latin for "the thing speaks for itself." What a terrific doctrine for plaintiffs! It means that a jury is allowed to find negligence when the only rational explanation is negligence. Just as in the human toe case, injuries like those suffered by George Bagre do not happen in the absence of someone's negligence. Even when defendants amass mountains of evidence of how careful they were, juries can still find negligence when it appears to them that negligence is the only reasonable explanation.

The Daggett Chocolate Company tried one more tack: because Mr. Bagre won the chocolates in an illegal bingo game, he should not be allowed to collect damages. The court was not moved; in the absence of any causal relation between the illegal act and the injury, the verdict would stand.[5]

During the 1930s, food manufacturers who found themselves as defendants in tort actions routinely argued lack of privity as a defense. The appellate courts sensed the grave injustice that privity worked on unwary consumers and gradually did away with privity as a defense, at least in cases of food and beverage. The food industry was changing, as Americans were now purchasing foods made by unseen and unknown corporations. The courts changed the law to meet the realities of the new American food industry. A shining example of that change was the California Supreme Court's decision in what we call . . .

The Case of the Creepy-Crawly Sandwich

On 21 July 1936, Mr. and Mrs. Klein were motoring about the California countryside when Mrs. Klein sent her husband into the Happy Daze Buffet for a ham and cheese sandwich. Mr. Klein purchased the sandwich and gave it to his hungry wife. She took a bite and tasted something odd and unpleasant. She inspected the sandwich and found that it was crawling with worms.

Mrs. Klein vomited, became ill, and suffered severe emotional distress. She also sued.

The problem for the Kleins was that the Happy Daze Buffet did not prepare the sandwich. The restaurant bought sandwiches already assembled by the Duchess Sandwich Company. So the Kleins sued both Happy Daze and Duchess. Duchess had delivered the infested sandwich only one hour before Mr. Klein bought it; it was unlikely that Happy Daze had done anything wrong. If anyone were to blame, it had to be the sandwich maker. When it came time for trial, the judge threw out the case by directing a verdict in favor of both defendants. Even though Duchess was probably to blame, there was no privity between Duchess and Mrs. Klein.

The California Supreme Court had no problem deciding that there was more than enough evidence to prove a case of negligence on the part of the Duchess Sandwich Company. The court could have resolved the case solely on that basis but addressed the privity issue and ruled once and for all that privity would no longer be a bar to consumers injured by unwholesome food, at least in cases where the consumer has bought a sealed package or container that could only have been rendered unwholesome when it was within the exclusive control of the manufacturer.[6]

Today, defendants rarely argue privity as a viable defense. (In a 1968 Rhode Island case, a bakery unsuccessfully argued privity in a case involving a loaf of bread containing baked machinery grease that the plaintiff mistakenly believed was a clump of rat droppings.[7]) It has become well settled that there is an implied warranty of fitness and wholesomeness that goes with every food item we eat and that it runs all the way to the ultimate eater. Plaintiffs may still wish to argue both breach of implied warranty and negligence and often do. Courts routinely permit litigants to argue alternative theories of liability and let the jury make the appropriate findings.

The Case of the Too-Hard Roll

Some call them submarine sandwiches, others call them hero sandwiches, torpedoes, hoagies, wedges, or po'boys. In New England they are grinders, and Thomas Scanlon loved them. He ate one on 12 June 1962. What exactly did he eat? Judge Kosicki described it in mouthwatering terms:

> If we pay regard to the testimony and to the common knowledge respecting the subject, a grinder may tersely be described as a gustatory extravaganza of regal dimensions and savor. It consists of an elongated roll or small loaf, either hard-crusted or soft, slit longitudinally and filled with an imaginative assortment of meats, condiments and vegetables. By an edible colloquialism, the word "grinder" is accepted as descriptive of the lacerated condition of the contents of the roll; it has no anthropomorphic meaning suggestive of the grinder's own violent tendencies toward an unwary consumer.[8]

Mr. Scanlon's first bite was memorable. He felt a sharp pain and discovered that he had broken a tooth and cut his gums. Two of his friends corroborated what Mr. Scanlon found: the grinder roll was as hard on the inside as it was on the outside. There was no dispute over the fact that the roll was stale and hard. The defendant (the maker of the grinder) countered with his plea that grinder rolls are supposed to be hard crusted and that the injury to Mr. Scanlon's tooth was due to his obviously weak teeth. Judge Kosicki addressed the issue of the proper hardness of grinder rolls:

> To the cognoscenti, scorning the pabulum of the soft roll, the hard roll would seem to be the only kind fit for and worthy of human consumption. No doubt it offers, among other things, to those endowed with hardy dental equipment, a welcome challenge to accomplish an ardent mastication; and thus it would seem to enhance the pleasure

of eating by imparting a sense of triumph in a task nobly done. The plaintiff, however, makes no pretense to being numbered among the elect. In effect he simply says that, whether stale or not, the grinder, as to him, was too hard for consumption; that he had the right reasonably to expect that what he bought was of the same kind and quality as the grinders he had been buying at the same place in times past; that he had placed his reliance on the defendant's skill or judgment; therefore, there was a breach of an implied warranty as to fitness for which the defendant is absolutely liable.[9]

The weak-teeth argument did not move the judge ("It took the plaintiff as it found him.") and the court entered judgment for the staggering sum of $200. Is that not an overwhelming example of the need for tort reform?

Granny, You Don't Want to Know!

On 3 September 1993, Dorothy Holloway took her granddaughter Nekisha to a Bob Evans restaurant for dinner. The waitress recommended the dinner special, a platter consisting of a chicken breast, stir-fry vegetables, wild rice, and Monterey Jack cheese. Dorothy ordered the special and Nekisha wisely chose a hamburger.

About halfway through dinner, Dorothy noticed that something had fallen off her fork. She then used her fork to push the object around on her plate and figure out what it was. Puzzled as to the object's identity, Dorothy asked Nekisha. "Granny, you don't want to know." Granny then realized that the mysterious object was a worm. She screamed, "There's a worm in my food!"

Nekisha paid for dinner as Granny went out to the car to "lose her dinner." Her physical problems continued for several weeks. She lost weight, missed work, and, understandably, suffered severe emotional distress. She sued, alleging both breach of contract and negligence, but never got to present her case to the jury. The trial judge granted summary judgment to the defendants Bob Evans (the restaurant) and Norpac Foods (supplier of the frozen vegetables, the apparent source of the worm). (Summary judgment is a legal procedure in which the court rules that there are no real issues of fact for a jury to decide.)

The case is important because the key issue on appeal was whether Dorothy Holloway's injuries should be compensated. Bob Evans argued that emotional distress is not a recoverable damage under a pure breach of contract theory. The Indiana Court of Appeals disagreed and ruled that you cannot go around grossing out grandmothers and get away with it.

The court accepted the defendant's argument that emotional distress by itself could not be compensated. Presumably, if Dorothy had noticed the worm when the waitress brought the dinner to the table but before putting a fork to it, she would not have had any case at all. Even if the sight of the worm on the plate intended for her had induced the same reaction, there would have been no "direct physical impact" and no lawsuit. Once she bit into the dish that contained the offending worm, her resulting physical and emotional distress would be covered. She did not have to present evidence that the food she consumed caused her to vomit or contributed to her physical illness in any way. All she had to do was show that she experienced a direct impact (eating some of the food that was in contact with the worm) and then suffered emotional trauma as a result of that impact.

The reasoning of the Indiana court is, of course, arbitrary but necessary. If Dorothy were not allowed to present her case to a jury, restaurants that do not bother to take every precaution to make sure that worms do not get into the food will have no incentive to implement the necessary procedures to safeguard against such unfortunate occurrences. While the Bob Evans restaurant may have exercised reasonable care in washing the vegetables and preparing the meal, the "modified impact rule" (as the court used the term) strikes a reasonable balance between the consumer's interests in getting wholesome food and the restaurant's interests in being free from frivolous lawsuits.

What if Granny had noticed the worm before she began to eat from the dish but still became so overcome by the very sight of it on the plate intended for her? She might well have reacted in the very same way, experiencing both physical and emotional trauma. Yet she would be without legal recourse and Bob Evans would have gotten away with serving a worm in its food. Unfair? Then again, what if several other patrons of the restaurant had rushed over to the table when Dorothy announced the presence of the worm? What if the patrons reacted with similar disgust and manifested both physical and emotional trauma?

Could they recover, too? Or would a court invoke some sort of perverse privity doctrine to restrict the damages only to the person who ordered the meal, even though she never touched it?[10]

The impact rule can produce strange results and leave some injured plaintiffs without recourse. Take the case of Marie Doyle, a Florida woman who opened a can of peas and discovered a large insect floating atop the surface of the contents. How gross! Marie jumped back in shock, fell over a chair, and suffered substantial physical injuries. She sued everyone, from the manufacturer to the grocer, alleging negligence, strict liability, and breach of warranty.

Although Marie's injuries were quite real, the Florida Supreme Court decided that her lawsuit must fail for the simple reason that she never ingested any of the peas. If she had put a spoon to the peas and taken one tiny taste before noticing the offending bug, she could have recovered. The defendants got off because Marie Doyle was attentive enough to inspect her peas before eating them. When the unhappy customer complains, "Waiter, there's a fly in my soup," the restaurant is in the clear so long as the unlucky diner has yet to put his spoon into the broth.[11]

The Tennessee Court of Appeals wrestled with the same issue in a graphic 1982 case.[12] During his lunch hour on a warm summer day in 1979, Carl Gentry opened a can of pork and beans. After a few bites he discovered a condom in the beans. He ran to the bathroom and vomited. But he never sought medical treatment, did not lose weight, did not miss any work as a result of the incident. He alleged a loss of appetite, a revulsion for pork and beans (an affliction which many people have even in the absence of any such revolting incidents), mental anguish, and embarrassment at the hands of his coworkers. You can imagine the names he was called.

The Tennessee court was satisfied that the plaintiff's nausea and vomiting constituted sufficient physical injury to sustain a jury verdict, even in the absence of expert medical testimony. Mr. Gentry got to keep his $2,500 jury award (hardly a "runaway jury verdict"). If he had discovered the condom before taking the first bite of the beans, recovery would not have been possible. The court quoted from a similar 1970 Maine case (a condom in a bottle of Coca-Cola):

> The foreign object was of such a loathsome nature it was reasonably foreseeable its presence would cause nausea and mental distress

upon being discovered in the place it was by a consumer *who was in the process of drinking from the bottle*. The mental distress was manifested by vomiting.[13]

How did these condoms find their way into the baked beans and Coca-Cola bottle? There was no "negligence" on the part of the manufacturers, at least in the usual sense of lack of care in the production process. Undoubtedly, some workers with either perverse senses of humor or anger at the employer put them there. The negligence was in having such workers on the assembly line. Whatever theory or factual context one chooses, recovery of damages was the only just option.

For the Love of Applesauce

It has become almost fashionable to poke fun at seemingly outrageous jury verdicts and court decisions, although upon closer scrutiny these cases may be more sensible than they first appear. That describes *Martel v. Duffy-Mott*,[14] a 1968 Michigan case that should strike a resonant cord with all food lovers.

Mrs. Martel served her two young sons some Mott's applesauce. After ten-year-old Gary took a few spoonfuls, he reported to his mother that it tasted "funny." Mom tasted and smelled the applesauce and agreed with her son's culinary report. She immediately called the poison control center and was advised to bring her boys—and the remaining applesauce—to the nearest hospital without delay.

Hospital staff examined the applesauce and decided that the most prudent course of action was to pump the boys' stomachs. The boys recovered from their ordeal quickly. They suffered no lasting ill effects from their bout with the "funny" tasting applesauce. Except for one thing: they refused to eat applesauce ever again. One boy testified: "I don't seem to trust it anymore." The other said, "I don't want to get my stomach pumped again."

The boys and their mother (as their guardian) sued, alleging both breach of implied warranty of merchantability and negligence. After putting their case to the jury, the trial court directed a verdict in the defendant's (Mott's) favor. On appeal, the Michigan Court of Appeals reversed and sent the case back for a full trial. There were two significant issues.

First, was there enough evidence to show that the applesauce was indeed deleterious or unfit? Mott's argued that in the absence of lab tests or expert testimony, it would be sheer conjecture for a jury to find anything wrong with the applesauce. The appellate court ruled that lay testimony that a food product tastes or smells bad can be sufficient for a jury to find that it is indeed unfit. Why didn't the hospital test the applesauce? Good question! It may be that on the night of the boys' ordeal, testing the applesauce in anticipation of a lawsuit was the furthest thing from everyone's minds. (What ever happened to the jar of applesauce? The record reveals that a Mott's representative cheerfully exchanged it for four new ones.)

What about the possibility that if recovery is allowed solely on the basis of a plaintiff's testimony that a manufacturer's food tasted bad or smelled bad, the floodgates will have been opened to countless spurious claims? "When that occurs, if it does, they can be closed." The court was confident that juries would be able to use their common sense is assessing the credibility of witnesses and somehow arrive at the truth.

The second issue concerned damages: should a jury be allowed to even consider putting a price tag on the boys' loss of enjoyment of applesauce? Yes!

It is a close question whether the plaintiffs should be permitted to recover as part of their consequential damages for past and future loss of enjoyment of applesauce. Applesauce is but one of a large variety of desserts, most of which other desserts can, no doubt, we take judicial notice, fill the gastronomical void created when plaintiffs lost their taste for applesauce. Plaintiffs do not claim permanent injury or loss of taste or appetite in general, or loss of ability to consume or enjoy a basic nutriment or variety of food substances. We could well draw a line—no recovery for loss of enjoyment of applesauce and put a label on it: the claimed damages are "remote," "uncertain," "conjectural," etc. But we decline to do so.

More and more of the food sold to the public comes in cans, frozen, prepared, and even precooked ready to eat. Whole meals can be bought all prepared, ready or almost ready to go on the table. We do not think it a sensible use of the time of the profession or of the bench to construct a body of law as to which foods are of such importance that loss of enjoyment is compensable and those which, as a matter of law, are not of that rank. We think it sounder to permit a plaintiff who can convince a jury that the food product he consumed was inedible and in consequence he no longer enjoys eating it, to recover damages, including damages for loss of enjoyment, if he can additionally convince the jury that a true loss was suffered and that it should add a dollar amount therefor. In some cases loss of enjoyment may be real and substantial, an injury not to be made light of.

We see no need to create rules of law in a narrow area that the good sense of the average jury can handle with greater dispatch and probably sounder results. If a recovery seems disproportionate, the corrective remedies for excessive verdicts are available.

A victory for food lovers everywhere!

Another applesauce case surfaced in 1995 when Steve Torba alleged that he hurt his lip on a plastic shard in a container of Santa Cruz Natural Organic Apple Apricot Sauce, manufactured by the Smucker Company. Mr. Torba could offer no explanation as to how the plastic shard got into the apple-apricot sauce and Smucker offered detailed evidence that showed that the plastic shard in question could not have come from its manufacturing process. Still, under the reasoning of the Michigan applesauce case, could not this still be a legitimate jury question?

There was one problem. Steve Torba was not a little boy who innocently lost his love for applesauce. No, Torba was an inmate in a federal prison who suggested that he would call as a corroborating witness another inmate, Ronald T. Williams. Judge Kathleen McDonald O'Malley did her homework and found that inmate Williams had a long and legendary history of filing frivolous lawsuits, including a product liability claim in which he alleged he was cut by a glass piece in yogurt resulting in paralysis of his lip. The similarity between Williams's yogurt complaint and Torba's applesauce complaint was, in the court's word, "compelling."[15]

Skeptics may view the case as evidence of discrimination against inmates but the more reasonable explanation is that Judge O'Malley was not a fool.

So where does this journey through the bizarre food cases of the last century lead? Where is the connection to Stella Liebeck and her cup of scalding-hot coffee? Did the case of the worm-infested sandwich, the case of the spoiled tongue, the case of the little boys whose love for applesauce evaporated in an instant, all foretell the jury's massive verdict in *Liebeck v. McDonald's?*

"Wait!" you may say, "the Stella Liebeck case is different." You are right; report directly to your nearest law school and enroll posthaste. It was a different kind of food injury case because the coffee that burned Stella was not poisonous, contained no foreign substances, and was prepared exactly the way McDonald's had been making it for years. On the morning that brought Stella her pain, suffering, and (eventually) sizeable monetary award, tens of thousands of people around the world were starting their day with the very same cup of steaming coffee, made fresh and hot, just the way McDonald's customers liked it. At least that was how McDonald's wanted everyone to see it.

At first blush, it seemed ridiculous. Not only did Stella receive exactly what she ordered—a cup of hot coffee—she was certainly to blame for foolishly putting the coffee between her legs. Besides, right on the coffee cup was an imprinted warning: "Caution: Contents Hot!"

Coffee drinkers feared that a "silly old woman" (Stella was seventy-nine) without the common sense to know that you don't put hot coffee between your legs when you are in a car would rob them of the simple pleasure of hot morning coffee.

The McDonald's hot coffee case made the news because it was the exception, not the rule. There have been hundreds of reported cases of customers injured by the accidental spilling of hot beverages. In the overwhelming majority of these cases, the defendant restaurant or food supplier, not the injured plaintiff, prevails.

Injured coffee drinkers have tried a variety of legal theories to press their claims. Some have argued that vendors have a duty to warn customers about the hot beverages; others claimed that a cup of hot coffee capable of causing burns is a defective or unreasonably dangerous product; still others have maintained that serving hot coffee constitutes negligence; and some have pushed for a rule requiring spill-proof lids. All have been valiant and creative efforts but few have prevailed.

How then did Stella Liebeck win her case? More important, does her victory signal a change in the way coffee will be served?

First, consider what got left off the sensational headlines. Despite the jury's verdict and award of $160,000 in compensatory damages and $2.7 million dollars in punitive damages, the trial judge reduced the total award to $640,000. McDonald's and the lawyers for Mrs. Liebeck then settled the case (rather than go through a lengthy appeal) for an undisclosed sum.

Despite the sobering touch of reality that set in after the verdict, we still must ask: how did Stella Liebeck's lawyers convince the jury to award her any damages? Stella never really wanted to sue McDonald's, at least at the beginning. Without any lawyers, she wrote to McDonald's and asked only for her out-of-pocket expenses and the lost wages of her daughter who had to stay home with her. Twenty thousand dollars—and an assurance that McDonald's would turn down the temperature of its coffee—would have staved off the lawsuit. McDonald's offered $800.

Stella Liebeck found a Texas lawyer who had previously obtained a sizeable settlement for another McDonald's "burn victim." The case survived McDonald's pretrial motions for dismissal and went to trial. Jurors who initially thought the lawsuit frivolous and a waste of their time were moved by photos of Liebeck's horrible injuries. An expert testified that coffee at 170 degrees could cause serious burns within four seconds of hitting the skin.

McDonald's fought back with its own experts. A safety consultant testified that 700 burn complaints out of 24 million cups over ten years was a good record. The jury was appalled, choosing to view each of the 700 burn cases as a serious matter. Nor was the jury swayed by the warning on the cup ("Caution: Contents Hot!").

McDonald's had one last shot, closing arguments. Its lawyer pinned the blame on Stella Liebeck for foolishly placing the cup of obviously hot coffee between her legs. The jury would have to decide whether society would further restrict what people really want—good hot coffee.

In the end, the jurors who initially felt insulted and inconvenienced by Stella Liebeck's "frivolous" lawsuit were now more outraged by the corporate giant's callous attitude toward its victims. One juror even pressed for damages totaling nearly $10 million dollars.

Even the trial judge, a self-described conservative, had no problems with the jury's verdict, although he did reduce the damage award. However, as legal doctrine, the case of *Liebeck v. McDonald's Restaurants* has no precedential value. It was a single jury's verdict that never made it to the appellate level. The body of case law (decisions of appellate courts across the country) suggests that Stella Liebeck would have likely lost if the appeal had gone forward.

According to industry experts, good coffee needs to be brewed at a temperature between 195 and 203 degrees Fahrenheit. It is possible to brew coffee at lower—and potentially safer—temperatures but it will probably not taste as good.

In a similar Virginia case, in which a customer purchased coffee at a drive-through eatery and spilled it when his car hit the dip in the road at the parking lot and street, the plaintiff argued that (1) the defendant restaurant impliedly warranted that the coffee sold was fit for consumption and that because of (*a*) its extreme heat and (*b*) an improperly attached lid, it was not as warranted; and (2) the defendant was negligent in failing to warn about the heat of the coffee and in improperly attaching the lid.

The trial court never let the case go to the jury. It granted "summary judgment" in the defendant's favor, meaning that there were no important factual issues for a jury to even consider. The court based its ruling on the fact that there was no evidence that the coffee was defective or that it violated any industry or government standards for heat.

"There is no evidence that either the heat of the coffee or the security of the coffee cup lid violated any applicable standard. Do other fast food restaurants serve coffee at a lower temperature, or with lids that will prevent spills even when passing over an obstruction in the road? Do customers expect cooler coffee, which may be less tasty, or cups which may be more secure, but harder to unfasten?"[16]

While there may be "no crying over spilt milk," there will continue to be rivers of tears when cups of coffee occasionally spill and burn. Considering the number of cups of coffee Americans drink each day (450 million, according to one authority[17]), spills and burns will be inevitable.

In ruling for the restaurants in the majority of cases, the courts have balanced the rights of individuals to be free from unwarranted harm in the beverages they innocently drink against society's interest in enjoying good coffee. So long as "good coffee" means "hot coffee," the courts will continue to find in favor of more flavorful coffee and against injured plaintiffs.

Now consider the case of Jack McMahon, who bought a cup of hot coffee from a mini mart at a Mobil station. He asked his wife Angela to remove the plastic lid while he drove. She decided to pour some of the coffee into a smaller cup to make it easier for her hubby. In the process, she flooded her lap with coffee and suffered painful second and third-degree burns. She sued both the manufacturers of the cup and the lid, claiming that the Styrofoam cup was poorly made or because the inordinately hot coffee weakened its structure. They settled with those defendants. But she also went after Bunn-O-Matic, the manufacturer of the coffee maker.

According to the McMahons, the temperatures at which the apparatus brews and serves the coffee (195 degrees during the brewing cycle and 179 degrees for holding in the carafe on the hot plate) were excessive. They had two theories of liability: (1) Bunn should have warned consumers about the severity of burns that hot coffee can produce; and (2) any coffee served at more than 140 degrees is unreasonably dangerous and therefore defective.

In the district court, the defendants prevailed. Then in the Seventh Circuit Court of Appeals, Judge Easterbrook wrote on behalf of the court, coffee lovers, and common sense.

Judge Easterbrook first wondered: why are these people suing the maker of the coffee pot and why isn't Bunn-O-Matic bringing that up. "If a restaurant fails to cook food properly and guest comes down with food poisoning, is the oven's manufacturer liable?"[18]

Judge Easterbrook was puzzled about going after Bunn but suggested a possible theory (one that the McMahons did not advance): vendors with a more-mobile trade and weaker cups must use machines that brew coffee at lower temperatures or require stronger cups.

As for the warnings—what kind of warnings? That the coffee was hot? That it can cause burns? Duh! The McMahons conceded that they knew these things.

Unusually hot? Judge Easterbrook refused to take judicial notice (a judicial ploy that permits courts to consider well-known facts without requiring them to be formally introduced into evidence) that 179 degrees is unusually hot for hot coffee and referred to other cases in which the evidence was that the industry-standard serving temp is between 175 and 185. According to the court, "most consumers prepare and consume hotter beverages at home." He even took Angela McMahon to task for her habits as a tea drinker—pouring boiling water over tea leaves.

Coffee served at 180 degrees by a roadside vendor, which doubtless expects that it will cool during the longer interval before consumption, does not seem to be so abnormal as to require a heads up warning.[19]

Judge Easterbrook then addressed the argument that Bunn should have provided a detailed warning about the severity of burns that hot liquids can cause—just not feasible. "Bunn can't deliver a medical education with each cup of coffee."[20]

Finally, is it negligent to serve coffee at 180 degrees when 140-degree coffee is safer? Although the plaintiff's expert testified that 140 degrees is the maximum temperature at which coffee should be served, Judge Easterbrook went on to lay out the good reasons for brewing coffee at temperatures near 200 degrees and serving it at around 170 degrees, not the least is the final flavor of the coffee and the satisfaction to the coffee drinker. He concluded:

It is easy to sympathize with Angelina McMahon, severely injured by a common household beverage—and, for all we can see, without fault on her part. Using the legal system to shift the costs of this injury to someone else may be attractive to the McMahons, but it would have bad consequences for coffee fanciers who like their beverage hot. First-party health and accident insurance deals with injuries of the kind Angelina suffered without the high costs of adjudication, and without potential side effects such as lukewarm coffee.[21]

The court did not know whether the McMahons carried such insurance but took the approach that the courts cannot make businesses like Bunn "insurers ... of the harms, even grievous ones, that are common to the human existence."[22]

Did Judge Easterbrook make America a better place for good coffee? Food lovers might applaud his bold pronouncements, but the trend of litigation in the face of food injuries will not go away so easily.

Although the Stella Liebeck case will fade into legal history as an interesting but insignificant bit of trivia, McDonald's lowered the holding temperature of its coffee by about ten degrees. It continues to brew its coffee at the same high temperatures but it will not be selling it to consumers as hot as it once did. For the coffee drinker who loves it scalding hot, for whatever reason, blame it on Stella.

BONES OF CONTENTION

Their monument sticks like a fishbone
in the city's throat.
—*Robert Traill Spence Lowell,* For the Union Dead

Aside from the famous McDonald's hot coffee cases, have there been any other "burning issues" in the area of food tort liability?

Pieces of glass, metal washers, worms, needles, and the like have all been found in food and, more often than not, they have provided the basis for successful lawsuits, whether under theories of negligence or breach of warranty. Those are the easy cases and we are hardly surprised to learn that plaintiffs come out on top. What about the tough cases, where the offending objects might not seem so outrageous?

Should a plaintiff be allowed to recover damages when she finds a chicken bone in a chicken pie, a fish bone in fish chowder, a piece of walnut shell in maple walnut ice cream, a piece of oyster shell in an oyster stew, or a cherry pit in a cherry pie?

American courts have struggled with these kinds of cases and have not always been uniform in resolving the underlying question: how do you deal with an object that harms people but seems to be "natural" to the dish or food that the plaintiff consumed?

All Mixed Up

The California Supreme Court is credited (or blamed!) for coming up with the "foreign/natural test" for determining liability.

On 17 December 1932, Harry Mix ordered a chicken pie at a southern California restaurant run by the Ingersoll Candy Company. He seemed to enjoy the dish until he swallowed a sharp piece of chicken bone. His injuries were not trivial and he sued to recover damages totaling $10,000. Harry alleged both negligence and breach of warranty. The trial court dismissed the case.

On appeal, the California Supreme Court had to deal with two significant issues. First, did the transaction between Harry and the restaurant even constitute a "sale of food" so that Harry could argue breach of warranty? If what transpired that day was not a "sale of goods" but only a "sale of services," then Harry Mix could not recover on a breach of warranty theory, only on a negligence theory. The second issue (to be reached only if the transaction was a "sale of goods") was whether the presence of the chicken bone in the pie breached any warranty that the dish was fit for human consumption.

The first issue (whether the restaurant sold food) may seem absurd and even trivial by today's standards but it presented a real barrier to Harry Mix. The courts of eight states and the federal courts adhered to the theory that restaurant keepers, like the innkeepers of old, merely furnish a service to their patrons when they provide meals to them. Food is just an incidental part of the meal.

The California Supreme Court reasoned that the "sale of services" argument did not comport with the modern-day realities of the food industry and could only work an unreasonable hardship on unwary consumers. After all, was there any real difference between the sale of food by a restaurant keeper and the sale of virtually the same food by a grocer? The first battle went to Harry Mix and he must have believed he would soon win the war.

The path was clear for Harry Mix to present his claim under a theory of implied warranty of fitness. He would maintain that when the restaurant served him the chicken pie, it warranted to him that it was reasonably fit for human consumption. He would argue that the presence of the dangerously sharp piece of chicken bone made the pie unfit, without having to show negligence on anyone's part.

The California Supreme Court began with the language of the statute imposing an implied warranty of fitness on the restaurant and keyed on the critical language: food must be "reasonably fit" for human consumption. In the court's view, that did not mean "perfect."

Thus, the court was able to distinguish the chicken bone from the nails, pieces of glass, wires, and noxious substances that rendered food totally unfit for human consumption. Such objects were far more than imperfections. They were definite defects.

Yet, Harry Mix's injuries were as severe as any he might have suffered if the offending object were a nail, a stone, or a piece of glass. Nevertheless, the California Supreme Court let the restaurant off the hook. Here is the court's analysis:

> It is not necessary to go so far as to hold that chicken pies usually contain chicken bones. It is sufficient if it may be said that as a matter of common knowledge chicken pies occasionally contain chicken bones. We have no hesitancy in so holding, and we are of the opinion that despite the fact that a chicken bone may occasionally be encountered in a chicken pie, such chicken pie, in the absence of some further defect, is reasonably fit for human consumption. Bones which are natural to the type of meat served cannot legitimately be called a foreign substance, and a consumer who eats meat dishes ought to anticipate and be on his guard against the presence of such bones. At least he cannot hold the restaurant keeper whose representation implied by law is that the meat dish is reasonably fit for human consumption, liable for any injury occurring as result of the presence of a chicken bone in such chicken pie.[1]

Thus was born the foreign/natural test for food injury cases. This judge-made law meant that juries could never even reach the question of liability when a person is injured by a bone that is natural to the dish the consumer has ordered. It would not matter how serious the injury was. Caveat diner!

The foreign/natural test was neat, tidy, and promoted judicial efficiency by keeping certain cases out the hands of juries who might otherwise be willing to award massive damages. On the one hand, it made some sense: how can we expect chefs to guarantee perfection? On the other hand, by imposing random hardships on unwary customers, would chefs have any incentive to do everything humanly possible to make sure unwanted bones do not find their way into pies, soups, and other culinary delights?

Courts across the country faced similar issues but had difficulty with the California foreign/natural test. The Wisconsin Supreme Court considered the topic in the case of . . .

The Chicken's Revenge

In 1957, Ed Bethia ordered a chicken sandwich at the Cape Cod Inn in Milwaukee, Wisconsin. Why there was a "Cape Cod Inn" in Wisconsin and why Mr. Bethia would order a chicken sandwich in a place we presume specialized in seafood we will never know. This was your standard 1950s kind of chicken sandwich: two or three pieces of sliced chicken meat and a layer of lettuce between two slices of bread, sliced diagonally and each half pinned with toothpicks.

The first bite was as Mr. Bethia expected—tender moist chicken. But the chicken bit back with the second bite. The unsuspecting diner felt a sharp pain in the back of his throat, caused by a sharp fragment of chicken bone, about one and one-half inches long and an eighth of an inch in diameter at its thickest point. The bone eventually made its way into Mr. Bethia's digestive system, causing severe laceration and infection. He needed surgery and then he sued. The trial court never let the case go to the jury but ruled in the restaurant's favor. Mr. Bethia appealed to the Wisconsin Supreme Court.

If this had been California, Mr. Bethia would probably have had no case against the restaurant because the chicken bone was obviously "natural" to the chicken sandwich.

Not so fast. The Wisconsin Supreme Court was not about to be swayed by the reasoning and logic of the California Supreme Court. The land of cheese and bratwursts would think for itself. But it faced the same preliminary hurdle that California had to clear: when a restaurant serves a meal, does it sell the food or does it render a service? This was important because if the transaction is a sale of food, there is an implied warranty that the food is reasonably fit for human consumption. If the meal is deemed to be a service, then the only liability the restaurant faces is for actual negligence.

Although it may seem self-evident that a restaurant does indeed sell the food rather than render a service, there was a line of cases, going back to old England, that held otherwise. The Wisconsin Supreme Court considered the matter and entered the twentieth century:

> This line of authority bases its decisions on the reasoning an innkeeper utters, rather than sells, the food, because food was generally combined with other services in the old, typical English inn, or the food was incidental to the service of preparing and serving it or title could not pass because the food was consumed in the process of delivery. These are old-fashioned concepts which do not fit modern-day practices. Food or meals may be sold in a restaurant or hotel not combined with any services such as lodging. The food furnished in a restaurant is paramount and the preparation and serving of it are incidental to the sale. Title under the sale theory passes when the food is put on the table, not piecemeal as it is consumed. The old boarding-house theory under which one could carry away as much of the food furnished as he could stuff in his stomach but could not put any in his pocket has no application to modern dining. Today if one takes home from a restaurant part of his steak for his dog, he could hardly be accused of larceny.[2]

(We wonder: what about those "all-you-can-eat" buffet places that do not allow patrons to take away food not consumed on the premises? Did my mother commit theft when she stuffed some of those cold shrimp into a plastic bag and then into her handbag at the bountiful salad bar at the Paxton Inn?)

Ed Bethia must have been nervous. He and his lawyers were familiar with the California *Mix v. Ingersoll Candy Co.* case and how it, too, gave the plaintiff the early advantage by holding that the sale of food in a restaurant is a sale of goods and not just a sale of service. Mr. Bethia knew that his case was factually similar to that of plaintiff Mix and knew that the Wisconsin Supreme Court could easily adopt the rule and reasoning of the California Supreme Court to deny him the opportunity to present his case to a jury.

The Wisconsin Supreme Court was not about to be swayed by California's cavalier approach to chicken bones. It recognized that four other courts had followed the *Mix* case but declined to follow its logic:

> This reasoning is fallacious because it assumes that all substances which are natural to the food in one stage or another of preparation

are, in fact, anticipated by the average consumer in the final product served. It does not logically follow that every product which contains some chicken must as a matter of law be expected to contain, occasionally or frequently, chicken bones or chicken-bone slivers because chicken bones are natural to chicken meat and both have a common origin. Categorizing a substance as foreign or natural may have some importance in determining the degree of negligence of the processor of food, but it is not determinative of what is unfit or harmful in fact for human consumption. A bone natural to the meat can cause as much harm as a foreign substance such as a pebble, piece of wire, or glass. All are indigestible and likely to cause injury. Naturalness of the substance to any ingredients in the food served is important only in determining whether the consumer may reasonably expect to find such substance in the particular type of dish or style of food served.[3]

Courts lined up on both sides of the issue; although, if you really are counting, the "reasonable-expectation" theory seemed to gather more credible support. Here are a few choice cases to brighten your day and make that next meal a more cautious one.

We begin with a cocktail, very dry. Mr. Philip Hochberg damaged a tooth when he bit into an olive pit embedded in an olive that was swimming in his martini at O'Donnell's Restaurant in the District of Columbia. Siding with the Wisconsin approach, the District of Columbia Court of Appeals reversed the trial court's decision to direct a verdict against Mr. Hochberg and let him have his day in court. Perhaps he could persuade a jury that he reasonably believed he could chew on that olive without worry of a lurking pit. At least he could try.[4]

The Supreme Court of Alabama wrestled with the issue in a 1983 case involving a precocious three-year-old lad named Rodney who ordered fish at Morrison's Cafeteria. Why any self-respecting three-year-old boy would ask for fish at a cafeteria where there were so many other fatty choices remains a mystery. Nevertheless, Rodney began to choke on a bone in his Spanish Mackerel and it had to removed by hospital personnel. Rodney's mother was furious because she could not get anyone to take her and little Rodney to the hospital and, adding insult to gagging, she was told at the checkout that she had to pay her bill before leaving.

A jury awarded Rodney and his mother the grand sum of $6,000.78 and the restaurant appealed. Morrison's tried to get the Alabama courts to adopt the foreign/natural rule and determine as a matter of law that a bone in a piece of fish does not breach any implied warranty that the food served is fit. The Alabama Supreme Court rejected the foreign/natural rule but held that even under the reasonable-expectation test, there was no way any jury could find for Rodney and his mother. The bone was one centimeter in length and the court was not about to let a jury award Rodney even a dime for his injury. The court went on:

> Courts cannot and must not ignore the common experience of life and allow rules to develop that would make sellers of food or other consumer goods insurers of the products they sell. As has been pointed out, "consumers do have rather high expectations as to the safety of the products which are offered for sale to them . . . [and] they have a rather low threshold for the frustration of these expectations." [citation omitted].[5]

One of the more colorful cases, both for its unusual subject matter and the elegance of its written opinion, is that of Yong Cha Hong who claimed that she bit into a worm while munching on a piece of fried chicken. She claimed great emotional and physical distress to the tune of $500,000. If it had been a worm, the plaintiff might well have been on her way to the half million dollars she sought. But it was not a worm. According to the experts, it was either a chicken aorta or a chicken trachea. The defendant restaurant moved for "summary judgment," trying to avoid the possibility of trial by getting the court to rule that there is no way any reasonable jury could find in the plaintiff's favor and tried to argue the foreign/natural rule.

This did not sit well with Judge Smalkin. Arguing that a chicken aorta or a chicken trachea is natural to fried chicken because it's from the same chicken is not the way to persuade a federal judge armed with the *Fanny Farmer Cookbook:*

> "The dream of the good life in America is embodied in the promise of 'a chicken in every pot.' Domestic and wild fowl have always been abundant and popular, and each wave of immigrants has brought along favorite dishes—such as paella and chicken cacciatori—which have soon become naturalized citizens."
>
> Indeed, as to fried chicken, *Fannie Farmer* lists recipes for three varieties of fried chicken alone—pan-fried, batter-fried, and Maryland

"A fly in your soup? Very good, sir! Will you be alleging breach of warranty, negligence, or strict liability?"

(Cartoon by Dennis Schmidt)

Fried chicken. As best this Judge could determine (and he is no culinary expert) the fast-food chicken served in Roy Rogers most resembles Fannie Farmer's batter-fried chicken. That is, it is covered with a thick, crusty (often highly spiced) batter, that usually conceals from inspection whatever lurks beneath. There is deposition testimony from the plaintiff establishing that she saw the offending item before she bit into it, having torn the wing asunder before eating it. A question of fact is raised as to just what she saw, or how carefully she might reasonably be expected to have examined what she saw before eating. It is common knowledge that chicken parts often harbor minor blood vessels. But this Judge, born and raised south of the Mason-Dixon line (where fried chicken has been around longer than in any other part of America), knows of no special heightened awareness chargeable to fried chicken eaters that ought to caution them to be on the alert for tracheas or aortas in the middle of their wings.

The plaintiff would have her day in court.[6]

The Nestlé company tried to convince the Illinois Supreme Court to adopt the foreign/natural test in a case brought by Elsie Jackson, who broke a tooth on a pecan shell in a Katydid candy. These delightful sweets contain pecans, so the foreign/natural distinction should have spelled certain victory for Nestlé. Unfortunately for the candy giant, the Illinois Supreme Court was not biting. In the new era of consumerism, the foreign/natural test, wrote the court, is an anachronism and goes back to the days of caveat emptor (let the buyer beware).

Nestlé tried to persuade the court to create some kind of exception for products that, in the present state of human knowledge, are incapable of being made safe for their intended and ordinary use. In effect, Nestlé argued that it was too difficult to remove all the shells from the pecans and its candy should get the same kind of treatment that the law gives to blood plasma, blood derivatives, corneas, and organs used for transplant. Sorry, wrote the court, Katydids are not in that league because they lack the "social utility" of those products that are sometimes exempt from strict liability.

Nestlé argued that consumers had an obligation to protect themselves by "thinking and chewing carefully." The court was not moved.

Although the majority opinion of the Illinois Supreme Court[7] favored the plaintiff, Elsie Jackson, Justice Heiple dissented with a stern prediction:

The effect of this decision will go far beyond the defendant Nestlé-Beich company, whose candy caused a broken tooth. It extends to all manufacturers and purveyors of food products including the neighborhood baker, the hot dog vendor, and the popcorn man. Watch out Orville Redenbacher!

The continued march toward strict and absolute liability for others (others meaning anyone not injured who has assets) and the absence of any responsibility by the injured for their own welfare takes yet another step with this majority ruling. Accordingly, I dissent.

Even California has backed off from its now infamous *Mix v. Ingersoll Candy Co.* decision. Sometime in the late 1980s, Jack Clark ordered a chicken enchilada at the Mexicali Rose Restaurant and sued when he was injured by a one-inch chicken bone in the dish. The foreign/natural test of *Mix* would seem to bar any chance at recovery, but the trial court refused to be bound by the decision. The court of appeal believed it had no choice but to follow *Mix* and ordered the case thrown out.

Judge Poché wrote a separate concurring opinion for the California Court of Appeal in which he recognized the futility of trying to distinguish a chicken bone in an enchilada (the case before him) from a chicken bone in a chicken pie (the *Mix* case). He concluded by writing that until and unless the California Supreme Court changed its mind on *Mix*, "I will explain to my luncheon companions why for sound legal reasons they should order a hamburger and pass up on the chicken enchilada."[8]

The California Supreme Court took the case to consider the continuing viability of the beleaguered *Mix* decision. The majority opinion defended *Mix* and its long and arduous history but ultimately modified it in a way that accepts the alternative reasonable-expectation theory without totally abandoning the rule of *Mix*. Justice Mosk, in a sharply worded dissent, would have been content to summarily overrule *Mix* and concede that it was a poor decision from the outset. It is a lengthy decision, worth reading if you have a few spare hours and have an insane wish to learn more than any human being needs to know about this topic.[9]

Does this seem pointless? What difference does it make which test the courts choose to apply as long as they get it right? The major difference is in how much faith you have in the jury system. The strongest point made in support of the foreign/natural test is that it promotes "judicial economy." That is legalese for "it lets judges instead of juries decide cases." The reasonable-expectation test gives more cases to the juries because reasonableness is ultimately a question of fact that only a jury can decide. Those who decry runaway verdicts should find comfort in the foreign/natural test; if you are comfortable with the jury system we have, the reasonable-expectation test is for you.

Before we leave this subject, there is one more case to consider. We will do more than consider it, we will read the entire decision because it is the greatest food decision ever written. Be careful not to try to classify it as a foreign/natural case versus a reasonable-expectation case. Although the plaintiff lost, it is a case that stands not for any specific legal principle but rather for the sanctity of good food. It is the case of ...

A Peculiarly New England Injury

The most "culinarily correct" court decision of all time is the case of *Webster v. Blue Ship Tea Room*,[10] decided in 1964 by the Massachusetts Supreme Court. Priscilla Webster ordered a bowl of fish chowder and became painfully aware of something caught in her throat. It was indeed a fish bone and she landed in the hospital.

Here is the text of the court's decision (complete with recipes), weighing the interests of the poor injured plaintiff, the quaint little restaurant, and the proud history of New England fish chowder. (A gentle warning is in order: do not think for one moment that all court decisions are this interesting or this well written. If you believe that law school is no more than luxuriating in this kind of wonderful prose, find a real lawyer and ask her about the many naps she took reading cases in preparation for those early morning lectures.)

> This is a case which by its nature evokes earnest study not only of the law but also of the culinary traditions of the Commonwealth which bear so heavily upon its outcome. It is an action to recover damages for personal injuries sustained by reason of a breach of implied warranty of food served by the defendant in its restaurant. An auditor, whose findings of fact were not to be final, found for the plaintiff. On

a retrial in the Superior Court before a judge and jury, in which the plaintiff testified, the jury returned a verdict for her. The defendant is here on exceptions to the refusal of the judge (1) to strike certain portions of the auditor's report, (2) to direct a verdict for the defendant, and (3) to allow the defendant's motion for the entry of a verdict in its favor under leave reserved.

The jury could have found the following facts: On Saturday, April 25, 1959, about 1 P.M., the plaintiff, accompanied by her sister and her aunt, entered the Blue Ship Tea Room operated by the defendant. The group was seated at a table and supplied with menus.

This restaurant, which the plaintiff characterized as "quaint," was located in Boston "on the third floor of an old building on T Wharf which overlooks the ocean."

The plaintiff, who had been born and brought up in New England (a fact of some consequence), ordered clam chowder and crabmeat salad. Within a few minutes she received tidings to the effect that "there was no more clam chowder," whereupon she ordered a cup of fish chowder. Presently, there was set before her "a small bowl of fish chowder." She had previously enjoyed a breakfast about 9 A.M. which had given her no difficulty. "The fish chowder contained haddock, potatoes, milk, water and seasoning. The chowder was milky in color and not clear. The haddock and potatoes were in chunks" (also a fact of consequence). "She agitated it a little with the spoon and observed that it was a fairly full bowl * * *. It was hot when she got it, but she did not tip it with her spoon because it was hot * * * but stirred it in an up and under motion. She denied that she did this because she was looking for something, but it was rather because she wanted an even distribution of fish and potatoes." "She started to eat it, alternating between the chowder and crackers which were on the table with * * * [some] rolls. She ate about 3 or 4 spoonfuls then stopped. She looked at the spoonfuls as she was eating. She saw equal parts of liquid, potato and fish as she spooned it into her mouth. She did not see anything unusual about it. After 3 or 4 spoonfuls she was aware that something had lodged in her throat because she couldn't swallow and couldn't clear her throat by gulping and she could feel it." This misadventure led to two esophagoscopies at the Massachusetts General Hospital, in the second of which, on April 27, 1959, a fish bone was found and removed. The sequence of events produced injury to the plaintiff which was not insubstantial.

We must decide whether a fish bone lurking in a fish chowder, about the ingredients of which there is no other complaint, constitutes a breach of implied warranty under applicable provisions of the Uniform Commercial Code [footnote omitted], the annotations to which are not helpful on this point. As the judge put it in his charge, "Was the fish chowder fit to be eaten and wholesome? * * * [N]obody is claiming that the fish itself wasn't wholesome. * * * But the bone of contention here—I don't mean that for a pun—but was this fish bone a foreign substance that made the fish chowder unwholesome or not fit to be eaten?"

The plaintiff has vigorously reminded us of the high standards imposed by this court where the sale of food is involved (see *Flynn v. First Natl. Stores Inc.*, 296 Mass. 521, 523, 6 N.E.2d 814) and has made reference to cases involving stones in beans (*Friend v. Childs Dining Hall Co.*, 231 Mass. 65, 120 N.E. 407, 5 A.L.R. 1100), trichinae in pork (*Holt v. Mann*, 294 Mass. 21, 22, 200 N.E. 403), and to certain other cases, here and elsewhere, serving to bolster her contention of breach of warranty.

The defendant asserts that here was a native New Englander eating fish chowder in a "quaint" Boston dining place where she had been before; that "[f]ish chowder, as it is served and enjoyed by New Englanders, is a hearty dish, originally designed to satisfy the appetites of our seamen and fishermen"; that "[t]his court knows well that we are not talking of some insipid broth as is customarily served to convalescents." We are asked to rule in such fashion that no chef is forced "to reduce the pieces of fish in the chowder to minuscule size in an effort to ascertain if they contained any pieces of bone." "In so ruling," we are told (in the defendant's brief), "the court will not only uphold its reputation for legal knowledge and acumen, but will, as loyal sons of Massachusetts, save our world-renowned fish chowder from degenerating into an insipid broth containing the mere essence of its former stature as a culinary masterpiece." Notwithstanding these passionate entreaties we are bound to examine with detachment the nature of fish chowder and what might happen to it under varying interpretations of the Uniform Commercial Code.

Chowder is an ancient dish preexisting even "the appetites of our seamen and fishermen." It was perhaps the common ancestor of the "more refined cream soups, purees, and bisques." Berolzheimer, *The American Woman's Cook Book* (Publisher's Guild Inc., New York, 1941)

p. 176. The word "chowder" comes from the French "chaudière," meaning a "cauldron" or "pot." "In the fishing villages of Brittany * * * 'faire la chaudière' means to supply a cauldron in which is cooked a mess of fish and biscuit with some savoury condiments, a hodge-podge contributed by the fishermen themselves, each of whom in return receives his share of the prepared dish. The Breton fishermen probably carried the custom to Newfoundland, long famous for its chowder, whence it has spread to Nova Scotia, New Brunswick, and New England." *A New English Dictionary* (MacMillan and Co., 1893) p. 386. Our literature over the years abounds in references not only to the delights of chowder but also to its manufacture. A namesake of the plaintiff, Daniel Webster, had a recipe for fish chowder which has survived into a number of modern cookbooks [The text of this footnote appears at the end of this paragraph.] and in which the removal of fish bones is not mentioned at all. One old time recipe recited in the *New English Dictionary* study defines chowder as "A dish made of fresh fish (esp. cod) or clams, stewed with slices of pork or bacon, onions, and biscuit. Cider and champagne are sometimes added." Hawthorne, in *The House of the Seven Gables* (Allyn and Bacon, Boston, 1957) p. 8, speaks of "[a] codfish of sixty pounds, caught in the bay, [which] had been dissolved into the rich liquid of a chowder." A chowder variant, cod "Muddle," was made in Plymouth in the 1890s by taking "a three or four pound codfish, head added. Season with salt and pepper and boil in just enough water to keep from burning. When cooked, add milk and piece of butter." [Foot-note omitted.] The recitation of these ancient formulae suffices to indicate that in the construction of chowders in these parts in other years, worries about fish bones played no role whatsoever. This broad outlook on chowders has persisted in more modern cookbooks. "The chowder of today is much the same as the old chowder * * *." *The American Woman's Cook Book, supra,* p. 176. The all embracing Fan-nie Farmer states in a portion of her recipe, fish chowder is made with a "fish skinned, but head and tail left on. Cut off head and tail and remove fish from backbone. Cut fish in 2-inch pieces and set aside. Put head, tail, and backbone broken in pieces, in stewpan; add 2 cups cold water and bring slowly to boiling point * * *." The liquor thus pro-duced from the bones is added to the balance of the chowder. Farmer, *The Boston Cooking School Cook Book* (Little Brown Co., 1937) p. 166.

[Footnote: "Take a cod of ten pounds, well cleaned, leaving on the skin. Cut into pieces one and a half pounds thick, preserving the head whole. Take one and a half pounds of clear, fat salt pork, cut in thin slices. Do the same with twelve potatoes. Take the largest pot you have. Fry out the pork first, then take out the pieces of pork, leaving in the drippings. Add to that three parts of water, a layer of fish, so as to cover the bottom of the pot; next a layer of potatoes, then two tablespoons of salt, 1 teaspoon of pepper, then the pork, another layer of fish, and the remainder of the potatoes. Fill the pot with water to cover the ingredients. Put over a good fire. Let the chowder boil twenty-five minutes. When this is done have a quart of boiling milk ready, and ten hard crackers split and dipped in cold water. Add milk and crackers. Let the whole boil five minutes. The chowder is then ready to be first-rate if you have followed the directions. An onion may be added if you like the flavor." "This chowder," he adds, "is suitable for a large fishing party." Wolcott, *The Yankee Cook Book* (Coward-McCann, Inc., New York City, 1939) p. 9.]

Thus, we consider a dish which for many long years, if well made, has been made generally as outlined above. It is not too much to say that a person sitting down in New England to consume a good New England fish chowder embarks on a gustatory adventure which may entail the removal of some fish bones from his bowl as he proceeds. We are not inclined to tamper with age old recipes by any amendment reflecting the plaintiff's view of the effect of the Uniform Commercial Code upon them. We are aware of the heavy body of case law involving foreign substances in food, but we sense a strong distinction between them and those relative to unwholesomeness of the food itself, e.g., tainted mackerel (*Smith v. Gerrish,* 256 Mass. 183, 152 N.E. 318), and a fish bone in a fish chowder. Certain Massachusetts cooks might cavil at the ingredients contained in the chowder in this case in that it lacked the heartening lift of salt pork. In any event, we consider that the joys of life in New England include the ready availability of fresh fish chowder. We should be prepared to cope with the hazards of fish bones, the occasional presence of which in chowders is, it seems to us, to be anticipated, and which, in the light of a hallowed tradition, do not impair their fitness or merchantability. While we are buoyed up in this conclusion by *Shapiro v. Hotel Statler Corp.,* 132 F.Supp. 891 (S.D. Cal.), in which the bone which afflicted the plaintiff appeared in "Hot Barquette of Seafood Mornay," we know that the United States District Court of Southern California, situated as are we upon a coast, might be expected to share our views. We are most impressed, however, by *Allen v. Grafton,* 170 Ohio St. 249, 164

N.E.2d 167, where in Ohio, the Midwest, in a case where the plaintiff was injured by a piece of oyster shell in an order of fried oysters, Mr. Justice Taft (now Chief Justice) in a majority opinion held that "the possible presence of a piece of oyster shell in or attached to an oyster is so well known to anyone who eats oysters that we can say as a matter of law that one who eats oysters can reasonably anticipate and guard against eating such a piece of shell * * *." (P. 259 of 170 Ohio St., p. 174 of 164 N.E.2d.)

Thus, while we sympathize with the plaintiff who has suffered a peculiarly New England injury, the order must be "Judgment for the defendant."

Curiously, the Massachusetts court never once mentioned either the California Supreme Court's decision in *Mix v. Ingersoll Candy Co.* or the foreign/natural test. In fact, legal scholars have never been able to pinpoint the precise theoretical basis for the court's decision. Judge Smalkin, who was also a professor of commercial law, commented in the chicken aorta case (above):

[Webster] can be read in several ways: (1) There was no breach because the bone was not extraneous, but a natural substance; (2) There was no breach because New England fish chowder always has bones as an unavoidable contaminant; or (3) The plaintiff, an undoubted Yankee, should have expected to find a bone in her chowder and should have slurped it more gingerly.[11]

Did the Massachusetts Supreme Court get it right? For all of its precious language and quirky style, the court recognized that if Priscilla Webster were to prevail, fish chowder as we know it and love it would end. As a native New Englander myself, I am happy to return to Boston and exercise the utmost care as I feast upon a bowl of New England fish chowder.

7

THE LEGACY
OF MR. PEANUT

A good name is better than precious ointment.
—*Song of Songs*

Once upon a time there was food. There was wheat and corn. There was beef and there were chickens. The land flowed with pure milk and sweet honey.

Today there is still wheat but it is Gold Medal "Best for Bread™" flour. There is corn but it is the Jolly Green Giant's Corn Niblets™. The beef is Black Angus™ and the chickens are Perdue™ roasters. The land flows with Golden Guernsey™ milk and Sue-Bee™ honey. You know what the ™ means: someone claims to own that word or phrase, at least as it applies to marketing that item. It is a trademark.

The food industry reminds us daily that the law recognizes three types of property: real property (as in land or real estate), tangible property (as in things you can touch, like boats and diamond rings), and the subject of this chapter, intellectual property (as in patents, trademarks, trade secrets, and copyrights).

Trademarks and trade names are a vitally important part of any food product. Millions of dollars of research and design go into naming and packaging before a cookie, ice cream bar, or pasta sauce ever gets to market. Millions of dollars of lawyers' fees are also spent on trade-name registration, protection, and litigation. And who do you think ultimately pays these costs?

A product's trademark and trade name are as valuable, maybe even more valuable, than the recipe for the product itself. How did we get here? How did we get to a place that seems to value the appearance of a food more than the food itself? When did we start to elevate the form over the substance of our sustenance? Has the legal system advanced the cause of good food or retarded it in pursuit of the defense of intellectual property?

A trademark is a word, a phrase, a design, a logo, or some distinctive symbol that identifies the source of a product and distinguishes the product from other items in commerce. It identifies the product.[1] Examples of food trademarks are Aunt Jemima, Oreo, Mr. Peanut (more about him later), and the golden arches that beckon us to McDonald's.

If you decide to make a tomato sauce and call it Ragú, if you manufacture a cookie and call it an Oreo, if you make a peanut candy and identify it with a humanized peanut caricature, or if you open a burger joint and call it McDonald's (even if your last name is McDonald), you have infringed on someone else's trademark. You should expect lawyers in expensive suits to bang on your door within moments of launching your product.

The first "trademarks" may well have been the mandatory imprints on the bottom of loaves of bread to identify old London's dishonest bakers who either short weighted their loaves or adulterated them with unwholesome ingredients. As the food industry developed, producers became known for their wares and made sure that their customers would know them by their package. The first registered trademark in the United States went to Underwood Deviled Ham in 1868.

Contrary to popular belief, it is not necessary to register a trademark with the government. However, it is good idea to do so because it will be easier to defend a mark against subsequent infringers if the mark has been registered with the U.S. Patent and Trademark Office. A "tm" next to a product name or symbol means only that the owner is claiming the mark or name. The symbol of a registered trademark is the letter "R" in a circle (®). The law of trademarks on the federal level—and that is where most trademark law is made and fought over—has come about through a set of statutes commonly known as the Lanham Act[2] and a body of judicial decisions interpreting the Act.

In every body of law there is a landmark case. In the area of school desegregation, it is the 1954 case of *Brown v. Board of Education*.[3] In the area of the procedural rights of criminal defendants, it is the 1966 case of *Miranda v. Arizona*.[4] And in the area of food trademarks, it is the 1962 decision by the U.S. Court of Customs and Patent Appeals in the case of *Planters Nut and Chocolate Co. v. Crown Nut Co.*[5] It is the famous Mr. Peanut case.

The story of Mr. Peanut began in 1899 when twelve-year-old Amedeo Obici came to America without money or promise. He searched out his uncle in Wilkes-Barre, Pennsylvania, worked at his fruit stand, and eventually bought a peanut roaster for $4.50. In 1912, he started the Planters Nut and Chocolate Company.[6]

In 1916, Obici ran a contest among high school students to find a catchy logo for the company. The winner, Antonio Gentile, won the $5 first prize for a sketch of a humanized peanut. Mr. Peanut was born.

Mr. Peanut was an American success story without equal. The August 1950 issue of *Modern Packaging* magazine described him as the "star salesman for Planters" and "the best known and most successful trade symbol of its kind to be found anywhere."[7] Although Mr. Peanut's popularity may have ebbed over the last few decades, Planters Nuts (now part of Nabisco Foods) remains a significant player in the marketplace, and Mr. Peanut collectibles often fetch high prices at auctions and antique shops. It may well be that Mr. Peanut remains as vibrant as he ever was but he now has more competition from so many other food symbols that have come on the scene and infiltrated the market. Consider just a few: Tony the Tiger, the Keebler elves, the California Raisinettes, Charlie Tuna, Cap'n Crunch, and the most seductive of them all, Chiquita Banana. But none has had more staying power than the dapper gentleman with the cane and monocle, Mr. Peanut.

In 1953, another peanut company appeared and began selling its goods in a way that caught Mr. Peanut's attention. The Crown Nut Company came up with its own humanized peanut and in 1956 tried to register it with the U.S. Patent Office. Planters opposed the registration.

The case wound its way slowly but inexorably through all the appropriate administrative channels. The Patent Office Trademark Trial and Appeal Board dismissed Planters' opposition to the Crown application and Planters appealed.

No testimony was given in the case. The court considered the symbols themselves and that is exactly what we can do. There is Planters' Mr. Peanut (we will call him "exhibit A") and the Crown Nut Company's little peanut king ("exhibit B").

What do you think? Does the newcomer, the little peanut king (exhibit B), infringe on the venerable Mr. Peanut (exhibit A)? The court split 3–2, ruling in favor of Mr. Peanut: "Engaging in the nut business does not entitle one to adopt as a trade mark a humanized version of the identical nut which has already been humanized and adopted as a trade mark, and made famous by the advertising expenditures of another."[8]

The essence of the Mr. Peanut case was whether, in looking at exhibits A and B, one sees the differences or the similarities? It is the classic case of judges seeing eight ounces of peanut butter in a jar that can accommodate a whole pound: is it half empty or half full? The majority focused on the similarities and found in favor of Mr. Peanut:

1. Each is a symbol in the form of a little man based on an unshelled, two-kernel peanut
2. Each is standing
3. Each has something on its head, either a hat or a crown
4. Each is holding something in one hand and the other hand is empty

In sum, each was a male version of a humanized two-kernel, unshelled peanut. The court disagreed with the administrative board's decision that the marks were different enough so that consumers would not likely be confused or deceived. Do you think you would be deceived? That, however, is not the test; whether the knowledgeable and sophisticated observer (you!) would be deceived is not the test in trademark law. Would the average Joe be confused and think the two came from the same corporate entity?

The large crown on the newcomer's head is an obvious difference but the majority dismissed that by suggesting that it was "not at all

Exhibit A   Exhibit B

improbable that [Mr. Peanut] should appear adorned with a crown."[9] This seems to have been a forced and curious distinction; the court might as well have said that even though the two are quite different, Mr. Peanut might change into something closer to the imposter.

The dissenting opinions of Judges Worley and Kirkpatrick are equally, if not more, persuasive. Judge Worley wrote: "Humanizing one's wares is as old as commerce itself and I had always thought was, or at least should be, free for all to do."[10]

Judge Kirkpatrick took the majority to task for dissecting the two characters in order to find technical similarities but believed that, taken as wholes, they were totally different: "The human being suggested by [Mr. Peanut] is a dude—a spindly legged creature, top hatted, spatted and monocled; that suggested by [Crown Nut Co.], a rather coarse-looking monarch, crowned, robed in ermine and carrying a mace." The judge was willing to accept Crown Nut's characterization of the two as a "tall and suave sophisticate" (Mr. Peanut) and a "stunted, midget-like gleeful king" (the newcomer).[11]

The real fire in Judge Kirkpatrick's belly burned when he accused the majority of thinking it the duty of a court to "protect the value of an opposer's extensively and expensively advertised trade mark and good will rather than a [newcomer's] right under a plain statutory provision to register his mark."[12]

The Mr. Peanut decision remains good law to this day. If the Hardee's fast food chain were to employ a clown in its promotional activities (perhaps they would call him Hardee Har Har?), Ronald McDonald could cite the Mr. Peanut decision for the proposition that trademark law permits only one fast-food clown at a time.

There is a certain silliness to all of this, isn't there? A trademark is a marketing tool, nothing more. It has nothing to do with the quality of the food beneath the label. In 1942, the U.S. Supreme Court wrote:

> The protection of trade-marks is the law's recognition of the psychological function of symbols. If it is true that we live by symbols, it is no less true that we purchase goods by them. A trade-mark is a merchandising short-cut which induces a purchaser to select what he wants, or what he has been led to believe he wants. The owner of a mark exploits this human propensity by making every effort to impregnate the atmosphere of the market with the drawing power of a congenial symbol.[13]

Fights over trademarks and trade names (they have the same legal status) can be nasty and costly. In the 1970s, a Milwaukee, Wisconsin, salad dressing company by the down-home name of Henri's Food Products introduced a new product called "Yogowhip," a salad dressing with a yogurt base. It was called Yogowhip because it was made with yogurt and it was whipped.[14]

Kraft Foods, makers of Miracle Whip, sent Henri's a letter demanding that they drop the Yogowhip name because of likely confusion with Kraft's product, Miracle Whip.

This was Goliath telling David to take his puny little slingshot and go home. In the real world, that is precisely what happens most of the time. When large companies claim trademark infringement by small companies, the little guys know that they cannot muster the financial resources to do battle with the giants. The cost of trademark litigation can be so enormous that a small business is usually better served by giving in and starting over with a new trademark, rather than risk financial ruin against the deep pockets of an industrial giant.

By all rights, Henri's should have resigned itself to finding some other name for its new product. Instead, Henri's chose to fight.

Henri's did not wait for Kraft to file a trademark infringement action but instead filed first in the Eastern District of Wisconsin, claiming fraud, mislabeling, unfair advertising, and antitrust violations. It was a good strategic move because it kept the case on Henri's home turf. At the very least, it kept Henri's travel expenses down.

The trial, in December 1981, lasted two weeks and saw an impressive parade of witnesses, from food technology experts to linguistic specialists, all presenting evidence as to what was a "whip." Judge Terence Evans dismissed Henri's proactive charges of fraud, mislabeling, and antitrust violations, but ruled that the trademark "Yogowhip" did not infringe on Kraft's "Miracle Whip" trademark. Henri's had "won."

The win was not final because Kraft appealed to the Seventh Circuit, a maneuver that, although not unexpected, added to the legal bills of both parties. In 1982, a split three-judge panel upheld Henri's victory in the lower court.[15] But it was a costly victory. The legal fees for Henri's alone surpassed $1 million. With victories like that, who needs defeats to ruin business? Amazingly, Henri's survived. (When we last checked, it had been bought out by a large international conglomerate.)

More typical was the case of Kim Wall's Sundance Foods, a tiny Midwest company started in 1991 to manufacture and market southwest-style specialty foods. When Robert Redford's Sundance Catalog Company threatened a trademark suit, the little food company barely hesitated in changing the name to SunWild, in order to avoid costly litigation. Relabeling and remaking the product line was expensive but not nearly as expensive as protracted litigation would have been. Even Kim's dog had been named Sundance, although the German shepherd apparently was spared the name change.[16]

Sometimes the cases are downright silly—to all but the parties involved. In 1983, General Mills, makers of the well-known cereal Wheaties ("Breakfast of Champions™"), went after the owners of a suburban Chicago hot dog stand named Wee-Dee's Wee-Nees. The

"Wee-Dees" part of the name came from the surname of one of the owners, Richard Wehde.[17]

A pizzeria in Clifton, New Jersey, incurred the wrath of the national pizza chain, Domino's, because its name came too close for corporate comfort. "Dom Knows Pizza" found itself the defendant in a trademark infringement suit because of the like-sounding name. Dom may know pizza but he did not know anything about trademark law.[18]

Litigation over the names of restaurants has been spirited and amusing. The famous Stork Club of New York successfully sued a ten-stool bar in San Francisco that had taken on the same name.[19] Key to the court's decision was that fact that the name "The Stork Club" was "fanciful." In trademark law, fanciful names are easier to protect than common or descriptive names. The court found: "It is in no way descriptive of appellant's [the original New York restaurant] night club, for in its primary significance it would denote a club for storks. Nor is it likely that the sophisticates who are its most publicized customers are particularly interested in the stork."[20]

The court also rejected the west coast infringer's argument that it was just a small and humble operation: "Humility is no doubt a virtue in many instances, but in a case of this type it affords no defense to a suit for an injunction against infringement of a trade name." Nor did the San Francisco ten-stooler convince the court with its argument that no intelligent person would think that its sleazy operation had any connection to the upscale New York establishment: "It may well be true that a prudent and worldly-wise passerby would not be so deceived. The law, however, protects not only the intelligent, the experienced, and the astute. It safeguards from deception also the ignorant, the inexperienced, and the gullible."[21] (See? I told you that you are not the test for confusing trade names and trademarks.)

What does the word "beefeater" mean to you? If you know nothing of distilled spirits (as in gin), you might think it refers only to one who eats beef. What a fine name that would be for a restaurant specializing in steaks and chops! The problem is that since 1909, James Burroughs Limited, a British corporation, has been using the name Beefeater in connection with its gin.

James Burroughs not only registered the name Beefeater with the U.S. Trademark Office, it also registered the symbol of a yeoman (a Tower of London guard) for use in connection with its Beefeater Gin product. When restaurants began using the name "Sign of the Beefeater," the English distillery objected and the battle was joined. Judge Frank McGarr, sitting in the U.S. District Court in Illinois, thought he could resolve the matter by simply looking at the two marks in chambers: "... for most of yesterday I stared at the Beefeater Gin bottle."[22]

Such is the unhappy lot of a federal judge. Judge McGarr stared and stared, and stared some more, and finally concluded that the distillery had an exclusive right to use the name "Beefeater" and its associated symbol but only in connection with selling alcoholic beverages. Thus, the restaurant did not infringe on the distillery's mark. James Burroughs Limited appealed and won.

The Court of Appeals found that the "Beefeater" restaurant had infringed on the distillery's "Beefeater" name and symbol because the public would likely be confused by the coexistence of the two names and marks pertaining to two different businesses. By comparing the two marks side by side in chambers, the lower court judge had approached the issue the wrong way. Although it was appropriate to compare the two marks, the comparison should take place in the marketplace, not in the courtroom.

It makes no difference whether an entirely different kind of business uses the trademark of another. For example, if a computer manufacturer were to name its hard drive a "Whopper," the Burger King chain would easily win an infringement suit, even though the computer maker might argue that it is in an entirely different line of business and could hardly take away from the sales of the fast-food giant. Trade names are valuable pieces of property and the law does not look kindly on those who reap where they have not sown.

Certain legal principles have evolved over the years as to what kinds of names are protectable and what kinds of names are not. Marks and names are usually classified in five categories, from not very distinctive to strongly distinctive:

1. generic
2. descriptive
3. suggestive
4. arbitrary
5. fanciful

Generic names are virtually impossible to protect as trade names because they are not at all distinctive. For example, a butcher shop may sell ground beef and can (and should) label it as "ground beef" but could not expect to get a trademark for "ground beef" or "ground chuck" or even "ground sirloin." It is what it is and the butcher needs a more imaginative name to get trade-name protection. That end of the spectrum is easy.

Up the ladder comes descriptive terms, such as "juicy ground beef." Can our neighborhood butcher protect his hamburger patties under the name Juicy Ground Beef? Not likely. The butcher is only describing the product or what the product will be after cooking.

Can a fast-food restaurant sell hamburgers and protect the name "Hamburger," so that no one else could use the term? No, it is generic. What if that same fast-food chain sold hamburgers weighing four ounces each and sold them as Four Ounce Hamburgers? Again, the answer would seem to be no, because the term merely describes the weight of the burger. What if a brilliant marketing executive decides to call it a "Quarter Pounder?" Is that not also merely descriptive of the weight of the product? Yes. And no.

The famous McDonald's Quarter Pounder is indeed descriptive but has achieved what the law calls "secondary meaning" and can be protected against all other four-ounce burgers. It acquired this secondary meaning through success over time. If a local butcher shop tried to sell premade four-ounce ground-beef patties as Quarter-Pounders, the McDonald's lawyers would jump to the front of the line with a sharply worded cease and desist (meaning "cut it out and don't even think of doing it again") letter.

The line between generic and descriptive is often blurred. A 1961 case is a good example. The Weiss Noodle Company had registered the name "Ha-Lush-Ka" as a mark for its egg noodle products. Along came the Golden Cracknel and Specialty Company, wanting to market egg noodles to the Hungarian American market. Much to its dismay, it found that Weiss had registered the name Ha-Lush-Ka. Why was that a problem? Because "Ha-Lush-Ka" is the phonetic spelling of the Hungarian word *haluska,* meaning egg noodle.

The U.S. Court of Customs and Patent Appeals did not hesitate in canceling the Ha-Lush-Ka trademark. "The name of a thing is the ultimate in descriptiveness. It is immaterial that the name is in a foreign language."[23] What about secondary meaning? Not!

> While it is always distressing to contemplate a situation in which money has been invested in a promotion in the mistaken belief that trademark rights of value are being created, merchants act at their peril in attempting, by advertising, to convert common descriptive names, which belong to the public, to their own exclusive use. Even though they succeed in the creation of de facto secondary meaning, due to lack of competition or other happenstance, the law respecting registration will not give it any effect.[24]

The noodle case illustrates a stark and frightening reality in trademark law: even if you successfully register a name or mark with the U.S. Patent Office, it can be canceled at a later time.

The Weiss Noodle company made one last pitch to the court, arguing that it had been the first to develop an egg noodle product 1 inch wide, .03 inch thick, and 5 inches long. How interesting! And how irrelevant!

The owners of Tom and Sally's Handmade Chocolates, a New England candy company, had been marketing a product called Chocolate Body Paint since 1993. When a San Francisco company tried to sell Chocolate Gourmet Body Paint just before Valentine's Day 2000, Tom and Sally went to court to stop them, but they lost. Even though they owned the trademark on their Chocolate Body Paint, the federal court judge applied basic principles of trademark law to find that their trademark was at best a descriptive term. After all, what is Chocolate Body Paint? It is exactly as the phrase suggests. Had Tom and Sally come up with a more creative, perhaps a more suggestive name, they could have owned a great trademark but not the concept of a chocolate body paint. (How about Leonardo's Masterpiece Chocolate Bawdy Paint?)

The third classification is the "suggestive" name. This is supposed to be a middle ground but one that should get trademark protection. The problem is that the courts have had great difficulty defining the term. It lies somewhere between the usually unprotectable descriptive mark and the almost always protectable arbitrary or fanciful mark. But a fine example is the 1924 case that gave a "crushing" defeat to a

California beverage company trying to take advantage of an American institution.

The California Crush Fruit Company began to market a product called "Suncrush." The Orange Crush Company objected, claiming that Suncrush infringed on its well-known soft drinks. The patent office ruled in favor of Suncrush on the grounds that the terms were merely descriptive. The court of appeals thought otherwise: "A person of average intelligence would not understand, when buying an orange crush drink, that he was getting a crushed orange."[25]

If the Orange Crush Company had been selling crushed oranges, the term "Orange Crush" would have been descriptive. But as applied to a beverage, it was only suggestive of crushed oranges and worthy of protection. It seems that if a trade name is descriptive of some other product, it has a stronger identity. The breakfast cereal Grape Nuts would undoubtedly fall into this category; the term describes something (nuts from grapes?) but that is not the product being offered.

The last two categories are often lumped together because there is little doubt that they deserve protection. Fanciful names evoke striking images in unexpected contexts. For example, the name "Wild Thymes" is both a clever play on herbs and a rousing invitation to brightly flavored foods; it is the fanciful name of a small New York condiment producer. (They make a terrific rosemary-garlic mustard.)

Arbitrary names are made-up names, even if we may not think they are made up. Häagen-Dazs brand ice cream is not from the Danish word for ice cream or anything at all; it is a brilliantly invented word that may conjure up images of Copenhagen but is as arbitrary as any trade name ever devised. Try marketing a computer program, a board game, a line of clothing, anything at all, using the name "Häagen-Dazs" without the permission of the Pillsbury Company (owners of Häagen-Dazs since 1983), and if you can beat the inevitable charge of trademark infringement, you are the finest legal mind of the twenty-first century.

What about the names of people? First names of people are especially weak in the eyes of the law. A "Joe's Diner" is an example of a weak name that would likely be unsuccessful suing another Joe's Diner in another state. However, if another Joe's Diner were to open its doors down the street, the court would undoubtedly recognize the unfairness of allowing a diner-come-lately to take advantage of the original Joe's local success.

Last names are also weak trade names, although perhaps not as weak. Smith's Restaurant, Wilson's Bar, and Johnson's Pub are not distinctive enough to warrant trade-name protection except in their own local trade area.

Sometimes "weak" names become strong when they acquire secondary meaning. This means that although the name started out weak, the business became so successful on a larger scale than originally anticipated that the law protects it. Denny's Diner and McDonald's are prime examples of common names that have taken on secondary meaning so as to warrant the full protection of the law.

Consider the name "Patsy's." At the beginning of the year 2000, there were six restaurants in Manhattan bearing that name. Two got into a fight over which could sell Patsy's pasta sauce in jars. The name "Patsy" may not seem Italian to some but in New York it is the soul of Italian food. It was an Americanized nickname for Pasquale, and for years two Patsy's coexisted peacefully in New York.

Patsy Lancieri's, famous for pizza, opened on First Avenue (near 118th Street) in 1933. Patsy Scognamillo's opened in 1944 on 56th Street near Broadway and was known for its pasta. For years, there was plenty of good Italian food for New Yorkers to savor and no one even thought about a lawsuit.

Then came the inevitability of deaths, changing neighborhoods, corporate buyouts, and licensing agreements. The pizza wars raged with what many consider the best of the lot changing its name to Grimaldi's (Patsy Grimaldi was supposedly the nephew of Patsy Lancieri) and locating in Brooklyn; place mats at Grimaldi's offer up a history of the sordid lawsuits as reported by the *New York Times*. But the storm over Patsy's Pasta Sauce would soon ravage the city.

Frank Brija bought the First Avenue Patsy's (the pizza Patsy's) and soon opened or licensed a few more. Sal Scognamillo and his cousin Frank DiCola continued to run the other Patsy's (the pasta Patsy's). In 1994, the cousins bottled their marinara sauce under the Patsy's name. In 1999, Frank Brija's Patsy's began to bottle its sauce—in a jar and with a label similar to the cousins' sauce.

It was time for the federal district court to sort it all out. When Mr. Brija claimed that the legendary Frank Sinatra had been a patron at his pizzeria, tempers flared; the Scognamillo family claimed Old Blue Eyes as theirs, and the Sinatra family backed them up. Ultimately, the court ruled for the Scognamillo Patsy's and issued an injunction barring Frank Brija and his group from selling Patsy's pasta sauce.

One can never say what swayed a court in any given case but Judge John Martin was obviously annoyed by Mr. Brija's claim that he had been bottling Patsy's pasta sauce before the Scognamillo Patsy's had ever done so. To support that claim, he had old invoices for the labels. The only problem was that these old invoices showed a telephone number with the area code 973; that area code began in 1997. Oops. And Mr. Brija's credibility was not exactly enhanced by his record of convictions for armed robbery and illegal possession of weapons back in 1977.

Courts try to avoid ruling in favor of liars or people they think are liars.

Although the name "Patsy" is a weak trade name, it will be strong enough to ward off copycats in its local market, at least when it comes to bottled pasta sauces. The product is rapidly gaining a national market and may well have already acquired secondary meaning.

Then we have the Wolfie case.

Yes, Wolfie. During the 1950s, there were two Miami Beach restaurants called "Wolfies," run by the same corporation. Why "Wolfie?" It was the nickname of one Wilfred Cohen.

Fourteen hundred miles away, in Brooklyn, New York, well after Wolfies of Miami Beach had gained quite the following in Florida, another Wolfies arose, but completely unrelated to its southern namesake. Aside from the identical name, the Brooklyn sandwich shop bore several remarkable similarities to Wolfie's of Florida. First, the menu was similar in style and color. As for the menu items in the Northern copycat—"Wolfies Floridian Style French Toast" and "Wolfies Floridian Style Sundae Delights" should give you a clue.

On the other hand, what is so distinctive about the name "Wolfies?" It had not taken on any kind of secondary meaning and was well known only in Miami Beach. So what if the Brooklyn Wolfie was an attempted clone of the Florida Wolfie?

Not when it comes to business. And not when the defendant in a lawsuit plays fast and loose with the court, for that is exactly what the Brooklyn Wolfie tried to do in the U.S. District Court when the Florida Wolfie sued to stop it from using the good name of Wolfie.

The Brooklyn Wolfie lost and the court of appeals agreed that there was only room for one Wolfies in the United States.[26] Once again, the dissenting opinion sheds light on what really happened. According to Judge Moore, the Brooklyn Wolfie should have come clean and admitted his deed: "I copied Wolfies of Miami; what's wrong with that?" He would have been honest with the court and might have won.

Instead, the Brooklyn Wolfie offered several unbelievable explanations of the origin of the name "Wolfie." First, it was named after the father of a friend, Wolf Pollack. Second, someone in the Brooklyn restaurant was a womanizer, a "wolf." The third strike for the court was an economic tall tale: the electric sign that bore the previous name "Jackies" could be cheaply altered by substituting "Wolf" for "Jack."

So he lied a little. Aren't appellate courts supposed to overlook these factual infirmities and make sure the law is applied correctly? In one of the great outpourings of judicial sarcastic wit of the twentieth century, the dissenting Judge Moore observed that there was no possibility of competition between the two restaurants:

> If the Brooklyn College student who seeks physical rehabilitation from his mental debilitation caused by a two-hour examination believes that he is walking across the street into Wolfies of Miami, he would truly be in a state of post-examination shock. Nor is it possible that a family from the midwest, anxious to visit Wolfies, would find itself in Brooklyn instead of Miami. Everyone gets lost in Brooklyn—but not that lost.[27]

Trade name litigation shows no signs of letting up, especially with the expansion of markets via the Internet. There may be no such thing as a neighborhood pub or restaurant any more, as nearly every business in the world has its own web site. The best strategy may be to toss a handful of letters into a blender (or a random letter generator) and rely on the law's pleasure at protecting arbitrary names. But do a trade name search to make sure no one else came up with such an improbable combination.

A more-difficult legal issue arises in the case of parodies. A young Floridian came up with a bright idea: put some unpopped kernels into a bottle that bore a strong resemblance to Dom Perignon Champagne and call it "Dom Popingnon Champop." Charge ten dollars a pop and laugh all the way to the bank. Dom Perignon, through its American distributor, was not amused and sued in federal court.

Dom Popingnon was a brilliant parody of one the most sophisticated symbols of upper-class consumption. Judge Bernard Newman reviewed the history of Cuvée Dom Perignon, from its humble origins in a sixteenth-century French monastery (Dom Perignon was the name of the monk credited with inventing the method of making what we now call champagne) to its arrival in the United States on the maiden voyage of the ship *Normandie* in 1936. It continues to be, in the judge's words, a "distinctive and highly prestigious champagne, and is associated in the minds of the purchasing public with wealthy and famous people."[28]

A bottle of Dom Perignon means success. Even when it appears in movies—and then only after the distributor approves the script in advance (a representative from Dom Perignon is on the set to make sure the bottle is properly treated and correctly opened).

Everyone is supposed to be impressed with Dom Perignon. John Calderaio was not impressed. He had worked as a valet parker at a Boca Raton hotel where he apparently developed a distaste for the condescension of the wealthy patrons of that establishment Calderaio, then twenty-one and newly married, was eager to form his own company and conceived of Dom Popingnon as a fun way of casting ridicule upon the tastes and pretensions of Dom Perignon purchasers.

Calderaio wanted to poke fun at the wealthy elite and figured that popcorn in a bottle that looked like a bottle of Dom Perignon would get a few laughs and maybe even make a few dollars. The execution of the idea was nothing short of brilliant. He captured the essence of the Dom Perignon look in all aspects, from the size and shape of the bottle, to the characteristic shield of the label, to a look-alike type script, and even to similar (but funnier) text. For example, instead of "Product of France," Calderaio's product read "Product of Iowa." What a great idea!

Parody has a long and honored tradition in art and literature. It is a sophisticated kind of humor that must convey two simultaneous—and contradictory—messages: that it is the original, but also that it is not the original. The traditional test of trademark infringement is likelihood of confusion but effective parody must convey at least an initial hesitation. "Is it real or is it Memorex™?"

Parody is more often the subject of copyright cases. The landmark parody case involved a rap song parody by Two Live Crew of the Roy Orbison classic "Pretty Woman." The U.S. Supreme Court held that the commercial nature of a work of parody does not necessarily mean that the work is presumptively an unfair use of the original.[29] Of course, the Two Live Crew case went to the question of fair use under the copyright laws, not under trademark infringement under the Lanham Act. It may well be that parody of a trademark is entirely different from parody of a song, a book, or a magazine as a purely legal matter.

Judge Newman heard from the witnesses and saw the evidence. He applied traditional trademark infringement legal principles and ruled in favor of Dom Perignon and against the parody. It wasn't that Judge Newman failed to see the humor in Dom Popingnon. To the contrary, one senses that the good judge was heartily amused by the cleverness of the parody! But he still found for the venerable champagne producer because the parody was not "sufficiently effective to eliminate a likelihood of confusion on the part of customers."[30]

The real problem was that the parody was too effective, too good, and too clever. Dom Popingnon did too good of a job poking fun at snobbery and conspicuous consumption. But that was what made it such a brilliant parody! When the champagne distributor first contacted John Calderaio and demanded that he stop marketing his product, Calderaio offered to put a disclaimer on its bottles, informing consumers that the popcorn-filled look-alike was not a Dom Perignon product or in any way connected with the real Dom Perignon.

If Calderaio had not paid such close attention to detail, and if his parody had been less stinging, he might have won. If the bottle had not been the same size as the real Dom Perignon bottle, the parody would not have been as sharp but the likelihood of confusion would have been less.

Judges are not comfortable with parodies of trademarks, especially in the food business. Too bad. We need to lighten up when it comes to good food and good drink. The Dom Popingnon case was decided by a single federal district court judge and never made it to the court of appeals. You probably know why John Calderaio, working out of his garage, never pursued the case any further. It makes the young satirist think twice about marketing that next brilliant parody, doesn't it?

The only good news for Calderaio is that Judge Newman refused to award the Dom Perignon distributor its requested legal costs. Imposing those costs—and they were undoubtedly substantial—would have been an unreasonable burden on both Calderaio and his young family. Dom Perignon won the case; there was no need for it to try to bury the young man who dared poke fun at its lofty image.

Has the public really benefited from the court's decision in the Dom Popingnon case? Or was the French champagne maker the only winner? Good food and drink need not be deadly serious to be attractive. If gourmets and gourmands cannot laugh at themselves, who even wants their truffles and beluga caviar?

The ultimate irony of the Dom Popingnon case is personal. When my wife and I were married in 1998, a good friend gave us a bottle of Cuvée Dom Perignon (vintage 1988). We decided to save it until the book-signing party for *Habeas Codfish*. Oh well, maybe it's too old to be any good.

McBULLY

Posterity waves no garlands for imitators.
—*Johann Christoph Friedrich von Schiller,*
Wallenstein's Camp

There is another aspect to infringement of intellectual food property, closely related to trademarks but not so clear and distinct. What if a restaurant copies the look and feel of another restaurant? What if an olive oil producer copies the style in bottling of another producer? This is not trade-name or trademark infringement. It is what the law calls "trade-dress" infringement and it is taken very seriously in the food industry. The seminal trade-dress case made it to the U.S. Supreme Court.

Felix and Mike Stehling opened a chain of Mexican-style restaurants in San Antonio, Texas. These "Taco Cabana" restaurants created a Mexican theme by their distinctive and colorful decor, described in court documents as:

> a festive eating atmosphere having interior dining and patio areas decorated with artifacts, bright colors, paintings and murals. The patio includes interior and exterior areas with the interior patio capable of being sealed off from the outside patio by overhead garage doors. The stepped exterior of the building is a festive and vivid color scheme using top

border paint and neon stripes. Bright awnings and umbrellas continue the theme.[1]

If that sounds unremarkable to you, it must have sounded pretty good to Marno McDermott and Jim Blacketer, two Texas businessmen who opened the Two Pesos restaurant in Houston, with a look and feel almost identical to that of the Taco Cabana experience. As one witness testified: "They look the same. Then you're inside they feel the same. They both have the same product."[2]

Taco Cabana sued Two Pesos in federal court and won. The court awarded nearly $2 million in damages plus nearly another $1 million in attorneys fees. The judgment was upheld by the U.S. Court of Appeals and then by the U.S. Supreme Court. The Supreme Court took the case to consider the narrow legal question of whether trade-dress infringement requires a showing of secondary meaning. (It does not; a showing of distinctiveness is sufficient.)

Trade dress is a slippery concept. It is the "total image" and "overall appearance" of a business or product. The law recognizes that certain elements of a business or product are more functional than dressy; these elements, no matter how clever they might be, cannot be protected as trade dress. That ends up being a jury decision and in the case of the dueling Mexican restaurants, the jury decided that the various elements of the Taco Cabana look amounted to more than function. It was indeed distinctive.

The jury made the call after visiting both establishments. Because the district court found that the infringement was both willful and deliberate, it chose to exercise its powers under federal law and both doubled the jury's damage award and assessed Two Pesos the cost of Taco Cabana's lawyer fees. And if that were not enough to teach the infringers a lesson, the court ordered Two Pesos to make changes in its restaurant design and to post for a whole year signs admitting that they had unfairly copied Taco Cabana's concept. As the U.S. Court of Appeals remarked, the imitation was "brazen."

Imitation may well be "the sincerest form of flattery" (an aphorism attributed to Charles Caleb Cotton) but in today's food marketing world, it is more likely to land you in court. Perhaps Cato the Elder had it right when he wrote: "Fools do not imitate the successes of the wise."[3]

It is very easy to poke fun at the many apparently frivolous lawsuits fought over trademarks. One must understand, though, that trademarks are more about business than cuisine. Businesses, be they food related or not, must go after all infringers, large and small, or they risk losing the legal status of an exclusive mark.

We have examined trademarks, trade names, and trade dress. There is one more "trade" item to be considered in this context: trade secrets.

A trade secret is information that benefits a business and is kept confidential. It may be a formula, a process, a physical device, a design, or even an idea. Lawsuits abound in which companies allege theft or unlawful disclosure of trade secrets. In the food world, there have been some choice morsels of trade-secret litigation.

In the late 1970s, Louis Hutchison came up with an idea for "skinless fried chicken." It would revolutionize fast-food restaurants as we knew them. Because so much of the fat in chicken comes from the skin, and because everyone loves fried chicken, the sky seemed the limit for Louis and his concept of a more healthful piece of fried chicken.

Louis worked hard to develop his skinless fried chicken. He test-marketed a prototype and put it into seven fast-food restaurants that he owned in the Las Vegas area. As far as Louis was concerned, his recipe and technique for preparing skinless fried chicken was a trade secret.

Louis Hutchison knew he had something big, something very big. He contacted a vice president at Kentucky Fried Chicken (KFC) about the possibility of KFC buying the rights to the new chicken concept. KFC wrote back to Louis in 1984 saying it was not interested in the skinless fried chicken because it did not fit into KFC's marketing plans.

Louis was persistent. He knew that if he could get KFC interested in his secret recipe, he could retire early. He convinced KFC to send someone to Las Vegas to evaluate his product. When Tony Wang arrived in Las Vegas, Louis had him sign an agreement not to disclose any trade secrets that might be revealed during the course of the visit. Mr. Wang then tasted some of the chicken and even watched the cooking procedure.

Louis again met with top KFC officials who finally told him they were not interested in the product. That was early 1985.

As it turned out, two years later KFC began working on a range of new products under its "Good For You" slogan. In late 1987, the head of Research and Development at KFC directed his staff to find a way to make skinless fried chicken. After months of testing and tasting, KFC came up with its version of skinless fried chicken and went nationwide with it in 1991. Needless to say, Louis Hutchison cried "fowl!" and sued.

The KFC chief researcher testified that he knew nothing of Hutchison's product and developed the KFC skinless fried chicken on his own. Hutchison claimed that KFC stole his trade secret. But what "trade secret" did KFC allegedly steal?

KFC argued that there was nothing secret about what Louis Hutchison ever had. Louis cut up the chicken, removed the skin, marinated it, dipped it, breaded it, and fried it. "Big deal," said KFC. That pretty well describes what everyone else in the fried chicken industry was doing, except for taking off the skin. Not much of a secret, is it?

Louis claimed that the process was much more involved than that. In his own words, his trade secret was a

> method/technique, and/or process of economically producing a skinless fried chicken product that looks and tastes like skin-on fried chicken cooked in the same manner, but which contains substantially less fat, calories, salt and cholesterol.... The procedures involved in this trade secret are skinning the chicken in a fast and economical manner; marinating the chicken to introduce the desired flavoring, moisture and to create a sticky protein gel which serves as a substitute skin; dipping and breading the chicken pieces; and the cooking procedure.[4]

The problem for Louis is that this description sounded more like a sales pitch than a legally defined trade secret. The court did not buy it.

If Louis Hutchison had claimed that KFC stole his breading recipe, the contents of the cooking oils, or even the precise cooking temperature, he might have had a case. But he alleged only that KFC stole something that was hardly a secret to anyone in the business.

As it turned out, Louis Hutchison's "secret" method for de-skinning the chicken was to remove the skin by hand. Ask any chef in America, Europe, or Asia: that's not much of a secret. Even if it were a secret, KFC never stole it because they used various mechanical means of skinning its birds. There's more than one way to skin a chicken, and Louis's way does not qualify as a trade secret. The legal principle is this: if something is obvious and not a secret, courts will not classify it as a trade secret. Also, being the first to introduce a product on the market does not necessarily mean you have a legally protected trade secret. The court pointed out that as early as 1981, Pudgie's, a New York chain, was offering skinless fried chicken on its menu. That was one year before Louis tried it out on his customers.

What about recipes in general? Can they be protected?

Old Country Buffet is one of those all-you-can-eat cafeteria-style restaurants, not known in culinary circles for exotic cooking but known by a lot of folks who like to stoke up on mountains of food. According to one of the founders of Old Country, its secret to success was "small batch cooking." This ensured freshness and higher quality.

The Klinkes (Paul, Carol, and Greg) had been in the restaurant business and wanted to buy an Old Country Buffet franchise. "Sorry, Klinkes, we're not franchising," said the Old Country owners. Not to be denied, the Klinkes went undercover and stole the Old Country Buffet recipes. They quickly opened up their version of Old Country Buffet and called it "Granny's." Old Country Buffet sued for theft of trade secrets.[5]

What exactly did the Klinkes steal? They ripped off recipes for basic American staples, such as BBQ chicken and that great gourmet delight, macaroni and cheese. There was nothing original in these recipes; they were so basic and obvious that they could not possibly qualify as trade secrets. The trial court also found that the recipes themselves, as found in the "secret" files of Old Country Buffet, were never used by the cooks in their original format. Because of the limited reading skills of the cooks, the recipes had to be dramatically simplified.

There was one more element to the case. The Klinkes also ripped off the Old Country Buffet employee manual. This, too, did not qualify as a trade secret for two reasons. First, they were hardly a secret, because employees could keep them when they left the employ of Old Country Buffet. Second, there was nothing of significant value in the manuals. Truisms like "follow each recipe exactly" and "when tasting foods, never use a cooking utensil," are hardly trade secrets.

The Klinkes may have been lazy and opportunistic, but in the eyes of the law, they were not thieves. At least, what they stole were not trade secrets. A similar case with the same result occurred when Claud

Henning accused Kitchen Art Foods of "stealing" his recipe for an angel food cake mix back in 1948; it was neither new nor novel and not worthy of protection.[6]

What if instead of taking recipes for BBQ chicken and macaroni and cheese, the Klinkes stole the recipes for the Old Country Buffet's "secret sauce" or "secret blend of herbs and spices?" That could have been a case of trade-secret theft.

In 1997, Scott Chen, owner and head chef of the upscale Empress of China restaurant in Houston, Texas, sued a rival restaurant, Hunan Paradise, for serving Chen's signature dishes. How did Hunan Paradise get the recipes? A former Empress employee went to work for Hunan Paradise and allegedly brought the recipes with him.

The similarities were apparent. "Filet Mignon la Empress" became "Filet Mignon la Paradise." "Beef la Scott" became (same dish) "Beef l'Orange." Even a food critic noticed an uncanny resemblance in Hunan's food to the well-known food of Chef Scott Chen at Empress of China. Mr. Chen sued but the case was settled out of court. Both restaurants seem to be thriving.

Had the case gone to trial, it is likely that Mr. Chen would have prevailed. If these recipes were original and distinctive (an example of one of his more imaginative creations is "Lobster with Avocado and Tangy Honey Radish Sauce"), they could have qualified as trade secrets. There would have to be something secret in the preparation. If Chef Chen had come up with a most unusual combination of ingredients that was easily identifiable, there would be no trade secret to protect. For example, if the chef paired smoked salmon with circus peanuts (a combination that the author himself devised in a drunken stupor one cold January night) and served it as a new and exotic appetizer, there would be no secret to protect. Any other restaurant could serve the same bizarre combination because, although novel, it was obvious.

If a recipe can be protected as a trade secret (which it can be if there is something original and not obvious and it is of definite economic value), can it receive protection under the laws of copyright? Probably not. Can it be patented? Probably not, but that is a more difficult question.

The great French food writer Brillat-Savarin wrote: "The discovery of a new dish does more for the happiness of mankind than the discovery of a star."[7] Unfortunately, neither contribution to civilization merits a patent or even a copyright. Build a better mousetrap and you can patent it. Come up with a better brownie and it's, "Thank you very much." You can patent an invention or an industrial process but, under most circumstances, you cannot patent a recipe.

Let's consider the issue of copyright first as it applies to recipes.

A copyright is the protection that the law gives to expressions of creativity. Books, songs, and works of art are usually given copyright protection. It is a fundamental principle of intellectual property law that you cannot copyright a fact or an idea, only the particular expression of that fact or idea.

Let's say that you publish a collection of fifty favorite family recipes, including Grandma Minnie's secret recipe for Baked Garlic-Dill Mustard Salmon. (By publishing it, you get copyright protection, even if you don't formally register it.) A year later, someone publishes the same recipe, including the color photo of the dish that appeared in your book. Can you sue for copyright infringement?

You can sue for infringing on your rights to the photograph but not for reprinting the recipe. The courts seem to view a recipe as a technical, noncreative listing of ingredients. If someone copies your introduction to the recipe, telling of your fond memories of Grandma Minnie, you probably have grounds for a lawsuit. But a claim of "That's my recipe!" will likely lose.

What about a compilation of recipes?

Two publishing giants locked horns in a bitter copyright fight over recipes using Dannon yogurt. Both Meredith Corporation and Publications International, Limited (PIL) produce cooking magazines and books commonly found on racks near the checkout lanes in supermarkets all across America. They are hard to miss.

In 1988, Meredith published *Discover Dannon—50 Fabulous Recipes with Yogurt.* Judge Kanne, writing for the Seventh Circuit Court of Appeals, obviously enjoyed his judicial deliberations (although we do detect a dollop of sarcasm):

> From "Simple Snacks" to "Dazzling Desserts," "Super Salads" to "Exciting Entrees," the array of offerings is enough to send anyone rushing to the fridge. Some highlights are "Chunky Chili Dip," "Crunchy Tuna Waldorf Salad," "Spicy Bean Tostadas," and for dessert, "Chocolate Fruit

Torte." As inspiration, Meredith offers pictorial representations of the final products upon which the yogurt devotee may longingly fixate.[8]

Publications International entered the Dannon yogurt cookbook scene with a dozen publications, beginning as early as 1992. Two of them, *Dannon Healthy Habit Cookbook—Great Tasting Recipes Lower In Fat And Calories* (1993) and *Taste Why It's Dannon—Collection Of Great-Tasting Recipes* (1995), each contained twenty-two recipes (though not the same twenty-two in each publication) that had first appeared in Meredith's *Discover Dannon* book.

Were the various PIL recipes exactly the same as the ones in Meredith's *Discover Dannon* compilation? The court had no difficulty in finding them to be "functionally identical." They even had the same titles. The only differences were in the listing of ingredients, directions for preparation, and nutritional information. As the court dryly observed: "[I]t doesn't take Julia Child or Jeff Smith to figure out that the PIL recipes will produce substantially the same final products as many of those described in *Discover Dannon.*[9]

Meredith stormed into the district court and convinced the judge to issue a preliminary injunction prohibiting PIL from publishing, distributing, or selling any books or magazines that contained one or more of twenty-six recipes. In the interests of culinary completeness and legal accuracy, and to satisfy your morbid curiosity, here are the twenty-six forbidden recipes:

Blueberry-Lemon Muffins	Mustard Pork Chops
Crunchy Tuna Waldorf Salad	Broccoli-Tuna Pasta Toss
Gingered Fruit Salad	Strawberry Brulee
Sunflower Herb Dressing	Yogurt Drop Cookies
Fresh Basil and Pepper Potato Salad	Fruit Trifle
Curried Turkey and Peanut Salad	Lemony Carrot Cake
Orange Poppy Seed Dressing	Lemon Yogurt Frosting
Spicy Bean Tostadas	Easy Fruit Shortcake
Chunky Chili Dip	Orange-Filled Cream Puffs
Creamy Tarragon Dip	Chocolate Fruit Torte
Savory Dijon Chicken Spread	Creamy Citrus Cheesecake
Swiss 'n' Cheddar Cheeseball	Nutty Cheese and Apple Salad
Italian Ham Lasagna	Creamy Vegetable Potpourri

Each and every one of these tempting recipes is made with Dannon yogurt and each was now off limits to the thieves at PIL, by virtue of the injunction issued by the honorable John Grady, federal district judge for the Northern District of Illinois.

The injunction did not last long. In dissolving the injunction, the court of appeals found that Meredith Corporation could not establish a valid ownership in any protectable copyright with regard to these recipes. The recipes before the court were simple listings of ingredients and directions for preparing the final product from the component ingredients; that is not an expression of artistic endeavor that deserves copyright protection:

> The identification of ingredients necessary for the preparation of each dish is a statement of facts. There is no expressive element in each listing; in other words, the author who wrote down the ingredients for "Curried Turkey and Peanut Salad" was not giving literary expression to his individual creative labors. Instead, he was writing down an idea, namely, the ingredients necessary to the preparation of a particular dish. "No author may copyright facts or ideas. The copyright is limited to those aspects of the work—termed 'expression'—that display the stamp of the author's originality." [Court's citation omitted.] We do not view the functional listing of ingredients as original within the meaning of the Copyright Act.[10]

The court left open the possibility of extending copyright protection to "recipes that might spice up functional directives by weaving in creative narrative."[11] The court followed up with this plausible scenario:

> There are cookbooks in which the authors lace their directions for producing dishes with musings about the spiritual nature of cooking or reminiscences they associate with the wafting odors of certain dishes in various stages of preparation. Cooking experts may include in a recipe suggestions for presentation, advice on wines to go with the meal, or hints on place settings and appropriate music. In other cases, recipes may be accompanied by tales of their historical or ethnic origin.[12]

Meredith had another argument, that its compilation of recipes was original and worthy of copyright protection, even if the individual recipes were not so worthy. That may be true, but the court found that the PIL publications altered the poached recipes just enough and put them in a different-enough order to escape the wrathful consequences of the judicial system. PIL was smart enough to vary ever so slightly what it had "borrowed."

Do you want to "assemble" a cookbook of your favorite recipes from the hundreds of cookbooks on your shelf? You can do it without violating the laws of copyright. You don't even have to identify the source. Be careful not to copy verbatim any of the introductory descriptive narrative. To be extra safe, vary the order of ingredients, just a little. Add your own narrative and you can get your own copyright. Just don't run into federal court when someone steals any of the recipes from your book of stolen recipes.

The court of appeals in the Meredith case got it right when it observed that "there can be no monopoly in the copyright sense in the ideas for producing certain foodstuffs. Nor can there be copyright in the method one might use in preparing and combining the necessary ingredients."[13]

As chefs have achieved celebrity status, the notion of a "signature dish" has developed. Some chefs have become famous for certain elaborate dishes. Can a chef sue a copycat who produces that same dish, in terms of both ingredients and appearance, in his upstart restaurant? The best bet might be a claim of trade-dress infringement or, if a former employee is responsible for the sudden appearance of the dish in a new location, a claim of theft of trade secrets.

What about a patent on a recipe? There are thousands of patents that have been granted to the food industry so why not one to a chef who comes up with a brilliant new dish? Perhaps the chef has discovered a new way to cook a veal chop. Perhaps he has invented a new chocolate sauce. Perhaps she has come up with a way to enjoy a vegetable that people have never before eaten. Consider the thistle-laden artichoke: who was the first person to think that such a fearsome piece of vegetation could be eaten?

A patent is a document that the U.S. Patent and Trademark Office issues for inventions that are new and nonobvious. The document is valuable because it grants a monopoly for a limited period of time on the use and development of the invention.

In the food industry, there might be patents for microwave pop-corn[14] or for something "relating to a process for preparing low DE starch hydrolysates and low DE starch conversion syrups." In case you did not know, "DE" is short for "dextrose equivalent" and we are talking about patent number 3,849,194.

Nearly all patents relating to food have to do with the technology of preparing food for mass-market use and distribution. They are more likely related to food processing than to small-scale cuisine. General Mills, Kraft Foods, and Nabisco are far more likely to be regular visitors to the patent office than are chefs Charlie Trotter, Emeril Lagasse, and Jean-Louis Palladin.

Food—in its purest form and as used to create dishes that we enjoy at home and in fine restaurants—does not lend itself to patents. Food utensils, such as knives, pots and pans, and kitchen tools that slice and dice, are inventions that are regularly patented. To the extent that celebrity chefs lend their names to kitchen hardware, the likes of the above-mentioned chefs may well stop in at the patent office.

You can patent a food processor but not the food you process in it. And you can patent the industrial technology and machines that make the food you put into your food processor, just not the food itself.

You will find few patent designations on products in grocery store aisles. This does not mean that the manufacturers have not patented anything related to their products. It means only that there is very little reason to post a notice of patent on a food product, especially when the patent relates only to the manufacturing process and not the food itself. We found on a box of Jell-O brand instant pudding the designation of patent number 4,280,851. What is this?

Jell-O has not patented the pudding itself but rather part of the technological process for manufacturing the instant version of its pudding. Patent applications are generally tedious documents and this one is no exception. It first provides certain necessary information such as the names of the inventors (Esra Pitchon, Joseph D. O'Rourke, and Theodore H. Joseph); then comes the all-important name of the company that will make money from it (General Foods, or the "assignee") and then pages and pages of detailed descriptions of the particular process that is new. In most cases, the process itself is not new but the improvement to existing technology is the new thing.

If you think patent law is fun and exciting, consider what a young patent lawyer had to draft for the patent office in the Jell-O instant pudding case. Here is an excerpt of the "summary" of the invention, as presented to the U.S. Patent Office (with my helpful comments):

Accordingly, the present invention broadly contemplates providing an improved process and apparatus for cooking or gelatinizing a material which is normally difficult to cook and spray dry because of the formation of high viscosities during cooking, so that an easily dryable, uniformly cooked and finely-sized product is obtained thereby. The material is initially liquified or mixed in an aqueous solvent (e.g. a slurry is formed), then atomized into an enclosed chamber to form a relatively fine spray which may be uniformly cooked or gelatinized. A heating medium is interjected into the atomized material in the chamber to cook the material. The chamber contains a vent aperture to allow the heated atomized material to exit the chamber, with the size and shape of the chamber and the vent aperture being effective to maintain the temperature and moisture content of the material for a period of time sufficient to cook or gelatinize the material. In accordance with a preferred embodiment of the invention, atomization of the liquified material is effectuated in a multi-fluid nozzle through which there is conveyed the material, and steam as the heating medium is interjected into the atomized material. [Is this boring or what?]

In accordance with a preferred embodiment of the present invention, the material is atomized through an atomization aperture within a nozzle, and steam is interjected into the atomized material through a second aperture in the nozzle. Preferably, the heating medium (e.g. steam) is interjected through a plurality of second apertures surrounding the atomization aperture. Furthermore, the chamber which surrounds the atomization and second apertures defines a vent aperture which is preferably positioned opposite the atomization and second apertures. The elapsed time between passage of the material from the atomization aperture, through the chamber and exiting thereof from the vent aperture defines the cooking or gelatinization time of the material. The process and apparatus of the present invention not only produces a uniformly cooked or gelatinized material with a minimum of shear and heat damage, but it avoids the formation of deposits, agglomeration or clogging of the cooked or gelatinized material and provides an apparatus that is easy to maintain and repair. [Sorry, but it doesn't get any better.]

Further, the present invention by subjecting the atomized material to a constant environment is able to gently, quickly, and uniformly cook or gelatinize the atomized material individually while avoiding overcooking, and even more surprisingly, provide such cooking or gelatinization at relatively high starch content (e.g. 15 to 50%). The present invention is particularly suitable for use in the gelatinization of starches, but is not limited thereto and also has a wide range of applicability to materials such as protein, and other types of cookable or gelatinizable materials. [Better than a sleeping pill, isn't it?]

When the teachings of the present invention are applied the processing of starch materials it is desirable that the resultant gelatinized starch, for products such as instant puddings, have a particle size wherein at least 90% by weight of the particles pass through a 100 mesh U.S. Standard Screen and preferably at least 30% by weight pass through a 400 mesh U.S. Standard Screen. The practice of the present invention should result in a uniformly gelatinized starch material having good solubility and dispersibility characteristics, with a minimum of heat damage and granule breakage resulting in a maximum amount of whole precooked granules in a dry useable powder form. The gelatinized starch granules are in the form of indented spheres and upon rehydration of the starch material individual granules swell. [Can you believe that lawyers make money writing this kind of stuff?]

Further, in accordance with the teachings of the present invention, the materials may be atomized by methods other than those specifically disclosed herein with regard to the two-fluid or multi-fluid nozzle (pneumatic), such as through centrifugal forces (spinning disc), pressurized atomization, or through the employment of sonic or ultrasonic techniques. Ideally, a uniform spray of uniformly-sized, small particles is obtained to thereby ensure uniform cooking or gelatinization, granulation and drying. Accordingly, it is a primary feature of the present invention to provide a novel method and apparatus for cooking or gelatinizing a material in an atomized state such that an easily dryable, finely-sized product is obtained thereby. [They probably get paid by the word.]

Another feature of the present invention is to provide a process and apparatus of the type described herein which is particularly suitable for uniformly granulating materials, such as starches, with a minimum of heat damage and whole granule breakage. [Hang in there, we're almost ready to land.]

A more specific feature of the present invention lies in providing a process and apparatus of the type described utilizing multi-fluid nozzle wherein atomization of the material is effected by the use of at least one atomization aperture and steam as the heating medium is interjected into the atomized material spray, preferably through a plurality of apertures. More particularly, in accordance with the teachings of the present invention, a chamber surrounds the atomization and steam interjection apertures and contains a vent aperture positioned preferably opposite relative to the aforementioned apertures, with the size and shape of the chamber and the vent aperture being effective to maintain the temperature and moisture content of the material for a period of time sufficient to cook or gelatinize the material. [Whew!]

You will not find that in the *Joy of Cooking*. As wearisome and long-winded as the summary is, it is absolutely necessary to the patent process. And patents are not cheap. The filing fee alone for a utility patent is either $625 or $1,250, depending on the size of the company applying for it. That does not include the legal fees.

Then we have the case of patent no. 4,455,333, granted to Proctor & Gamble for the first soft store-packaged cookie. It was a new and revolutionary process but led to one of the strangest and most hotly contested cases in the annals of the cookie industry. It came to be known as "The Cookie War of 1984."

Not long after Proctor & Gamble came out with its Grandma's Cookie, its competitors tried to discover the secret of soft cookies. According to Proctor & Gamble, the Nabisco, Keebler, and Frito-Lay companies engaged in illegal industrial espionage. Nabisco sent a spy to a contract manufacturer where the new cookies were being produced; Frito-Lay directed one of its employees to pose as a supervisor of a potential customer and gain entrance to a confidential sales meeting; Keebler allegedly rented an airplane and took photographs of Proctor & Gamble's Jackson, Tennessee, plant while it was under construction. It was the new CIA—Cookie Intrigue of America.

Nabisco came up with a strategy: invalidate the patent. If Nabisco could prove Proctor & Gamble's "process" was no more than a minor variant of a previously published recipe, it might have a chance.

Nabisco researchers thought they had found the Holy Grail when they discovered a recipe for "Rigglevake" cookies (railroad cookies) in a 1968 Canadian cookbook. The recipe was based on a process developed by an order of Mennonites. Nabisco found several old Mennonite women who knew all about the process. Their testimony would sink the P & G patent! There was one minor problem: the religion of the Mennonites prohibited the women from giving testimony in court. The case was finally settled in 1989, with the defendants reportedly shelling out $125 million, at that time the largest settlement in a patent infringement case.[15]

Proctor & Gamble was lucky. Think of the damages it would have had to pay if all of the grandmothers in America had sued them for infringing on their good name?

Could the first person to discover that boiling an artichoke makes it edible have received a patent for his discovery? No. There may have been a discovery but not an invention. Newly discovered substances that occur naturally in the world do not qualify for patents and that is how the Patent Office would treat the adventurous soul who first figured out how to eat an artichoke.

A whole new area of patent law is developing over the emerging field of genetically modified foods. Plant patents have been around for years (relating to new reproducible plants that are both novel and nonobvious) but the brave new world of genetically modified substances will involve patent applications for years to come.

Chefs routinely invent great and glorious dishes every day. Why would they even bother to think of trying to patent their creations? Chefs would rather spend their time working on their next dish or improving the last one instead of meeting with the lawyers to figure out how to obtain a monopoly. Besides, chefs are usually eager to share their discoveries, knowing that it is their skills and passions that make their dishes so successful. No one can patent passion in the kitchen.

Of course, it is unlikely that the U.S. Patent Office would grant a patent for any culinary masterpiece and it is equally unlikely that a chef would try to patent the technique used to create it. This only illustrates the point: patents belong in the world of business where money is made, not in the kitchen where great food is served.

So it is with the complex field of intellectual property law. When you consider food as "property" and the subject of commerce, you need lawyers. When you think of food as aesthetics and the subject of nourishment, you need only chefs.

So why did I choose to call this chapter "McBully"? First, does not the made-up word "McBully" conjure up the image of a certain fast-food hamburger chain? Of course it does, and that is no accident. Could you call your bagel business "McBagel"? You could try, but I suggest you first talk to Ken McShea of Fishkill, New York.

With an annual advertising budget of between $10,000 and $15,000 (compared to McDonald's advertising expenditures in 1985 of $350 million, not including another $125 million for in-store promotions), Ken McShea's little bagel shop was a modest enterprise. I have never tasted Ken McShea's bagels but with a name like McShea they must be great.

You get the picture. McDonald's is Goliath and Ken McShea is a speck of dust on David's nose. For some reason, Ken thought the name "McBagel" would be cute. It was the only thing he did with the prefix "Mc." At the time Ken McShea started using the term "McBagel," McDonald's was using a whole host of "Mc" or "Mac" terms, with thirty-four of them registered with the U.S. government.

McDonald's was not amused and asked Ken McShea to stop using the term "McBagel" even though the fast-food giant was not then using the word. When McShea learned of McDonald's opposition to McBagel's, he ran a contest to select another name. His adoring public came up with "McSheagels." That would have been fine with McDonald's but McShea chose to fight. The court record does not reveal what mind-altering substances Mr. McShea was taking that clouded his judgment and led him to believe that he would have the slightest chance of winning a lawsuit against McDonald's. Perhaps Mr. McShea thought the publicity would bring thousands of sympathetic people to his door.

McDonald's seems to have been willing (at that time anyway) to accept the position that it could not object to someone's use of the prefix "Mc" or "Mac" in connection with nonfood products but was willing to fight to the death over its monopoly of the magical "Mc" on any food-related product. The federal district court sided with McDonald's because it found the prefix fanciful and arbitrary and therefore "strong." What about the likelihood of confusion? Would visitors to Ken McShea's humble little bagelry, devoid of golden arches or any of the

"There's a Mr. Egg McMuffin here who says we've been using his name without permission."

trappings of the usual McDonald's establishment, be confused? The court considered the "sophistication of buyers" and concluded: "In this case, both McDonald's and McBagel's cater to purchasers of fast food or other inexpensive restaurant services. Consumers in this market do not make sophisticated restaurant choices...."[16]

Apparently, McDonald's would have been content to let the Fishkill bagel shop operate under the name "McSheagel's." Don't you think McSheagel's is a far better name than McBagel's anyway? No matter, Ken McShea's stubborn persistence forced the court to decide the matter and it enjoined Ken McShea from using the prefix "Mc" with any food item. The court was unwilling to conclude that McDonald's "has a boundless monopoly on the 'Mc' formative."[17] Of course, that issue was not in front of the court that day. It arose in two subsequent cases, involving a national hotel chain's attempt to use the name "McSleep" for a low-priced subchain and a dental group's use of the name "McDental."

Quality Inns prepared to launch a new group of budget-priced hotels by the clever name of "McSleep." McDonald's objected, claiming that Quality Inns was trying to take advantage of the good will McDonald's had created over the years for the combination of "Mc" with just about anything. Here it was not a food item but McDonald's decided to fight for its monopoly over all fanciful words that begin with the prefix "Mc."

Quality Inns argued that the prefix "Mc" has become such a common part of the English language that McDonald's has lost its right to enforce its mark against those who would combine it with a nonfood generic term. The court rejected that argument and enjoined Quality Inns from using the term "McSleep," seemingly clearing the way for McDonald's to go after any and all users of the prefix "Mc" with any generic term.[18]

When a dental practice in Plattsburgh, New York, chose the name "McDental," guess who sued. The word "dental" is generic, has nothing to with food (except for the connection between candy and cavities), and would not ordinarily make people think of a national food chain. Still, a federal court enjoined the New York dentists from using the prefix "Mc."[19]

McDonald's trademark battles are international. In 1995, a South African man opened a burger restaurant by the name of "MacDonald's." complete with golden arches. The courts ruled in favor of the real McDonald's and forced the closing of the Johannesburg copycat.[20] In the Philippines, the fast-food giant did not fare so well; an appeals court reversed a lower court decision that had forced the closing of four branches of "Big Mak Burger." The owners claimed that the name was innocently derived from the names of the owners' parents, Maxima and Kimsoy.[21]

In Denmark, McDonald's tried to shut down a one-man hot dog stand by the name of "McAllan." The Danish Supreme Court ruled in favor of the little guy because there was no risk of confusion between the humble hot-dog stand and the burger megachain.[22] When McDonald's went after a Vilnius restaurant bearing the name "McSmile," opened before McDonald's even opened a single outlet in Lithuania, the tiny Baltic restaurant retained the law firm of McDermott, Will, and

Emery and wondered whether McDonald's would demand that attorney McDermott drop the prefix "Mc" from his name.[23]

Is McDonald's a bully? Trademarks are valuable properties and companies must be diligent in protecting them from all infringers, real and imaginary. Still, the idea that a fast-food giant owns the prefix "Mc" (and its variant "Mac") is more than a little disturbing. McDonald's has already appropriated "McWisconsin," McIllinois," and "McMichigan" in its marketing arsenal. What's next? I suspect I shouldn't even try to market "McMustard."

So what does this all have to do with food? How does the law of intellectual property affect food safety, food honesty, food nutrition, and food taste? I am sorry to report that it does not affect these core food values. All these cases, interesting as they are, have little to do with real food. But they are fun to read, aren't they?

LADLE AND SLANDER

A critic is a bundle of biases held
loosely together by a sense of taste.
—*Whitney Balliet,* Dinosaurs in the Morning

Can a restaurant sue a newspaper for libel arising out of a disparaging review?

When it comes to food, everyone is a critic. The difference between the paid restaurant reviewer and Joe Blow may be no more than a degree in journalism (if even that). Although some restaurant critics have some formal training in food service, most do not. No license is required, no credentials are needed, and no standards have to be met in order to criticize the offerings of the fanciest or plainest restaurant.

Bad reviews have been known to close restaurants in less time than it takes a soufflé to fall. Great reviews can mean years of vitality and profit. The stakes (if not the steaks!) are high. In the fine tradition of American litigation excess, there are scores of reported cases matching the maligned restaurateur against the opinionated reviewer. In an 1887 Massachusetts case, a newspaper printed this "report" of a catered dinner:

> Probably never in the history of the ancient and honorable
> Artillery Company was a more unsatisfactory dinner served
> than that of Monday last. One would suppose, from the elab-

orate bill of fare, that a sumptuous dinner would be furnished by the caterer, Dooling, but instead a wretched dinner was served, and in such a way that even hungry barbarians might justly object. The cigars were simply vile, and the wines not much better.[1]

Dooling sued and the Suffolk County judge ruled that without any showing of "special damages," the plaintiff could not prevail. The Massachusetts Supreme Court agreed and Dooling could only stew in his defeat.

Dooling v. Budget Publishing Company was not a free-speech case of even the slightest constitutional dimension. Not once did the court mention the First Amendment. Dooling lost because the article disparaged only the dinner, not Dooling himself. The paper reported one dreadful dinner; no more and no less. No matter that this single crucifying report would likely mean the kiss of death for Dooling's business. Sorry, Dooling. Your food stinks. But don't take it personally. (Remember this case; we will encounter the opposite situation nearly a century later and the result may surprise you.)

There were few reported cases of restaurants suing for libel over the next eighty years. Perhaps it was because baseball remained the beloved national sport, only to be replaced by litigation in the 1970s. An exception was a 1961 New Jersey case in which two restaurants sued to stop the distribution of the Mobil Travel Guide on the grounds that they received one-star (better than average) and two-star (good) ratings. Nothing in the ratings criticized or found fault with Mayfair Farms or Pal's Cabin. These two eateries were miffed because they did not receive the highest five-star rating (outstanding).

Superior Court Judge Herbert ruled in favor of the Mobil Travel Guide. "The proprietor of a restaurant exposes it to public criticism. It may come from one who writes professionally about eating places or from an ordinary patron who merely talks to his friends."[2] The court applied the principle that there is no such thing as a wrong opinion and easily disposed of the case.

Something happened to the American restaurant scene in the early 1970s. Julia Child and other well-known food personalities made great food more accessible to the people. "Gourmet" became fashionable; the age of fine dining had arrived. The age of the restaurant critic came with it.

Although a few publications had paid attention to upscale restaurants in the past, now even small newspapers and magazines began reviewing local eateries. No standards governed a publication's choice of a critic. Perhaps it was the feistiness of the times that led to the hard-hitting and often nasty reviews. Perhaps the would-be Woodwards and Bernsteins needed to find their own local Watergates and the new interest in "serious" food presented opportunities for journalistic excess. Perhaps the new fashionable restaurants were just an easy target for writers seeking to vent their rage and show off their craft.

On the legal scene, the Warren Court had created a new activist jurisprudence. Indeed, the Warren legacy is often associated with the rights of criminal defendants (e.g., *Miranda v. Arizona*,[3] requiring the police to advise suspects in custody of their rights, and *Mapp v. Ohio*,[4] applying the exclusionary rule of evidence to the states for Fourth Amendment violations). But the court also expanded the contours of the First Amendment guarantee of a free press to new frontiers as well.[5] Journalists could go after restaurants with virtual impunity.

The 1972 case of *Steak Bit of Westbury v. Newsday* in Nassau County, New York, was one of the first reported cases in which freedom of press under the First Amendment was a significant factor in the court's decision.

Stan Isaacs, columnist for *Newsday* (a daily Long Island newspaper), penned an article entitled "The Eat-Out on Old Country Road." It was a somewhat tongue-in-cheek review of twelve inexpensive take-out restaurants in Westbury. The plaintiff's business, the Lollypop Drive-In, came in dead last in the "Gluttons' Report," a comparative evaluation of the restaurants for "food quality" and "food quality adjusted for other factors."[6]

Lollypop claimed that the article's general assessment that the food at the various restaurants ". . . was mostly all fake food, ground-up schmutz [a Yiddish word that can be most charitably translated as dirt or filth]," coupled with its own low ranking, amounted to defamation. The article's helpful comment that there was also "a cemetery and a medical center on the route in case we need them" only added salt to Lollypop's wounds.[7]

The court ruled that the objectionable comments were protected opinions about the quality of the food and could not provide a basis for recovery. They did not impute to the defendant restaurant any deceitful or fraudulent business practices (which could have been grounds for a lawsuit). Even if the unflattering remarks were defamatory in nature, the Lollypop would still have to lose under the age-old doctrine of "fair comment."

Judge Harnett began his reasoning with the general premise that activities of public figures or private individuals involved in matters of public interest are protected. He then found that restaurants that serve food to the general public are involved in a matter of public interest. Therefore, restaurant reviews are protected by the constitution. How protected are they?

According to Judge Harnett and courts that would later apply this broad doctrine, newspapers were immune from defamation liability unless the plaintiff could prove that the offending reviews were motivated by malice or "made with wanton disregard."

How could a restaurant prove actual malice or "wanton disregard?" Restaurants would learn that their burden was nearly impossible to carry and that lawsuits were virtually an exercise in futility.

In 1973, Mary Mazza was a reporter for the *Daily Athenaeum,* the student paper at West Virginia University. An assignment to review the Morgantown restaurant scene brought her to the Havalunch on Pleasant Street. Mary ordered a bacon, lettuce, and tomato sandwich. She did not order a cockroach but got one anyway. She did not like either. And she did not much care for the ambience of the restaurant.

Mary's article covered more than twenty local establishments, including this choice morsel on the Havalunch: "Havalunch—Bring a can of Raid if you plan to eat here. And paint your neck red; looks like a truck stop. You'll regret everything you eat here, especially the BLT's."

Havalunch sued for libel in the Monongalia County Court. Local business owners and professionals testified as to the quality of the food and clientele of the Havalunch. The jury awarded $0 in general damages (since there was no proof of actual financial harm to Havalunch) but slapped Ms. Mazza with $15,000 in punitive damages.

The victory did not last long. On appeal, the West Virginia Supreme Court reversed. Because Havalunch could not show that Mary Mazza bore any actual malice against the restaurant, the doctrine of fair comment shielded her from any punitive damages.

As food law goes, *Havalunch v. Mazza*[8] is hardly a landmark decision. Restaurant critic wins, restaurant loses; that's the way the scales of justice usually tilt. Except Havalunch got the last word.

Justice Robert L. McGraw had disqualified himself from deciding the case, because of a prior relationship with one of the litigants. Disqualified or not, that did not stop him from issuing a separate opinion, not on the legal merits of the case, but on his memories of the Havalunch:

> I recall an eating establishment with standards of service and hygiene beyond reproach. I recall Mr. Veasey, quiet and friendly, at the cash register. I remember the delicious meals served at the spotless, immaculate, formica-covered, diner-type counters by cheerful waitresses in starched white dresses and mitres, well supervised by Mrs. Veasey.
>
> I have fond memories of delectable slices of apple, peach, lemon meringue, butterscotch and coconut cream pie. In addition to these delightful pastries, hearty, delicious meals of roast beef, ham, meat loaf or brown beans with tasty, attractive vegetables were consumed by countless students. As a compliment [*sic*] to every meal, ice cold sweet milk came from shiny stainless steel dispensers, and homemade light bread was sliced from large round loaves. For those who liked it, sweetened northern style corn bread was also baked.[9]

This may be the only recorded instance of a judge recusing himself from a case—and then proceeding to issue a lengthy opinion on the underlying cause. What led Justice McGraw to embark on this most extraordinary act of judicial activism?

As Justice McGraw pointed out in his opinion, the Havalunch had once baked cakes for the "Happy Birthday Company," a clever and successful venture that brought birthday cakes and smiles to many happy university students. It also helped finance the legal education of one Robert McGraw. As in *Justice* McGraw.

Havalunch v. Mazza was fairly typical of restaurant libel cases in one sense: the restaurant won on the trial level, only to lose on appeal. Trial judges are often reluctant to dismiss doubtful cases. It is usually more expedient to let a jury decide a case rather than erroneously dismiss a case and have an appellate court send it back for trial. Besides, if the judge gives the restaurant its day in court and the restaurant loses, there may be no appeal at all.

Restaurant critics continued their stinging attacks throughout the 1970s. In 1974, Richard Collins, writing in a New Orleans paper, ripped the Maison de Mashburn. The sauces were "hideous," the menu was a "travesty of pretentious amateurism," the oysters Bienville were a "ghastly concoction." The escargots were "simply pretentious failures that leave a bad taste in one's mouth." Mr. Collins was only getting started. He suggested that the poached trout under a crawfish sauce would be better named "trout à la green plague." The duck should have been called "yellow death on duck." The conclusion: "The restaurant as it stands now is a burlesque."[10]

Maison de Mashburn sued both Collins and the newspaper for $2 million. The paper blinked and settled out of court. Collins would not budge. The trial court granted summary judgment (a legal term meaning that because there are no genuine issues of fact for a jury to consider, the court, acting by itself, would decide the case) for Collins. The Louisiana Supreme Court upheld the trial court's decision and Maison de Mashburn could only lick its wounds (covered by whatever sauces it cared to serve).

Applying the general principle that expressions of opinion by the press concerning matters of public interest or concern are absolutely privileged unless published with knowing or reckless falsity, the Louisiana Supreme Court held that (1) the offending statements were expressions of opinion; (2) the review was written by a member of the press; (3) Maison de Mashburn was a public restaurant and a subject of public interest; and (4) the restaurant could not prove malice or reckless falsity.

Justice Summers dissented and eloquently presented the case for the beleaguered restaurant, in an opinion based not so much in constitutional doctrine but in fairness and sympathy:

> No food could reach the depths of degradation heaped upon Mashburn's menu by this column.
>
> Mashburn's restaurant represents a conscientious undertaking by a private individual in a harmless enterprise. It has no broad impact upon the public. . . . Why the author would employ the power of the press and embark on such a vicious and sustained attack defaming and maligning virtually all of Mashburn's culinary efforts is unexplained. One thing is certain. The composition on its face is

undoubtedly designed to strike at the heart of Mashburn's business causing him injury, untold humiliation and embarrassment.

In my opinion the tenor of this publication offends any ordinary standard of decency and fair comment. It constitutes a degrading, malicious and unprovoked attack which no privilege or right should condone.

...In my view this publication demonstrates a total lack of restraint in the use of the awesome power of the press against a small private business man engaged in an honest and conscientious effort to earn a living—an enterprise with a very limited effect upon the public interest.[11]

Eloquent? Yes! Persuasive? No. It was the lone dissenting vote.

In 1981, the *Gault/Milau Guide to New York* reviewed Mr. Chow, a Manhattan Chinese restaurant:

While his London restaurant enjoys an honorable reputation (although it is clearly overrated), the branch which the clever Mr. Chow has just opened in New York is simply astounding from a culinary point of view. In a pinch, you might not care that you have to wait ten minutes to obtain chopsticks instead of forks, that it is impossible to have basic condiments (soy sauce, hot sauce, etc.) on the table, that the principal concern of the waiters (Italians) is to sell you expensive alcoholic drinks, but the last straw is that the dishes on the menu (very short) have only the slightest relationship to the essential spirit of Chinese cuisine. With their heavy and greasy dough, the dumplings, on our visit, resembled bad Italian ravioli, the steamed meatballs had a disturbingly gamey taste, the sweet and sour pork contained more dough (badly cooked) than meat, and the green peppers which accompanied it remained still frozen on the plate. The chicken with chili was rubbery and the rice, soaking, for some reason, in oil, totally insipid.[12]

The review criticized Mr. Chow's version of the venerable Chinese classic, Peking Duck, which had only one course and offered pancakes "the size of a saucer and the thickness of a finger." The reviewer suggested that Mr. Chow send his cooks to Chinatown for instruction. The review finished with a flourish: "It is, however, true that when one sees with what epicurean airs his customers exclaim at canned lychees, one can predict for him a long and prosperous life uptown."[13]

Mr. Chow sued for compensatory damages in excess of $10,000 and punitive damages in excess of $250,000. He took exception to the entire review but the trial judge narrowed the jury's task to evaluating six allegedly false and defamatory statements:

1. "It is impossible to have the basic condiments ... on the table"
2. "The sweet and sour pork contained more dough ... than meat"
3. "The green peppers ... remained still frozen on the plate"
4. The rice was "soaking ... in oil"
5. The Peking Duck "was made up of only one dish (instead of the traditional three)"
6. The pancakes were "the thickness of a finger"[14]

Jury duty was never so much fun as that day in the district court for the Southern District of New York. The jurors must have been salivating as they watched a video of Mr. Chow's eager chefs preparing sweet and sour pork. Flour chef Kooh Hong Kim then gave an in-court demonstration of his method of making Chinese pancakes.

The jurors were duly impressed—sort of. They found in favor of Mr. Chow, awarding $20,000 in compensatory damages but only $5 in punitive damages. On appeal, Mr. Chow lost and went home with nary a fortune cookie.

The Second Circuit Court of Appeals carefully distinguished between statements of fact and opinions. As a general proposition, one cannot be found liable for expressing an opinion. Of course, the difference between an opinion and a statement of fact is not always clear. For example, the statement that the sweet and sour pork contained "more dough than meat" might seem at first glance to be a factual assertion. It's either more dough than meat or it's more meat than dough (or exactly the same), and one can measure by weight or volume and find out if the statement is true.

The court was unwilling to take such a literal approach. The reviewer obviously meant that in his opinion the sweet and sour pork was just too doughy. That Monsieur Bridault chose to express that opinion by means of hyperbole and exaggeration did not make it any less an opinion. So, too, did the reviewer mean only to opine that the service was bad, the peppers were too cold, the rice was too oily, and the pancakes too thick. These opinions were matters of personal taste and protected by the First Amendment.

Only the statement that the Peking Duck came in one dish instead of the traditional three could be considered a statement of fact. But Mr. Chow still could not prevail. Statements of fact, even if false, are not actionable unless they are made with malice. Mr. Chow could not prove that the reviewer knew that his statement about the Peking Duck was false or that he entertained serious doubts about its truth.

Curiously, Mr. Chow never contested that as a restaurant open to the public it was a "public figure," for purposes of First Amendment analysis.

The Second Circuit summarized the uphill battle restaurants face in suing for libel:

> Appellee [Mr. Chow] does not cite a single case that has found a restaurant review libelous. Appellants and *amici,* on the other hand, cite numerous decisions that have refused to do so. Although the rationale underlying each of these decisions is different, they all recognize to some extent that reviews, although they may be unkind, are not normally a breeding ground for successful libel actions.[15]

Amici, for those not familiar with this term of legalese, is the plural of *amicus* and it stands for *amici curiae,* meaning friends of the court. Courts often permit organizations to file briefs in support of particular litigants, especially where those organizations have broad public-policy perspectives that may help the court. No one filed "friend of the court" briefs in support of Mr. Chow. In support of the publications was an all-star cast of high-priced law firms representing some very heavy hitters, including CBS, ABC, NBC, the Association of American Publishers, the National Association of Booksellers, the National Association of Broadcasters, and Time, Incorporated.

Writing for the *Columbus Monthly,* Vivian Witkind reviewed the Aspen Inn and Tamarack, two Ohio eateries with Colorado decor. The introduction to the review did not bode well for these restaurants: "For a substantial cash outlay, you get a ritzy decor, something to eat and waiters who aren't surly. What you also get is a thinly disguised effort to milk you for every penny of profit. One way this is done is to cut corners on the preparation of the food."[16] The Tamarack was "saved" by the reviewer's assessment that some of the entrées were very good, including the "superb" baked spareribs. The Aspen Inn did not fare so well and it sued.

The review found two basic problems with the Aspen Inn: geographic schizophrenia and mediocrity. After all, could anyone explain why a Key West fish platter was on the menu of a Colorado-style ski resort motif restaurant? A more serious problem for the Aspen Inn was the comment that the Key West platter tasted "like old ski boots." Other menu items did not come off very well either. The escargots were "dull." The scallops ("coquilles St. Jacques") were "outrageously bad" and an "atrocity."[17]

These assessments were obviously opinions and could hardly be the basis of a serious lawsuit. Other parts of the review seemed to be more fact laden and presented a challenge to the court. Ms. Witkind wrote that the salad ingredients were "overwhelmed by croutons from a can and dressing from a bottle." She also panned the prime rib ("no flavor itself") which got all of its seasoning "from the Lawry's seasoned salt in the juice."

Were these statements of fact or exaggerated and fanciful expressions of opinion? The Ohio court could have held that the ordinary reader would read these comments as meaning that, in the reviewer's opinion, the croutons tasted *like* canned croutons, that the dressing tasted *like* bottled dressing, and the flavor of the prime rib tasted *like* Lawry's seasoned salt.

That approach would have been consistent with the wide latitude other courts (like the court in the Mr. Chow case) have afforded the literal language of restaurant reviews. The Ohio court chose the direct route, treating the offending words as statements of fact, and the restaurant still lost!

The restaurant lost because the testimony showed that the croutons did indeed come from a can and the salad dressing (at least most of it) from a bottle. As for the prime rib, the night manager testified that Lawry's Seasoned Salt was not used, at least not on the night that Ms. Witkind visited the Aspen Inn. However, he could not explain the restaurant's recent purchase of a large amount of—you guessed it, Lawry's Seasoned Salt.

The court gave us some insight into Ms. Witkind's method of review. She was paid $200 per review, plus expenses. She wrote the article on the basis of one visit. With her on that Saturday night were her husband and two friends. She also engaged in a twenty-minute telephone conversation with the restaurant's manager.

Is a single visit to a restaurant a sufficient basis for a negative review that is likely to severely damage the business of that restaurant? After all, it is possible that the reviewer hit the restaurant on a rare off night. There are no standards in the "industry," although most reviewers at the larger newspapers (e.g., the *New York Times*) will not pan a restaurant on the basis of only one visit.

The Ohio Court of Appeals made a broad statement about restaurant reviews: "By its very nature, an article commenting upon the quality of a restaurant or its food, *like a review of a play or movie,* constitutes the opinion of the reviewer."[18] Is that a fair comparison?

Roger Ebert, movie critic for the *Chicago Sun-Times* and one-time partner with the late Gene Siskel of the *Chicago Tribune,* is as famous as the movie stars he critiques. Millions watch his television show and eagerly await his verdicts of "thumbs up!" or "thumbs down!" But negative reviews from Roger Ebert do not necessarily mean financial ruin for a movie studio. There have been scores of critical flops that turned out to be box office smashes. Why are movie reviews different from restaurant reviews?

Restaurants are usually small businesses and generally have small advertising budgets. They can do little to counter the effects of a negative review. Movies are made by big studios with huge advertising budgets that can create enough prerelease hype to override any negative reviews. Studios can make millions from product licensing. Kids will pay big bucks for superhero action figures. When was the last time your child asked for a famous chef action figure (chef's toque and wire whisk sold separately)? Although a few chefs have achieved national fame (e.g., Paul Prudhomme, Emeril Lagasse) and have translated that fame into revenues apart from their restaurants, most restaurant owners depend only on what their chefs turn out from night to night.

Another difference: people may be more willing to go to a movie that has received negative reviews than to a restaurant that has been similarly slammed. Let's face it: some people enjoy "bad" movies; "slasher" movies, dumb sequels, and formula retreads of old themes can still attract lots of customers if the right star is in it, if the special effects are particularly dazzling, and if the national marketing is right. Besides, a "bad" movie experience may be disappointing but involves less of a risk (financially and emotionally) than a bad dining experience.

Movies make their money from one-time visits (some fans will see a movie twenty-eight times but the movie industry does not count on repeat customers) while restaurants rely on their customers returning over and over again. A potential customer who is dissuaded by a bad review from visiting a restaurant once is a potential lost repeat customer. Even movies that do not do well at the box office can make up part of their lost sales in revenues earned from video release. Restaurants do not have that second chance possibility. From a legal standpoint, a restaurant review may raise the same free-speech issues as a movie review, but the economic impact is potentially far more serious.

How far can the media go? Pretty far. In 1976, David Brudnoy was the host of a Boston radio talk show. He was also a well-known restaurant critic. When the topic of his September tenth show turned to tipping at restaurants, Brudnoy slammed the "dodin-bouffant" (the lower case is consistent with how the restaurant named itself) as one of two restaurants in the Boston area that followed the European practice of including the gratuity in the bill.

When a guest tried to defend "dodin-bouffant," Brudnoy explained that he thought the food was excellent. His complaint was with the service and the owners:

> the people who run the place are unconscionably rude and vulgar people. And the attitude they communicate is awful. But the food is fine. And it kills me to say this because I would like to be able to dump on their restaurant. I keep going there hoping it will decline and it doesn't. The food is fine, the people who run it are pigs.[19]

Pigs? Surely, a clear-cut case of libel. Remember the 1887 Massachusetts case in which the court refused to find libel because the report criticized only the food but not Dooling personally? Here, Brudnoy loved the food but called David and Karen Pritsker "rude" and "vulgar" and "pigs." Under the *Dooling* decision, the Pritskers would certainly prevail. But no! Now even these comments were protected under the First Amendment because, as the court "reasoned":

we think that the average listener would assume that Brudnoy's comments were based only on his observations of conditions at the restaurant, such as its service, decor, and atmosphere, and would regard his comments simply as his opinion of conditions which he, as a professional restaurant critic, found unsatisfactory or distasteful and which he reasonably attributed to the owners of the restaurant.[20]

Therefore, the reference to the Pritskers as "rude and vulgar" and as "pigs" was only in their capacity of restaurant owners, not as people. Indeed, Brudnoy had never even met the Pritskers. A little bit of legal sleight-of-hand? Perhaps. The bottom line was that the restaurant had again lost.

What about misstatements of fact? Restaurants have succeeded in getting newspapers to print retractions or corrections in only a handful of cases. One restaurant did prevail in a hotly contested case in New York City. In 1987, Maryann Terillo, owner and chef of Le Café de la Gare, sued *Newsday* because its food critic wrote that the café's cassoulet contained lamb, hot and sweet Italian sausage, pork pieces, and a parmesan cheese topping. Chef Terillo was outraged because those ingredients were "completely alien" to her creation. Her cassoulet contained white beans, tomato sauce, pork and garlic sausage, and duck confit. It was topped with bread crumbs and duck fat for browning.

Le Café de la Gare had tried to be an authentic French-style bistro, serving traditional French fare. Cassoulet, if prepared the way the food critic said it was prepared, would be an affront to food purists and certainly damaging to the Greenwich Village restaurant's reputation as a bastion of authentic French food. The food critic had even taken a copy of the menu listing the actual ingredients but she stood by her comments and raised the First Amendment flag.

Manhattan Small Claims Court Judge Norman C. Ryp ruled[21] that readers would consider the listing of ingredients as fact, not as opinion, and were therefore libelous:

> Integrity is not only standing up for one's rights of free expression but also owning up to one's wrongs, even if eating humble pie (cassoulet). This is especially true for food critics, whose words, ingested by a gullible public, can mean life or death to a restaurant.

Although Judge Ryp found that the critic's words were libelous, he refused to award the $1,500 in damages that the restaurant had sought (for lack of proof of harm). No matter. Chef Terillo was thrilled. She had taken on a major newspaper and gotten it to eat its words. A most fitting dessert.

In 1992, Marilyn Alva, writing in *Restaurant Business*,[22] concluded that the heyday of the scathing restaurant review was over and that there was now "no need to fear your local restaurant critic." Many restaurant critics (or as some prefer to be called, "reviewers") no longer want to be the bearers of bad news. To some degree, local writers now see themselves as part of the "team" that promotes the positive aspects of the area. This optimistic view (from the restaurants' perspective) may be premature.

Do food critics ever trade favorable reviews for money? Federal authorities investigated one Pittsburgh food writer for doing just that. Before charges could be filed, the writer committed suicide. Although this was an isolated case (in terms of how close it came to criminal charges being filed), the ethics of food writers is a legitimate question. Some restaurants sense a certain pressure to advertise in the paper if they want to get a review. Food writers will steadfastly deny any connection between advertising contracts and reviews but if the perception is there, does it matter?

One restaurant that suffered a negative review (the steak "appeared to have been cooked in a blast furnace") argued that its advertisement commitment to a newspaper precluded the newspaper from publishing any negative reviews about it. A Florida Circuit Court rejected this preposterous argument that somehow an advertising contract prevented the newspaper from expressing an opinion on an advertiser's business. It may not be good business for a newspaper to publish a negative review of an advertiser's establishment but it is hardly the basis for a legal argument precluding the criticism.[23]

Restaurants victimized by negative media reviews will continue to find little relief from the courts. Unfortunately, those unlucky eateries will suffer greatly because consumers endow restaurant critics with enormous credibility. But think of it: it's only one person's opinion. Are we so easily swayed by the opinion of someone we've probably never met?

The answer is that we are indeed easily—too easily—influenced by food critics.

Restaurant reviewers wield enormous power. They can shut down restaurants with a few strokes of their pens or clicks on their word processors. Restaurants have no recourse. They have no effective right of rebuttal.

The problem is an imbalance of power and economic resources. Restaurants can't fight back. There is a solution. Food writers need to be aware of their enormous power and the need to be fair. Consumers need to take the review they read with—well, with a grain of salt (seasoned or not).

As passionate as I am about good food, I am equally passionate about the First Amendment and the freedom of the press. The relatively few abuses that have harmed a handful of restaurants do not justify the greater harm of restricting the press in its legitimate role of reviewing the new theater of the day, the restaurant scene.

Although food reviewers have mellowed in some circles, they have become even more ruthless in others. The rise of the Internet has meant that would-be food critics can publish their opinions on self-made web sites with virtual impunity. They need not answer to anyone, especially not to an editor or a publisher.

Even mainstream food reviews have been surprisingly vicious. Writing in the *San Francisco Chronicle,* reviewer Michael Bauer trashed a Bay Area seafood restaurant (I'll not name it) in the most unforgiving terms: "On four visits . . . the story was pretty much the same: poor service and ill-prepared food. . . . We could have gotten through most of *Moby Dick* waiting for our first course to arrive." Mr. Bauer went on to lament the poor quality of the individual dishes and ended with a flourish: "If I've had a more disappointing experience in the past decade, I can't remember when. In fact, my idea of hell would be to spend another evening at [X's]."[24]

I asked Mr. Bauer if he had ever been sued over any critical reviews. He replied: "I've been threatened lots of times, and our lawyers have responded, but nothing's ever gone to court. I try to be very careful, but I know it's the things you don't think about that get you in trouble. As for [X's], I've not heard anything."[25]

What was the reaction of the X restaurant, bruised and battered by Mr. Bauer's review? I interviewed a corporate officer of the company that owned the restaurant (the corporation is not located in the Bay Area) who, while obviously unhappy with the review and critical of the reviewer, understood the futility of filing a lawsuit.

It seems to be a simple and straightforward rule of law: the press is immune from liability when it criticizes restaurants. When it comes to entire industries and the press, you would think that the principles should be the same. In practice, though, things are different. In the next chapter, we will see what happened when a major television network questioned the safety of apples in the northwest, when a major television talk show personality took on one of the most powerful food industries, and when a television news show sent its reporters undercover to reveal a parade of horribles in the meat department of a major supermarket chain. Stick around!

10

FROM BAD APPLES
TO MAD COWS

Free speech not only lives, it rocks!
—Oprah Winfrey,
in her press conference
after the jury's verdict
in the lawsuit brought by
the Texas Cattlemen's Association

On 26 February 1989, the popular CBS news show *60 Minutes* aired a segment on the chemical commonly known as "Alar" that was then being used in the apple-growing industry. The story was based on a Natural Resources Defense Council report that linked Alar to cancer, especially in children. The segment opened with a shot of a red delicious apple emblazoned with a skull and crossbones.

According to *60 Minutes*, growers sprayed Alar (the trade name for the chemical compound daminozide) on apples to keep them on the trees longer and to make them look more appetizing. Then came the zinger: children are most at risk for getting cancer from Alar when it breaks down into another chemical. The demand for apples dropped, prices plummeted, and many apple growers lost a lot of money. The growers sued CBS, claiming "product disparagement." They lost in federal court before the jury could even consider the evidence because the judge ruled that the growers could not possibly produce any evidence that CBS broadcast anything that was false.[1]

Judge Nielsen summed it up well:

That incident provoked what has come to be known as the "Alar Scare." Apples had not received such bad press since Genesis. The shock value of learning that a product universally considered so wholesome and all-American as apples could give children cancer galvanized parents nationwide into a boycott which had an immediate financial impact on Washington growers.[2]

Judge Nielsen ruled in favor of CBS and the court of appeals affirmed,[3] leaving the Washington State apple growers angry, frustrated, and, in some cases, financially ruined. The growers were furious that the courts never even allowed them to present their case to a jury. The problem was that, according to the courts, no reasonable jury could find for them. It was not a question of whose science you wanted to believe but whether CBS had any legitimate scientific evidence to back up the report that was the basis for their story.

The apple growers claimed that in the absence of any direct evidence that Alar caused cancer in humans, they should be able to present their case to a jury. The problem was that there was evidence of animal laboratory testing that the court held was a legitimate means for assessing cancer risks in humans. In short, the growers could not possibly prove the falsity of the underlying claims of the CBS show.

Alar soon disappeared from the agricultural scene. Uniroyal, the maker of Alar, voluntarily requested a withdrawal of Alar's food-use registrations. The EPA later canceled all food-use registrations for Alar in November 1989.[4]

Were the Washington state apple growers treated badly by the media and then by the legal system? According to Nicholas Fox's 1997 book, *Spoiled,* consumers reacted reasonably and responsibly to the scientific information available at the time. Furthermore, argues Fox, apple sales had been declining since 1984 (when the Environmental Protection Agency first announced that it would review Alar) and the drop in sales after *60 Minutes* was not all that great.

Depending on where your sympathies lie, the apple growers (*a*) were treated badly by journalism bent on sensationalism and high ratings, or (*b*) got what they deserved because they were using a chemical that was only questionably safe in order to increase their profits.

No matter. Agricultural interests across the country were terrified that what happened to the Washington apple growers could happen to them. In response to the Alar fiasco, or rather in anticipation of some future similar catastrophe, the agriculture industry, led by the American Feed Industry Association, came up with a brilliant new idea—agriculture disparagement laws.

Known informally as "veggie libel" laws or "banana bills" or "veggie hate crimes," these laws are (as of the beginning of 2000) on the books in thirteen states and under consideration in at least a dozen more. They allow food producers to sue when their products are unfairly criticized. They make it possible—at least theoretically—for agricultural interests to sue individuals and groups that make false claims about the safety of various agricultural and aquacultural products. The beauty of these laws (or the terror of these laws if you are on the other side) is that they get around some of the barriers that traditional defamation laws erected.

The first hurdle that the usual defamation laws put up is the "of and concerning" requirement. Translation: the party claiming injury must be the specific target of the defamatory statement. For example, if I tell a tasteless joke about blonds without naming any specific blond, no one blond can sue me. If I give an opinion about the safety of white bread without naming any specific bakery, the makers of Wonder Bread can't touch me.

The veggie libel laws addressed a basic problem that kept the Washington apple growers from successfully suing CBS: they could not win under traditional trade libel law. The usual trade libel is when one company tries to badmouth a competitor by spreading lies or other false information. That model did not fit when the speaker was someone like Ed Bradley, representing a major news organization.

The purpose of these new laws is no secret, namely, to protect the agricultural and aquacultural industries of the various states. For example, the Alabama, Arizona, Florida, Georgia, Louisiana, Mississippi, Ohio, and South Dakota statutes all use the exact same language: "to protect the agricultural and aquacultural economy . . . by providing a cause of action for producers to recover damages for the disparagement of perishable product or commodity."[5]

These statutes allow lawsuits for damages arising out of disparaging statements or the dissemination of "false information" about the safety of various foods. Is this kind of statute a "special interest" law? Certainly. Agricultural interests may argue that these laws are necessary "to level the playing field" but they are special-interest laws nevertheless, passed at the behest of powerful economic groups to protect their own interests.

Most legal scholars have argued that the various veggie libel laws are unconstitutional because they do not take into account any measure of "fault" on the part of the speaker and because they place an impermissible burden on speech that is protected under the First Amendment. The kind of speech here is vital to public safety and of great public concern.

Remember Upton Sinclair's damning indictment of the meatpacking industry? Would his writings have landed him in court under these agricultural disparagement laws? No matter that *The Jungle* was fiction, it is arguable that his inflammatory descriptions would have made him a defendant in a lawsuit. What about President George (the elder) Bush's famous remarks about broccoli? Could the broccoli farmers have sued him?

Although no one has been successfully sued under the veggie libel laws, their very presence can make publishers, broadcasters, and writers think twice about disseminating information or expressing opinions about the safety of food. That is exactly what legal scholars mean when they refer to the "chilling effect" that laws can have on speech. One case came close.

On 16 April 1996, Oprah Winfrey, the acknowledged queen of daytime talk television, aired a show about "dangerous foods." One of the topics was the possibility of the spread of bovine spongiform encephalopathy, or "mad cow disease," in the United States. Mad cow disease had claimed several lives in England and created a major panic in British markets.

In researching the show, staffers for Oprah Winfrey learned that most experts, including the Center for Disease Control and leading professors, believed that it was most unlikely that mad cow disease could ever become a problem in the United States (for an update, see chapter 15). However, Howard Lyman, a former cattle rancher turned vegetarian activist, believed that mad cow disease could produce a major epidemic on American soil.

Contrary to what many now believe, the show was not just about the possibility of mad cow disease and the alleged unsafe feeding practices of the U.S. beef industry. The program also covered other food issues, including the dangers of meat tainted with *E. coli* bacteria, food-handling tips, a discussion about raw oysters, potential problems associated with diet herbal teas, a tour of a Chicago restaurant, and a discussion of public water supplies. But it was the discussion of the threat of mad cow disease that provoked a major lawsuit.

Although Howard Lyman made several inflammatory statements about the safety of the U.S. beef supply and the possibility of a mad cow disease epidemic, other guests disagreed with Lyman's assessment of the problem. What finally aired was an edited version of the show that was originally taped on 11 April 1996. Edited out of the final program was Lyman's admission that American beef is generally safe and some statements (deemed "redundant" by the show's editors) by other guests.

Immediately following the 16 April 1996 broadcast, the cattle market in the Texas Panhandle and in national markets dropped dramatically. In the week before the show aired, the price of finished cattle ran at about $61.90 per hundred weight. After the show, the price dropped to the mid-50s and sales volume dropped as well.

Here is another not-so-well-known fact: in response to accusations of unfairness, Oprah Winfrey invited Dr. Gary Weber from the National Cattleman's Beef Association and a cattle rancher to a show aired one week later to refute the charges made by Howard Lyman. Dr. Weber explained, as he had briefly done on the original show, the voluntary ban on ruminant-to-ruminant feeding (the apparent cause of mad cow disease) and reassured the American public that American beef was safe.

The president of the National Cattleman's Beef Association sent Oprah Winfrey a letter thanking her for letting his organization "present the truth" about cattle-feeding practices, calling the rebuttal show "a service to consumers and a great relief to many of my fellow cattlemen."[6] Great relief or not, within a matter of weeks, a group of cattlemen sued Oprah, her production studio, and Howard Lyman, claiming that the show violated the Texas False Disparagement of Perishable Food Products Statute. They also charged the common-law torts of business disparagement, defamation, and negligence.

There were four key elements to the cattlemen's claims: (1) Oprah's exclamation during the original show that she was "stopped cold from eating another burger"; (2) Lyman's assertion that mad cow disease could make AIDS look like the common cold; (3) Lyman's accusation that the United States was treating the possibility of an outbreak of mad cow disease as a public relations issue without taking substantial steps to prevent it; and (4) the unbalanced editing of the original show.

Oprah Winfrey had more than enough money to meet the challenge of the Texas cattle interests. She was ready to challenge the constitutionality of the Texas False Disparagement of Perishable Food Products Statute with full vigor. The only problem was that the district court found that live cattle did not fit within the meaning "perishable food products" and the case proceeded on more traditional libel issues. The court never reached the greater constitutional issue of whether food libel laws violate the First Amendment.

Oprah Winfrey took her show to Amarillo where she was defendant by day and talk show host by night. During the five-week trial, a ticket to the Oprah Winfrey show was the toughest ticket to find in Amarillo. Of course, Oprah could not comment on the case during the trial, under strict court order. But when the jury returned its verdict in Oprah's favor, she was jubilant, calling the jury's decision a great victory for freedom of speech.

Was it? Oprah Winfrey may be one of the few Americans with the resources to fight a protracted legal battle with a powerful special interest group. Her legal fees were certainly in excess of one million dollars. Could you afford that kind of bill from your lawyer? While the outcome of the case may offer comfort to free-speech advocates, the fact that the beef industry was ready, willing, and able to press ahead with the litigation must create concern for anyone with a lesser bank account who might consider criticizing the safety of beef.

Oprah Winfrey won her case because the cattle ranchers could not convince the jury that anyone on the show knowingly made false statements about the safety of American beef. What about Howard Lyman's extreme comments that mad cow disease could make AIDS look like the common cold? Lyman was undoubtedly exaggerating but, in the eyes of the law, exaggeration does not equal defamation.

Lyman's opinions, although strongly stated with passion and emotion, did have some basis in fact. At the time of the show's broadcast, there was some ruminant-to-ruminant feeding going on in the United States.

As for the unfair editing job that the Oprah Winfrey show did on the taping, there was no way the court was going to find defamation simply because the show did not present the mad cow issue in the most favorable light to American beef.[7] When it was all over, plaintiff Paul Engler remarked: "It's very difficult to fight a celebrity."

Another important free-speech food case arose out of the ABC television show *PrimeTime Live*'s story on unsanitary meat-handling practices at the Food Lion supermarkets in North Carolina and South Carolina. What ABC told the nation was shocking. What the jury in Winston-Salem did to ABC was, to many observers, equally if not more shocking.

Producers at *PrimeTime Live* wanted to investigate reports that Food Lion stores were grinding out-of-date beef together with new beef, that they were bleaching rank beef to remove its foul odor, and that they were redating out-of-date (expired) meat. These allegations, if true, would make for a powerful segment on the popular show.

With the blessings of ABC superiors, reporters Lynne Dale and Susan Barnett went to work for Food Lion. They used false identities, false references, and false local addresses in applying for their jobs. Not surprisingly, they did not reveal their connection with ABC. They also misrepresented their educational backgrounds and employment histories. But Food Lion hired them.

Armed with hidden cameras and microphones, Dale and Barnett gathered a bonanza of information that confirmed most of the allegations of improper meat handling. The story ran on 5 November 1992, and it was as explosive as Upton Sinclair's fictionalized account of the beef industry eighty years earlier. The report included videotape footage of Food Lion employees repackaging and redating fish that had passed its expiration date, grinding expired beef with fresh beef, and applying barbecue sauce to chicken that was past its expiration date and selling it as fresh in the gourmet section of the store. Dale and Barnett also taped statements of former Food Lion employees alleging even more serious examples of meat mishandling.

Food Lion was devastated by the show and, predictably, it sued. Yet, it never denied the truth of ABC's claims that it had engaged in what most people regarded as despicable behavior. It sued because it objected to the methods that ABC used in obtaining and gathering the information that formed the basis for the story. Food Lion wanted to recover the costs and wages paid in connection with the employment of the two undercover employees, even though they only worked at

Food Lion for a very short time (Barnett for two weeks and Dale for only one week). Food Lion also requested damages for loss of good will, lost sales and profits, and diminished stock value. It also requested punitive damages.

Food Lion tried every legal maneuver, including a claim that ABC had engaged in racketeering in violation of the federal RICO Act (Racketeer Influenced and Corrupt Organizations Act). The company also alleged intentional misrepresentation, fraud, deceit, negligent supervision, trespass, breach of fiduciary duty, violations of federal wiretapping laws, civil conspiracy, and violation of the North Carolina Unfair and Deceptive Practices Act. About the only thing Food Lion did not allege was a violation of the Second Amendment (the right to bear arms).

The jury found ABC liable to Food Lion for fraud and found the two reporters liable for breaching their duty of loyalty to Food Lion as their employer and also for trespass. The judge would not allow the jury to even consider Food Lion's request for damages based on lost profits, lost sales, or diminished stock value. Things looked pretty good for ABC, as the jury awarded Food Lion a whopping $1,400 on the fraud charge, and assessed damages against the two undercover reporters at one dollar each.

The jurors were obviously not outraged by Food Lion's behavior; or they found ABC's behavior in going undercover to find the story more outrageous than the story itself. The jurors nailed ABC with punitive damages to the tune of $5,545,750. The trial judge reduced the punitive damages award down to $315,000. To no one's surprise, both sides appealed.

The battle was joined. For the fraud claim, on which Food Lion had requested more than $2 million, the jury had awarded a paltry $1,400. It may not seem like much money to a major media conglomerate, but ABC appealed anyway—and won! Because Dale and Barrett never made any misrepresentations about how long they would work, there was no fraud. Food Lion knew that all of their new hires were a risk; some might quit after only a few days.

Didn't Dale and Barnett breach their duty of loyalty to Food Lion? Only if Food Lion did not receive value for the wages it paid to the undercover reporters. As it turned out, Dale and Barnett were very good employees; both of their supervisors thought their performances were more than adequate. Didn't their use of hidden cameras and microphones breach a duty of loyalty to Food Lion? Perhaps, but the jury awarded damages of only one dollar each and Food Lion agreed that it could not prove damages in excess of this nominal amount.

The court of appeals did find that Dale and Barnett did commit the tort of disloyalty against Food Lion because they intended to do things that were against Food Lion's interests, that is, uncovering dirt and going public. Unfortunately for Food Lion, this tort did not translate to any real money.

What about the trespass theory? The court of appeals upheld the jury's verdict that Dale and Barnett trespassed but again, not much money would go to Food Lion on this element of the case.

The long and the short of the decision of the court of appeals is that Food Lion got two dollars in damages. That is not a misprint. Not two million dollars. Not even two thousand dollars. Two dollars—as in eight quarters. Barely enough to buy a package of ground beef, if that's how you want to spend it.[8]

So what have we? It is the food industry versus the media. In one case, the apple growers took on CBS and lost because there was nothing untruthful about what CBS said about Alar and its risks to children. In another case, the cattle raisers took on Oprah Winfrey and lost because they could not prove that Oprah's remarks or those of her guests were recklessly false. In the third case, a grocery chain took on ABC and lost (winning two dollars is a big loss in our book) because as deceitful as ABC was in gaining access to the Food Lion meat departments, it was the Food Lion food-handling practices that caused them to lose public confidence, not ABC's methods in getting the story.

On one level, it is easy to be sympathetic to the plight of the apple growers and the cattle ranchers. After all, they were engaged in perfectly legal activities and lost money. The apple growers probably knew that Alar was a risk and that its days of usage were numbered. But how can you not feel bad for someone who grows apples? For the most part, the cattlemen were not engaged in the dangerous ruminant-to-ruminant feeding that could create the risk of mad cow disease, but the practice had not been completely banned. Surely, the media cannot be expected to ignore the possibilities of harm to the public.

The Food Lion case is the most troubling because it asks the fundamental question: how far can the media go in exposing dangers in the food industry? ABC's conduct was certainly more deceitful than that of CBS or Oprah Winfrey, but so was Food Lion's conduct more reprehensible than that of the apple growers or the cattlemen. Frankly, it is very difficult to be at all sympathetic to a grocery store that intentionally sells bad meat. Give Food Lion credit for one thing: it must have hired some terrific lawyers because that's the only explanation I have for the jury's willingness to award more than $5 million to a company that was willing to package and sell rotten meat.

Do the ends (protecting the public from unsafe food) justify the means (fraud, deceit, and trespass in gaining access to a private business)? I am not at all sympathetic to photojournalists who engage in illegal or ethically questionable activities in order to gain access to a Hollywood celebrity just to get a sensational picture for a tabloid. But food safety is different, isn't it? Food safety is a matter of great public interest and perhaps we need to cut the media more slack when it comes to exposing dangers and abuses that affect our health.

Freedom of speech, as embodied by the First Amendment, is much easier to apply in the cases of restaurants miffed by unfavorable food reviews. One might assume that the same reasoning and result should apply in the case of larger corporate entities similarly wounded by the press. It would seem, at first glance, that the only difference is size. Then again, size does matter.

Who can argue with freedom of speech and freedom of the press? If your business has been harmed by an irresponsible though legally protectable story, you may well take issue with the broad protections given the press under the Constitution. Remarkably, though, the First Amendment has worked to protect the consuming public from fraud, deception, and unsafe products.

The dangers of an irresponsible press in the matter of food safety are certainly substantial. The dangers of a muzzled press are certainly greater.

11

IT'S NOT NICE TO DEFRAUD MOTHER NATURE!

"It was the *best* butter," the March Hare meekly replied.
—*Lewis Carroll*, Alice's Adventure in Wonderland

It is said that every writer has a bias, perhaps not even easily identified by the writer himself. But I freely admit to a strong bias on the topic of this chapter. When it comes to butter versus margarine, it's no contest. I adore the taste of sweet butter on a hard-crusted baguette or a slice of toasted rye. There is no way I would tolerate margarine on my bread. As for the commercials that claim I won't believe that a particular margarine is not butter, or tastes like the high-priced spread, or that it isn't nice to fool Mother Nature—I've tried them all and (*a*) I believed, (*b*) it didn't, and (*c*) she wasn't.

I have done blind taste tests with friends and they have unanimously selected butter as their preferred spread. The finest restaurants in the country use butter. On top of all that, I live in Wisconsin, proudly known as the Dairy State.

You won't find one stick of margarine in my refrigerator.

So do not say that I am "anti-butter."

Now let's get on with this chapter about laws and lawsuits that concern the dairy industry. We begin with butter and its sudden competition in the nineteenth century.

The French Emperor Louis Napoleon III had a problem: butter was scarce, especially for his soldiers and sailors who dearly loved it. That scarcity spread to the home front, and the French masses, though not exactly to the point of revolution over the shortage of pure dairy butter, were unhappy. So the king offered a prize to the person who would come up with a palatable and cheap substitute for butter.[1]

An enterprising and resourceful chemist named Hippolyte Mege-Mouriez took the prize with his invention of "oleomargarine," a refinement of an earlier nineteenth century discovery by Michel Eugène Chevreul of a fatty acid called "margaric acid." The "oleo" part refers to the oleic acid found in beef fat that Mege-Mouriez attached to Chevreul's margaric acid. The "margarine" name comes from the Greek word *margaron*, meaning "pearl," because Chevreul thought the substance formed pearl-like drops. In 1867, Mege-Mouriez began manufacturing his new spread, the very same year that the Illinois and Wisconsin Dairymen's Association was formed.[2]

It was only a matter of time, a very short time, before margarine came to the United States. The first U.S. patent was granted on 30 December 1873. Depending on whose point of view you choose to adopt, this event heralded (*a*) a low-cost and healthy choice for consumers or (*b*) the beginning of a wave of fraud on the public. Not surprisingly, the margarine industry championed the first view while the dairy industry pushed the latter.

The half-century following margarine's first appearance on American soil is full of legislative and judicial activity pitting the powerful dairy industry against the upstart margarine makers. Indeed, a review of the reported food cases from 1880 to 1930 reveals an almost obsessive preoccupation on the part of the dairy industry to make margarine as unattractive and difficult to obtain as possible. One state, New Hampshire, even required that margarine be colored pink; the U.S. Supreme Court overturned that law on the grounds that the restriction was so extreme as to amount to a total ban.[3] Yet, the same court upheld a ban on yellow margarine against a claim that it imposed an unconstitutional burden on interstate commerce because it bought into the argument that margarine might be a threat to public health.[4]

When a plaintiff in a lawsuit claims to represent the best interests of the consuming public, it is always best to ask one simple question:

does that party have a monetary stake in the outcome of the case? If so, the chances are good that the plaintiff doesn't give one whit about the public but cares only about its own financial interests.

That does not necessarily mean that the dairy industry cared only about its own survival and protection when it lobbied to have the state and federal legislatures pass laws that made the distribution and sale of margarine more difficult than it might have been otherwise. And it does not necessarily mean that the dairy industry was selfishly motivated when it brought hundreds of lawsuits against margarine makers and those who favored the "other spread." Not necessarily. But it does make you wonder. (Remember: I am a big fan of butter.)

Not long after margarine began to be made in the United States, the dairy farmers sensed a threat. Although they were not a well-organized political force in the early 1870s, they banded together to fight a common enemy and what they believed was unfair competition from margarine. They began their campaign at the state level. New York was at the time the leading dairy state so it was only fitting that the first state law regulating the sale of margarine was New York's "An act for the protection of dairymen, and to prevent deception in sales of butter," taking effect in 1877.[5]

Other states followed suit and by 1886, thirty-four states and territories had in place some kind of margarine laws on the books.[6] These initial laws made life difficult for the margarine makers but they survived. The public wanted margarine because it was cheaper. Furthermore, the first-generation margarine laws were not always effective. There was even one reported New York case in which the experts could not agree on whether the main exhibit was butter or margarine.[7] (I would have told them which was which.)

Although the courts were generally sympathetic to the plight of the dairy farmers and may have compromised judicial integrity in the process of upholding some very questionable legislation, it was inevitable that a major state court would break ranks. The New York Court of Appeals (New York's highest court) struck down the state's antimargarine law on the grounds that it interfered with freedom of contract. The law amounted to a virtual prohibition on the sale of margarine "such that the people of the State as cannot afford to buy dairy butter must eat their bread unbuttered."[8]

It was time to take the cause to the national level. In many ways, this was the first major attempt by a special interest lobby group to effectuate protectionist legislation. It changed Washington politics forever.

The first major piece of federal legislation addressing the "margarine issue" was the Margarine Act of 1886, imposing a tax of two cents per pound on margarine and expensive licenses for manufacturers and wholesalers. Two cents a pound may not seem like much but when one considers the price of butter in those days (around fourteen cents a pound in Wisconsin),[9] it should be obvious that this gave meaning to the old adage that the power to tax is the power to destroy. As bad as that was, it could have been worse; the original bill called for a tax of ten cents a pound.[10]

The dairy interests were not entirely satisfied with the federal Margarine Act of 1886 because the margarine industry was still around. They turned back to the states for further protection.

Before exposing the extremes of the antimargarine laws, it should be noted that there were many reported cases of fraud and deception. Because margarine was cheaper to make than butter, the opportunity for big profits meant an inevitable temptation to pass off yellow margarine as butter. It was a problem that would not go away by itself. But it created a tightrope challenge: how could laws be drafted to prevent fraud but still allow consumers the choice of a lower-cost butter alternative?

We will examine a handful of representative cases that show what can happen when powerful special-interest groups get their way in the legislature. If nothing else, these cases illustrate the importance of an independent judiciary. I have deliberately chosen Wisconsin as an example of a state whose dairy interests were strong and influential enough to create a wide range of laws and lawsuits that might fairly be called "protectionist." Do not assume that Wisconsin is unique in that respect. In 1969, forty-seven of the fifty states had laws applicable specifically to margarine or margarine-like products.[11]

Wisconsin, however, as the Dairy State, warrants special scrutiny. Don't worry, I will pick on a few other states, too. We can dedicate these cases to Wisconsin's Congressman Hudd, who, in the debate over the federal Margarine Act of 1886, pushed for the highest tax possible with these stirring words: "... I fly the flag of an intent to destroy the manufacture of the noxious compound by taxing it out of existence."[12] At least he was honest.

Our first case out of Wisconsin is a sad-but-true tale of a man who will forever be branded a criminal.

On 23 February 1909, William Welch did a terrible thing and paid a heavy price for his transgression. Welch was a waiter in charge of a lunch counter owned and operated by the Wisconsin Central Railway Company. When one R. B. Southard sat down for a meal, Welch did the unthinkable: he served Southard oleomargarine without telling him that the substance he was serving was not butter. It was not William Welch's lucky day: R. B. Southard was a dairy inspector for the state. Perhaps Welch should have suspected something because the "meal" that Inspector Southard ordered consisted of bread, butter, and coffee.[13]

On cross-examination, Welch's lawyer grilled the state's expert witness, the assistant chemist for the Dairy and Food Commission: "It is a fact, isn't it, that oleomargarine, much of it is a more wholesome food product than a great deal of the butter on the market?"[14] Brilliant trial tactics but wholly ineffective in Wisconsin.

Welch testified that as a humble lunch-counter worker making only $45 a month he had no control over what was ordered for the lunch counter. He further testified that he always asked that butter be sent and that he assumed that what he had served to Inspector Southard was butter.

In the Dairy State not only was it not nice to try to fool Mother Nature, it was against the law. Welch, who was but a lowly employee of the railway, was fined $100, more than double his monthly salary of $45. This was 1909, and a $100 fine then was the equivalent of a fine of about $5,000 at today's prices.

Welch appealed his fine to the Wisconsin Supreme Court. His lawyer argued passionately that justice was not done:

> The defendant is fifty years of age; a husband and a father; a sober, industrious, simple and guileless man. The fact that at the time of the commission of the alleged offense he was engaged in the modest occupation of a waiter at a salary of forty-five dollars a month is sufficient proof that he did not possess a keen and inquiring mind. He had no control whatever over the lunch counter where the food in question was served.... He was little more than a mere automaton.[15]

Welch lost. *State v. Welch* is barely a footnote to legal history, a case never cited as precedent for any important legal principle, and a case all but forgotten. But for its total absurdity, it seems hardly worth a mention. Yet it illustrates how serious the dairy interests regarded the margarine threat: it persuaded the legislature to criminalize the very serving of it.

Although early laws may have been subtle in their efforts to make it difficult to sell margarine, in 1925, Wisconsin enacted a law that outright banned the manufacture, sale, and even possession of margarine. Violation of the law carried the possibility of fines up to $500 and jail time up to six months. The John F. Jelke Company, a Chicago margarine manufacturer, sued the Wisconsin Dairy and Food Commissioner to stop enforcement of the law.

The trial judge agreed with Jelke that Wisconsin's new antimargarine law was defective on a number of grounds. It was (*a*) arbitrary, unreasonable, and discriminatory; (*b*) it denied Jelke the right to operate a lawful business; (*c*) it was an unlawful interference with interstate commerce; and (*d*) it was in violation of the Constitutions of the United States and Wisconsin in every way you could imagine. The case then landed in the Wisconsin Supreme Court where the law was exposed for what it truly was: a protective measure for the dairy industry:

> We are next urged to hold the act valid on the ground that the Legislature, in order to protect the Wisconsin dairy industry from unfair competition, may prohibit the manufacture and sale of oleomargarine. There is no basis in the evidence upon which a claim of unfair competition can be based. The argument is addressed to the proposition that, in order to promote one important industry, the Legislature may ... cripple or destroy another competing industry.[16]

One senses that the Wisconsin Supreme Court was more than a little impatient with the state's continued efforts to subvert the Constitution in the name of the dairy industry. It threw out the State's antimargarine law with a vengeance.

The hard-working and compassionate Wisconsin legislature, ever loyal to the dairy industry, was not done. It passed another antimargarine law and it, too, was declared invalid.[17] But while that law was being tested, J. D. Beck, then a commissioner at the Wisconsin

Department of Agriculture, took it upon himself to circulate to the press lists of merchants who sold margarine. Beck also assured the farmers that his inspectors would pay special attention to stores that sold margarine. Even after the new antimargarine law was overturned, Beck continued his crusade. The John F. Jelke Company (the same margarine maker involved in the earlier litigation) and others involved in making and selling margarine went to court to stop Beck from spreading his antimargarine message.

The lower court issued a restraining order against Beck but Beck ignored it. The court then found him in contempt, fined him $250, and sent him to jail when he refused to pay the fine. The Wisconsin Supreme Court upheld the contempt finding.[18]

This pattern would repeat itself again and again over the next thirty years. The Wisconsin Legislature and state bureaucrats would do their part to support the dairy industry by excluding all nondairy rivals and the courts would intercede to protect the legitimate rights of the competing industries.

On the national front, the Margarine Act of 1950 ultimately led to the end of taxation and licensing fees at the federal level. (The U.S. Supreme Court had upheld a steep state excise tax on margarine during the depression.[19]) Many states still restricted yellow margarine and many states, especially Wisconsin, saw numerous challenges to the reign of the dairy industry.

Longtime Wisconsin residents remember the 1950s and early 1960s for bootleg runs to Illinois for yellow margarine because its sale remained illegal in Wisconsin. There was an alternative—white margarine came with tiny packets of yellow coloring that the homemaker could mash into the margarine to make it look like butter (or just plain yellow margarine, if that was the goal).

Today there are few serious legal obstacles to selling margarine. Both products are fighting for an ever-smaller market, as consumers seem to be shifting away from fat-based spreads. In 1930, per-capita consumption of margarine and butter combined totaled more than 20 pounds (2.6 pounds of margarine, 17.6 pounds of butter). In 1997, although margarine had overtaken butter in the marketplace, the combined total had dropped to under thirteen pounds (8.6 pounds margarine, 4.2 pounds butter).[20] Both products must now compete for an ever-shrinking market.

Believe it or not, even Dairy Queen became a target of the dairy interests. Although the main products of the well-known Dairy Queen chain are milk-based, they were outlawed in Wisconsin because they did not contain enough milk fat. Although no one disputed the fact that the semifrozen product called Dairy Queen was healthful and nutritious, its 6 percent fat content put it into a no-man's-land under Wisconsin law. To be called "ice cream," a product had to contain at least 11 percent fat. The fat content of sherbet and ices was a maximum of 3.5 percent. Even though Dairy Queen was not sold as either "ice cream" or "sherbet" (and even had signs posted at its establishment so advising the public), a county court found that Wisconsin law barred the sale of Dairy Queen as an imitation of ice cream and as an adulterated product.

It took a 1952 Wisconsin Supreme Court decision to legalize the sale of Dairy Queen cones, dishes, and sundaes in Wisconsin.[21] Even though the Supreme Court was initially unanimous in its decision, the court took the unusual step of considering in great detail the dairy industry's motion for rehearing. Although the court ultimately let its initial decision stand, two justices went on record as willing to change their votes. Justice Currie's dissenting opinion echoed the fears of the dairy industry:

> Dairy Queen is sold in competition with ice cream and for every sale of a cone of Dairy Queen to a customer there is the likelihood that there has been lost the sale of a cone of ice cream. The farmers receive a higher price for the milk and butterfat than they do for Dairy Queen because of the much higher price they receive per pound for butterfat than for milk solids.[22]

The protectionist walls gradually began to crumble. In 1967, amidst the turmoil of the Vietnam War, Wisconsin became the last state to permit the sale of colored margarine. That did not mean the end of all hostilities, as a number of other laws stayed on the books.

A serious challenge to one of these laws came in the 1970s when Coffee-Rich, maker of a nondairy creamer used mostly as a whitener in coffee and tea but also on breakfast cereals and desserts, attacked Wisconsin's law that completely barred the serving of Coffee-Rich and other nondairy creamers in restaurants. Joining Coffee-Rich was Crandall's Restaurant, a Madison institution that had been serving Coffee-Rich to its customers for several years, in flagrant violation of the law.

Judge Norris Maloney, sitting in the Dane County Courthouse only a few blocks away from Crandall's Restaurant, declared the law unconstitutional because he saw the same wrongful intent on the part of the legislature to offer up yet another protectionist law for the benefit of the dairy industry. The Wisconsin Supreme Court took the appeal.

This case was obviously different from the other protectionist cases the court had previously decided. Fraud and deception were apparent because Crandall's never told its customers they were getting a nondairy creamer instead of "the real thing." As the Supreme Court astutely and perhaps even sarcastically noted:

> Instead of "coffee with cream" as they presumably requested, they received a blend of water, vegetable fat, corn syrup solids, vegetable protein, polyglycerol esters of fatty acids, polysorbate 60, dipotassium phosphate, disodium phosphate, carrageenan, and beta-carotene.[23]

If that's not fraud, what is? Yet, argued the state, there was no record of even a single consumer complaint. That was hardly surprising, responded the court; it just went to show how good a deception the Coffee-Rich was. Besides, even if a customer had figured out that the cream in the coffee was fake, was that worth even a phone call to the authorities?

No, said the Wisconsin Supreme Court, the purpose of the law was indeed to prevent fraud and deception. Besides, the legislature had not chosen the totally draconian solution of barring all sales of Coffee-Rich, as it tried to do to margarine and to Dairy Queen once upon a time. Coffee-Rich could still be sold by retail stores and used by institutions like schools and hospitals or dispensed with posted notices in vending machines. The limited prohibition made sense in the restaurant setting, where deception is greatest.

It looked as if the State of Wisconsin would prevail in upholding its ban on Coffee-Rich in restaurants. Not so fast! It was still unconstitutional because it was "an excessive burden on interstate commerce." Wisconsin had gone overboard in its blanket ban on nondairy creamer in restaurants because it did not even permit customers the choice of using these products in their tea and coffee. Besides, if deception is the evil to be remedied, why not let restaurants post a prominent notice on a wall or on the menu informing the customers that they will be served a nondairy creamer?

Curiously, the state, ever the champion of requiring businesses to post all kinds of labels and notices, feebly argued that labeling was not effective.

The hostilities have subsided except for a few minor skirmishes and laws that remain on the books. For example, yellow margarine can only be sold in one-pound units.[24] If a recipe calls for a stick (four ounces) of butter, you could run down to the corner grocery and buy a single stick of butter. If you need a stick of margarine, you have to buy the whole pound or put the grocer at risk of prosecution.

Remember William Welch, the poor lunch-counter worker who had the bad fortune to serve margarine to a state dairy inspector in 1909? That would still be a crime in Wisconsin. The current law provides: "The serving of colored oleomargarine or margarine at a public eating place as a substitute for butter is prohibited unless it is ordered by the customer."[25]

Does this really protect the customer? Would not a law that simply requires all spreads to be clearly marked be sufficient? If a restaurant wants to serve margarine and is honest and up front with its customers, will not the free-market forces determine whether serving margarine instead of butter is a good idea? The state of Wisconsin does not think so.

Wisconsin law also prohibits the serving of margarine to students, patients, and inmates at state institutions unless so ordered by a doctor "when necessary for the health of a specific patient or inmate."[26] (Apparently, school children cannot be served margarine under any circumstances.) The penalty for violating this law and the ban on serving margarine at restaurants unless the customer requests it can be stiff. First offenses are punishable with fines from $100 to $500 or imprisonment up to three months (or both!); subsequent offenses are punishable by fines from $500 to $1,000 or imprisonment from a minimum of six months to a maximum of one year (or both!).

We need to divert our journey to Washington State for a most interesting lawsuit.[27] In 1975, Washington had an unusual law on the books: "Advertising of oleomargarine—Dairy terms prohibited. It shall be unlawful in the connection with the labeling, selling or advertising of oleomargarine to use dairy terms ..."

Consider what this meant: a manufacturer of margarine could not advertise its product as "just like butter" or "tastes like butter." It could not even mention the word "butter." Not unless it wanted to go to jail! Marketers of margarine went into federal court to throw out this apparent violation of free speech. Washington State fought hard but the federal district court struck down the law.

In Kansas, another state dairy law came under attack, this time as late as 1983. The makers of Cool Whip, the famous and very successful nondairy topping, introduced some frozen whipped toppings that contained both dairy and nondairy ingredients. Although Kansas law allowed the sale of original Cool Whip, it would not allow the sale of the new dairy/nondairy product because it was a "filled dairy product" under Kansas law. This meant that it was, in effect, an adulterated dairy product or, at the very least, "a product in imitation of a dairy product."[28]

The federal district court did not hesitate in striking down the Kansas law. The court found the absurdity of the Kansas laws, allowing nondairy toppings but not allowing a mixture of the two kinds of ingredients, persuasive. Of greater interest to us is the court's observation that these so-called filled-milk laws (laws prohibiting the adding of nondairy ingredients to milk) "are no longer viable today." The court further noted: "Problems of fraud and deception regarding filled dairy products are a thing of the past."[29] Really?

In the scheme of things, these laws that served the dairy interests may seem like "small potatoes" but they are small *buttered* potatoes. Besides, things have not always gone so well for the dairy farmers of America. If you think that the price of milk is set by the laws of supply and demand, think again. The prices are fixed.

If the term "price fixing" strikes you as something that is illegal, you are right. It violates the antitrust laws and the whole premise of a free-market economy. But since 1937, milk prices have been regulated by the federal government. The Agricultural Marketing Agreement Act[30] authorizes the secretary of agriculture to issue milk marketing orders that regulate the minimum price producers of raw milk receive. The orders are regionally based. Some regions involve multiple states, like the New England, Middle Atlantic, Upper Midwest, and Southwest Plains regions. Others involve only areas of a single state such as

Chicago Regional, Upper Florida, Puget Sound-Inland, and Black Hills, South Dakota.

Doesn't this violate the antitrust laws? No. The Agricultural Marketing Agreement Act contains a section that says the antitrust laws do not apply to the provisions of the Act.[31] It is a kind of disclaimer but a very necessary one because the Act clearly sets up "cartels," the purpose of which is price fixing, exactly the activity the antitrust laws were designed to prohibit.

The intricacies of the milk marketing laws and regulations are mercifully beyond the scope of this book. Here is a quick summary, just in case you are dying to know more:

> The federal minimum price paid to producers is a "blend price," which is determined, in part, by the ultimate use of the raw milk. Fluid milk is currently divided into four classes. Class 1 milk is basic beverage milk and generally fetches a higher price than the remaining classes. Classes 2–4 include milk destined for "other uses" ranging from sour cream and yogurt to ice cream and hard cheeses.[32]

As complex and sometimes unfathomable as the milk pricing laws are, they have a laudable basis in history. During the depression, commodity prices plummeted. The federal government had no choice but to restore some kind of order to the dairy industry and to the entire agricultural world. The law it enacted to do so, the Agricultural Adjustment Act, may not always make sense to the casual observer. For example, one part provides: "For the purposes of this subsection, hogs and field corn may be considered as one commodity."[33]

The problem for dairy farmers is that prices in some areas have been inadequate. One state, Massachusetts, tried to help its own struggling farmers with an assessment/rebate scheme that seemed to tax all milk sold in Massachusetts, no matter where it came from, and then to rebate the money collected to Massachusetts dairy producers only. The U.S. Supreme Court struck it down as an unconstitutional burden on interstate commerce.[34] Congress is trying to come up with solutions to the plight of dairy farmers in various regions and the final chapter is far from being written.

Did you ever wonder how the dairy industry can afford its brilliant "Got Milk?" and "milk-mustache" ads? If you think the millions of dollars spent on these ad campaigns are voluntary advertising expenditures by thousands of dairy farmers, think again. The money for the various milk marketing boards comes from mandatory assessments, based on the amount of milk that individual farmers bring to market, and is a matter of federal law, the Dairy Production Stabilization Act of 1983.[35] Congress has embraced the dairy industry with gusto:

7 U.S.C. SEC. 4501 CONGRESSIONAL FINDINGS AND DECLARATION OF POLICY

(a) Congress finds that—

(1) dairy products are basic foods that are a valuable part of the human diet;

(2) the production of dairy products plays a significant role in the Nation's economy, the milk from which dairy products are manufactured is produced by thousands of milk producers, and dairy products are consumed by millions of people throughout the United States;

(3) dairy products must be readily available and marketed efficiently to ensure that the people of the United States receive adequate nourishment;

(4) the maintenance and expansion of existing markets for dairy products are vital to the welfare of milk producers and those concerned with marketing, using, and producing dairy products, as well as to the general economy of the Nation; and

(5) dairy producers move in interstate and foreign commerce, and dairy products that do not move in such channels of commerce directly burden or affect interstate commerce of dairy products.

(b) It, therefore, is declared to be the policy of Congress that it is in the public interest to authorize the establishment ... of an orderly procedure for financing (through assessments on all milk produced in the United States for commercial use) and carrying out a coordinated program of promotion designed to strengthen the dairy industry's position in the marketplace. . . .[36]

In case you were wondering, federal law defines dairy products as "products manufactured for human consumption which are derived from the processing of milk, and includes fluid milk products."[37] What about goats' milk cheese and goats' milk as a beverage? No. Federal law defines milk as "any class of cow's milk produced in the United States."[38] Instead of "Got Milk?" the goat farmers will just have to ask "Goat Milk?"

That's the law. But do not think that only the dairy industry is being forced to pay for generic advertising. Producers of wheat,[39] honey,[40] pork,[41] beef,[42] watermelons (!),[43] and eggs[44] (but only eggs from chickens) are all subject to similar mandatory payments by virtue of specific congressional action. Federal law (the AMAA) authorizes forced paid advertising for an amazing range of products, including onions (but not garlic), tomatoes (but not cucumbers), and Tokay grapes[45] (but not other grapes).

One might think this compulsory assessment—some might even call it a tax—is illegal, but in the context of agricultural commodities, it seems entirely lawful. The U.S. Supreme Court addressed a challenge from a group of California growers, handlers, and processors who objected to mandatory assessments for generic advertising of California nectarines, plums, and peaches.[46] By a slim one-vote majority, the court upheld the fruit advertising assessment and there is no reason to believe that a challenge to milk assessments would fare any better.[47]

Why doesn't a mandatory assessment to fund generic advertising offend the First Amendment's free speech guarantees? First, the marketing orders under which the fruit growers were assessed do not restrict them from delivering any message they want to deliver. Second, the orders do not compel anyone to engage in actual or symbolic speech. Third, the orders do not compel anyone to endorse or finance any political or ideological views. The court presumed that the growers, being in that business, would agree with the central message of the program (eat more of what we grow).

As is often the case with so many Supreme Court decisions, the dissenting opinion is stimulating and well considered. Justice Souter points out many areas of the law that are contradictory and absurd. For example, can anyone explain why only California-grown peaches can be made subject to mandatory assessments? Justice Souter could not.

As logical and persuasive as we might find the dissenting opinion in the California fruit case, it is not the law. Dairy farmers will continue to pay for the brilliant and ubiquitous "Got Milk?" program and whatever else the dairy industry's advertising firms develop. For small producers, it may be a question of "Got Money?" but they do reap the benefits of the program. And no one markets milk better than the National Fluid Milk Processor Promotion Board, recipient of all those assessments on the dairy farmers. In March 2000, DC Comics joined with the milk industry to let Batman and Superman pitch the product. According to a DC Comics vice president: "We're very excited about pairing Batman and Superman with Milk. Milk is associated with wholesome, all-American ideals and behavior... this attitude is the foundation of what motivates our characters to be heroes."[48]

There is a new target for the dairy industry: soy. In February 2000, the National Milk Producers Federation filed a complaint with the Food and Drug Administration seeking enforcement action to stop the product known as soy milk from being called any kind of "milk."

Is milk a generic term, usable by any product as a mean of identifying the liquid extract or liquid form of a product? Or must it mean only the lactic secretions of the cow? Referring to the highly successful ad campaign "Got milk?" Chris Galen of the National Milk Producers Federation purportedly said, "Unless you can demonstrate that the product comes from a cow, you don't got milk."[49]

Although the dairy industry remains strong, the soy industry has grown into a powerful lobby itself (though it does not have Batman and Superman on its side). Of course, there is no mandatory assessment for soy advertising, as there is for milk marketing. As for the legal merits, the dairy industry is stretching the point. What about goat's milk? Coconut milk? Milk of Magnesia? What about the "milk of human kindness"?

Wisconsin has not given up the fight. Even today, state law requires that school children be taught about the "values of dairy products and their importance for the human diet."[50] (In the same statute, students are to be taught the "value of frugality" as well.) The law is silent as to the teaching about possible health problems (lactose intolerance, excessive fat) associated with dairy products. Want to take bets that the downside receives little play in Wisconsin schools?

One judge, Federal Appeals Court Judge Jerome Frank, got it right many years ago:

> The city-dweller or poet who regards the cow as a symbol of bucolic serenity is indeed naive. From the udders of that placid animal flows a bland liquid indispensable to human health but often provoking as much human strife and nastiness as strong alcoholic beverages. The milking of animals in order to make use of their lactic secretions was

one of the greatest human inventions, but the domestication of milk has not been accompanied by a successful domestication of some of the meaner impulses in all those engaged in the milk industry. The difficulties described as "the milk problem" revolve in some considerable measure about the complex relations between the farmers and "handlers" who buy the milk from the farmers and sell it, in fluid or altered form, directly or indirectly through others, to the ultimate consumers. The resultant intricacies of milk-marketing have frequently led farmers and consumers—sometimes justifiably and sometimes not—to believe that they have been dealt with unfairly. The difficulties have given rise to much legislation and are reflected in many judicial decisions. The pressure of milk is indeed powerful.[51]

Did I mention that I'm totally nuts about butter?

12

NOT SO STRICTLY KOSHER

There is a story about a pious Jew who was suffering
from a rare disease that was curable only by eating pork.
He managed to have the pig slaughtered by a *shochet*,
a ritual slaughterer of traditionally kosher animals.
Discovering some questionable blemishes on the animals
lungs, the pious Jew took the dead pig to a rabbi and asked
if the pig were kosher. The rabbi examined the pig and
pronounced judgement: "It may be kosher but it is still a pig."
—*Richard J. Israel,* The Kosher Pig

If you are looking for a complex and comprehensive system of
laws regulating food in all aspects of human existence, you
need look no further than the laws of *kashrut,* the body of rules
that govern certain observant Jews in their daily lives. For centuries, Jews have adhered to the laws of *kashrut,* to "keeping
kosher," as a strict and all-encompassing code of conduct in
the kitchen and at the table.

It would be easy to dismiss the laws of *kashrut* as simply
tradition and time-honored customs. Yet they are indeed laws,
as strict and demanding of compliance as any federal statute.
Although one does not go to jail for violating the laws of
kashrut, the penalties for breaching these laws are in many
ways even more harsh than a long prison sentence. For the
observant Jew, to knowingly eat pork, to mix meat with milk,
to eat chicken that has not been slaughtered in accordance
with Jewish law, or even to eat a piece of candy that is not certified kosher, is an affront to God and a total abdication of con-
science. It is virtually unthinkable.

We are interested in the laws of *kashrut* for two reasons. First, they are a magnificent example of how a well-developed body of law has shaped a cuisine over the centuries. Second, and of more immediate concern, the laws of *kashrut* have recently collided with civil law to create a kind of kosher constitutional crisis. Keeping kosher may no longer be as simple as it once was if certain trends in the U.S. courts continue.

Kosher 101: An Introduction to the Laws of *Kashrut*

The word "kosher" is an English transliteration of a Hebrew word meaning "fit" or "proper."[1] The laws of *kashrut* are based on text found in the Torah (the first five books of the Bible) but have developed in the writings of the Talmud (commentaries and debates on the Torah) and rabbinic interpretations over the centuries. The seven basic principles of *kashrut* follow.

1. All fruits and vegetables are permitted. There is no such thing as a "kosher" as opposed to an "unkosher" banana. The source of this universal allowance is Genesis 1:29: "Behold, I have given you every plant yielding seed which is upon the face of all the earth and every tree with seed in its fruit; you shall have them for food." Being a true and complete vegetarian (a vegan) means never having to say that tonight's dinner may not be kosher. Go ahead: invite the rabbi. Lest one leap to the conclusion that this basic premise of *kashrut* is a guide to health, consider the many varieties of poisonous mushrooms in the field. Kosher? Yes. But still deadly.

2. Some animals are permitted and some are forbidden. When it comes to meat, the animal must be a ruminant and have split hooves.[2] Cows, sheep, goats, and deer are allowed while pigs and camels are not. Chickens, geese, ducks, and turkeys are permitted. Vultures and others birds of prey (scavengers) are not. Rodents, reptiles, and amphibians are forbidden, so the "delicacies" of rattlesnake meat and frogs legs can never be kosher.

3. Any fish that has fins and scales can be eaten.[3] Salmon, tuna, flounder, and herring qualify. Shrimp, lobster, and clams are out. As for swordfish, that depends on who's making the rules.[4]

4. Mammals and birds that are not on the forbidden list do not automatically become kosher meals because they must also be

slaughtered in strict accordance with Jewish law *(shechita)*. This means cutting the animal's throat with a perfectly sharp (no nicks or unevenness) knife so as to cut the trachea and esophagus in a swift, continuous motion. Theoretically, this ritual slaughter of animals, performed by trained personnel, is humane.[5] For some reason, fish do not require this same technique of ritual slaughter. Even after slaughter, further steps are taken to qualify the animal as kosher. Because of the biblical command that blood should not be eaten,[6] all blood that does not drain from the animal upon slaughter must be removed, either by broiling or soaking and salting. Inspection of the dead animal is also required, with the ritual slaughterer (the *shochet*) looking for a variety of possibly disqualifying conditions.[7] Those who desire to keep kosher do not eat meat from the hindquarter of mammals because the sciatic nerve (and the adjoining blood vessels) is deemed forbidden. The origin of this prohibition is the biblical story of Jacob's struggle, told as a wrestling match, in Genesis 32:25–33, in which "the hollow of Jacob's thigh was strained." It is technically possible to remove the sciatic nerve but difficult and costly; hence, the tenderloin, the sirloin, and the T-bone are, for all practical purposes, nonkosher cuts of beef.

5. Meat and milk cannot be eaten together. This is based on the biblical prohibition against "boiling a kid in its mother's milk."[8] Alas, the cheeseburger is forbidden. The rabbis extended this prohibition to mixing poultry with dairy; poached chicken breast in a tarragon mustard cream sauce may be delicious but it is definitely not kosher. The milk versus meat distinction plays an important role in kosher eating. It means two sets of dishes for a kosher household: one for meat, a separate set for dairy. It also means waiting a specified period of time between eating meat and dairy; opinions vary, from three to six hours. Because even the smallest amount of dairy product renders an entire dish or product "dairy," the kosher consumer must be careful in purchasing various items. Margarine, for example, may not be "parve" (or neutral, meaning neither meat nor dairy) if it contains whey or other dairy products. Commercial yogurts often contain gelatin that is sometimes obtained from animals, which themselves may be kosher or not.[9]

6. Kosher cheese, kosher wine, kosher grape juice, and other foods raise issues that are beyond the scope of this book but serve to give

notice that the laws of *kashrut* are complex, evolving, and not always universally accepted.

7. There are also special rules that govern foods eaten and prepared during the festival of Passover. No leavening (as in yeast or baking soda) is permitted. This is based on the story of the Passover, found in the book of Exodus, in which the Hebrews left Egypt in such a hurry that they had no time for their bread to rise.

So why do Jews accept the laws of *kashrut?* The overwhelming consensus in support of keeping kosher has little to do with physical health but is instead regarded as a spiritual journey. It is a question of ritual and holiness. The famous and revered twelfth-century Jewish scholar/physician Moses Maimonides saw a possible hygienic justification for the laws of *kashrut,* although he never argued that hygiene was the principal purpose behind these laws of holiness.

Scholars have offered a variety of explanations for the historical basis of the laws of *kashrut.* John Cooper, in his fascinating study of the social history of Jewish food, *Eat and Be Satisfied,*[10] details two of these approaches, the "structuralist approach" and the "ecological approach."

Briefly stated, the "structuralist approach" tends to identify the traits of the particular animals with its likelihood of being kosher. For example, fish that scavenge on the bottom are not exhibiting true "fish behavior" because they are not swimming gracefully through the waters. The "ecological approach" looks more to the societal and environmental demands of biblical days to figure out what was kosher. Hence, the pig, whose milk was not useful, was seen as a threat to the way of life of not only the ancient Hebrews but other societies as well.

Many consumers may perceive that kosher food is "healthier" than nonkosher food but Jewish scholars have by and large abandoned all health claims in support of *kashrut.* A kosher corned beef sandwich tastes great but is hardly the basis for a heart-healthy diet. Chopped chicken livers made with real *schmaltz* (rendered chicken fat) is a culinary delight but a cardiologist's worst nightmare.

The intricacies of the laws of *kashrut* mean that the kosher consumer must pay careful attention when shopping for food, when preparing food, and when eating out. To those who do not keep kosher, these laws inevitably appear as a hardship and a deprivation of culinary delights. No scallops, no crown roast of pork, no Porterhouse steak. To the observant Jew, the laws of *kashrut* represent a gentle yet firm guiding force of spirituality that leads to an even greater appreciation of food.

Have the laws of *kashrut* in any way stifled the development of a significant cuisine? Not at all. Certainly no more than our own cultural aversion to foods such as horse meat, dog meat, and caterpillar.[11]

Gourmet kosher cuisine is *not* an oxymoron; it is a reality. Kosher French, Chinese, Mexican, and ethnic restaurants of all types flourish in larger cities. Without doubt, the laws of *kashrut* have narrowed the choices of food available to those who adhere to its strictures. But there remain so many good and viable choices that the impact on cuisine has been only positive—kosher food, well prepared, is a treat and not a denial of anything.

But there is another side to kosher food, a controversial side that brings it from the kitchen into the courtroom.

Big Business

Make no mistake about it: the kosher food industry in the United States and around the world is big business. The Orthodox Union estimates the magnitude of the kosher food industry in the United States at $135 billion as of early 2001.[12]

Who is responsible for this booming industry? Observant Jews are only one part of the multi-billion-dollar kosher food industry. Adherents to other faiths, including Moslems and Seventh-Day Adventists, look to kosher certifications for a variety of reasons (including making sure that the product is pork free). Some may buy kosher believing that kosher means healthy. To some degree, the impressive dollar numbers reflect the simple fact that many brand-name products have found it a matter of good business to be certified kosher; most consumers buy a number of popular products completely unaware of the fact that these goods are indeed kosher.

The dark side of this rather uneventful marketing fact is that some anti-Jewish hate groups have developed the bizarre and baseless theory that there is a "kosher tax" levied on food, a kind of Jewish conspiracy to extort money from the population at large.

Kosher certification of brand-name packaged goods is usually a simple process. The manufacturer contacts a certifying agency. The most prominent agency in the United States is the Orthodox Union and its symbol is the letter "U" in a circle (often called the O-U). A rabbi will inspect the plant and the manufacturing process (a fee is charged). If the inspecting rabbi is confident that the process and finished product satisfy the laws of *kashrut* (no improper mixing of meat and milk, no introduction of forbidden substances), then the agency will allow the manufacturer to affix its trademark seal of kosher certification. A trip to the supermarket found the "O-U" symbol of the Orthodox Union on a wide variety of common and readily available prepared items, from Grey Poupon Mustard to Nabisco Graham Crackers, from Lawry's Seasoned Salt to Chicken of the Sea Tuna Fish, from Log Cabin Maple Syrup to Cracker Jacks. It even appeared on a container of McCormick Bac'n Pieces, artificially flavored (we hope) bits of vegetable protein that were, according to the label, "bacon flavored."

The Orthodox Union may be the most prominent certifying organization in the United States, claiming that foods bearing its "O-U" mark represent more than $1 billion in annual sales.[13] But there are other certifying agencies and other symbols.

Our trip to the grocery store also found the "Circle-K" of the Organized Kashrus Laboratories (New York) on Post Bran Flakes, Snapple Beverages, and Kraft Miracle Whip. The "KOF-K" Kosher Supervision mark (New York) appeared on Breyer's Ice Cream. A half-moon-K mark of the Kosher Overseers Associates of America (California) was on Campbell's Tomato Juice. The KVH letters stacked in a rectangle certified as kosher a host of Sara Lee products, representing the Vaad Harabonim of Massachusetts.

A leading magazine of Jewish life has listed 366 *kashrus* symbols and organizations, from the "Cap-K" of Nebraska, to the Texas-K International, from the Diamond-KA of New South Wales, Australia, to the Black Box NSK of Nova Scotia, from the Star-Menorah of Costa Rica, to the HKK of Hong Kong.[14]

The legal status of each of these kosher certification marks is that of a protected trademark, similar to the golden arches of McDonald's or the famous Planter's Peanut man (see chapter 7). If a company places an "O-U" on its product without an actual current certification by the Orthodox Union, it has infringed on the Orthodox Union's trademark. Make no mistake about it: the Orthodox Union will do whatever it takes to protect its trademark. Kosher trademark violators are subject to prosecution as are other trademark violators. One should not assume that these different marks live together in perfect kosher harmony. In at least one reported case, one certifying agency (Organized Kashrus Laboratories) sued another agency (Kosher Overseers Association of America), claiming infringement of its mark.[15]

Kashrus Magazine publishes consumer alerts and notices of unauthorized uses of certification marks. Some improper uses are honest mistakes while others are undoubtedly intentional efforts to defraud the kosher consumer. One can only speculate as to why a company would put an "O-U" on a package of dried shrimp and think it could get away with it.[16]

In examining a package for a kosher mark, you might see only the letter "k." Because one cannot get a trademark for an unstylized letter of the alphabet, the "k" on a food product is not really a certification of *kashrut*. It has come to mean that the manufacturer is representing to the consumer that the product is kosher but without the mark of authority of any listed certifying agency. It means: "Trust us, it's kosher, but we have no proof other than our good name."

The letter "k" may also mean that the product has been certified by a legitimate kosher certification but that the manufacturer, for one reason or another, has chosen not to list it. A company may choose to have the flexibility in packaging to put the naked "k" on its label and switch certifying agencies without having to recall product. A telephone call to the manufacturer should inform the consumer of who has certified the product as kosher. It is then up to the consumer to accept or reject the representation that the item is kosher enough for his or her standards. Some observant Jews will accept the plain letter "k" (depending on the product), but many do not. One Internet site claims that Jell-O brand gelatin "puts a K on its product, even though every reliable Orthodox authority agrees that Jell-O is not kosher."[17]

Kosher certification of meat and fowl is more complicated because each and every animal must be individually inspected. The process of producing a kosher chicken or a kosher cut of beef is more expensive than the more heavily mechanized process of bringing a nonkosher chicken or side of beef to market. While there may be suspicion among kosher consumers as to how expensive this process really is (so as to justify the higher cost of kosher meat), the higher prices that kosher meats fetch in the marketplace leads inevitably to the temptation and opportunity for fraud. After all, if the kosher/nonkosher differential is, for example, ten cents a pound, an unscrupulous vendor stands to pocket a handsome profit by selling nonkosher meat as kosher. Fraudulent, but profitable.

As early as 1796, when there was only one Jewish *shochet* (ritual slaughterer) in all of what was then New York City, a non-Jewish butcher by the unlikely name of Smart put the distinctive seal of the *shochet* on his unkosher meat. The New York Council hauled Smart before it and suspended his butcher's license for fraud.[18]

Repetitions of that fraud over the years prompted the state of New York to pass the nation's first statewide kosher fraud law in 1922:

> A person who, with intent to defraud, sells or exposes for sale any meat or meat preparations, article of food or food products, and falsely represents the same to be kosher or kosher for Passover ... or as having been prepared under, and of a product or products sanctioned by, the orthodox Hebrew religious requirements ... is guilty of a class A misdemeanor.[19]

The existence of a strong kosher fraud statute in New York was important to the growing Jewish population of the city. Many of the kosher consumers were recent Jewish immigrants from Eastern Europe and were very much at the mercy of the big-city merchants. The kosher fraud laws meant these new citizens could practice their faith with the assurance that the ability to follow the Jewish dietary laws would be the least of their worries as they tried to adjust to their new lives.

Undoubtedly, the kosher fraud laws of New York provided a safe haven for Jewish refugees determined to keep kosher and they sustained a thriving Jewish cuisine. Had these laws not been in effect, it is probable that Jewish cuisine in America would not be as vibrant and notable as it is. But its existence was not without trial and controversy.

Shortly after its passage, the New York law came under attack and found its way to the United States Supreme Court. In the case of *Hygrade Provision Co. v. Sherman*[20] the high court faced a challenge to the constitutionality of New York's kosher food law. The primary claim of the suit was that the terms "kosher" and "orthodox Hebrew religious requirements" were vague and therefore in violation of the due process clause of the Fourteenth Amendment. Not so, wrote the court. Everyone knew what was meant by those terms. Besides, the essential element of the statute was an intent to defraud.

Hygrade Provision is notable for two reasons. First, as a minor historical note, Justice Brandeis, then the sole Jewish member of the court, did not participate in the decision (he gave no reason for his recusal). Second, the court never considered any First Amendment issue (unconstitutional entanglement of church and state). The reason for this is obvious to constitutional scholars: the issue was never raised because the First Amendment was not held to apply to state laws until fifteen years later.[21]

The First Amendment to the United States Constitution—since 1940 applicable to the states as well as to the federal government— provides: "Congress shall make no law respecting an establishment of religion or prohibiting the free exercise thereof." These sixteen words have spawned hundreds of passionate lawsuits on diverse controversial topics ranging from a state's "released time" statute (allowing public schools to release students early to go to religious instruction)[22] to a city's zoning statute that gave a church veto power over certain liquor license applications.[23] It was only a matter of time before someone challenged a kosher fraud statute as a violation of the First Amendment.

In 1971, the City of Miami Beach prosecuted the Blackstone Hotel for fraudulently selling cakes as "kosher for Passover" when in fact those cakes were not. This was in violation of a municipal ordinance that prohibited the sale of any article of food that is falsely represented to be kosher or "as having been prepared in accordance with the orthodox Hebrew religious requirements."[24] The Blackstone Hotel raised the constitutional claim that the ordinance was invalid as a violation of the First Amendment. The Florida Court of Appeals gave the argument short shrift:

> We are unable to view this ordinance as a legislative enactment establishing or respecting the establishment of a religion, or as one prohibiting the free exercise of a religion to which it has reference. Rather than to prohibit the free exercise of the religion, the ordinance serves to safeguard the observance of its tenets, and to prohibit actions which improperly would interfere therewith.

No one had expected the Blackstone Hotel to win. Kosher fraud statutes were on the books in many jurisdictions and were seen as a reasonable protection against unscrupulous food vendors. But the seeds of doubt had been planted. Twenty years later they bloomed in the Garden State of New Jersey.

On five occasions during the late 1980s, investigators employed by the New Jersey Bureau of Kosher Enforcement found several violations at Ran Dav's County Kosher, a seller of kosher food in Union County, New Jersey. On one occasion, an inspector found calves' tongues that had not been deveined soaking in a brine solution. Another inspector found on the premises six boxes of a particular brand of chicken that had recently lost its kosher status. (The storage of nonkosher food with kosher food was prohibited.) Another violation was the apparent observation of blood and a vein in meat to be ground for hamburger. Yet another violation involved improper labeling of meat.

An orthodox rabbi on the premises at County Kosher claimed that everything at County Kosher complied with the laws of *kashrut*. Nevertheless, the state brought consumer fraud charges against the company. County Kosher argued vigorously that New Jersey's regulatory scheme violated the Establishment Clause of the First Amendment. In a split decision, the New Jersey intermediate appellate court upheld the constitutionality of the regulations.[25] The New Jersey Supreme Court reversed the lower court and declared the state's kosher fraud statutes unconstitutional.[26]

The New Jersey statute was designed to prevent fraud in the selling of food represented to be kosher. The key issue was whether the statute established a religious preference for one branch of the Jewish faith, Orthodox Judaism, when it defined kosher as "prepared in strict compliance with the laws and customs of the Orthodox Jewish religion."

The problem for the State of New Jersey, trying valiantly to save its kosher fraud statutes, was that the Supreme Court found that there are considerable differences of opinion both within Orthodox Judaism and between Orthodox Judaism and other branches of Judaism (Conservative and Reform). Further complicating the case was the fact that the State Kosher Advisory Committee (created by statute) consisted of ten rabbis appointed by the attorney general, all of whom were Orthodox.

Defending the Orthodox standard proved to be more than the State of New Jersey could handle. During the early stages of the law-

suit, it had tried to argue that the law permitted different interpretations of the laws of *kashrut*. It abandoned that untenable position and
maintained instead that a uniform standard (Orthodox) had to be
applied. That signaled the end of the New Jersey kosher statutes as
they were then written.

The New Jersey Supreme Court applied the three-pronged test of
the U.S. Supreme Court's decision in *Lemon v. Kurtzman*.[27] In order
for a state law to be valid, against a claim that it violates the Establishment Clause of the First Amendment, it must first have a secular
purpose. Second, its primary effect must be one that neither fosters
nor inhibits religion. Third, and most important, the statute must not
foster "an excessive entanglement with religion." It was this third
prong, the "entanglement" criterion, that doomed the New Jersey
kosher fraud statute.

There was no getting around the fact that businesses in New Jersey
had to meet strict religiously defined standards in order to claim that
they were "kosher." These standards were defined in terms of Orthodox Judaism and Orthodox Judaism alone. The New Jersey Supreme
Court wrote: "As a result, Jewish law prescribing religious ritual and
practice is inextricably intertwined with the secular law of the State."

New Jersey had no choice but to argue that its regulations incorporated a religious standard; indeed, that was necessary to protect consumers of kosher products from misrepresentation. But the corner into
which New Jersey was busily painting itself grew smaller and smaller
when the court found that the regulations "do not police the nutritional
quality or sanitary purity of kosher food, but only its religious purity."[28]
That, held the court, was excessive entanglement and that was the conflict with the First Amendment that could not be reconciled.

Part of the problem for the then existing kosher fraud laws was that
the New Jersey Supreme Court found that there could well be doctri-
nal disputes even within Orthodox Judaism. How could the state rec-
oncile these inevitable, albeit infrequent, differences of opinion? The
differences would be religious in nature and by putting its stamp of
approval on any one opinion, the state was obviously endorsing one
religious sect over another.

What if a merchant, perhaps with a supervising rabbi's stamp of
approval, sold "kosher pork?" Even if the merchant acted in the good-
faith belief that his pork was "kosher," the New Jersey "kosher police"

would undoubtedly go after him. As ridiculous as that scenario may sound, it illustrates the inevitable entanglement between religious dogma and the government.

Commentators have split over whether the traditional kosher fraud laws are constitutional.[29] Nevertheless, the tide has turned against the traditional kosher enforcement laws that allow the state to enforce the standards of Orthodox Judaism in defining what is and is not kosher. In 1995, the United States Court of Appeals for the Fourth Circuit affirmed a federal district court's order that struck down Baltimore's kosher fraud laws on First Amendment grounds.[30] That decision put in jeopardy the kosher laws on the books in twenty-one states.

The court of appeals could not help but point to apparent disagreements within Judaism as to interpretations over the laws of *kashrut* and gave as an example the differing views over swordfish.

The New York law has been under similar attack and was declared unconstitutional by federal district court Judge Nina Gerson in July 2000.[31] New York plans to fight the ruling and has appealed. I suspect that the New York law will probably not survive in its present form. It is likely that New York will go the way of New Jersey and other states and modify its kosher fraud laws to make them more into strict trademark enforcement and notification laws. The revised New Jersey statute[32] emphasizes the importance and strength of the kosher certification agencies and their symbols. It further requires businesses serving or selling food represented to be kosher to post the basis on which that kosher claim is being made.

If a New Jersey butcher claims to sell kosher chickens it need only post a notice stating what rabbi or what organization has supervised the operation and determined its kosher status. For example, a butcher might claim its meats are kosher because Rabbi X has said the meats are kosher. If the consumer is confident in the credentials of Rabbi X, the butcher has complied with the law so long as Rabbi X has actually certified the meats. The State of New Jersey is powerless to contest Rabbi X's qualifications and cannot, as it once did, overrule the rabbi's judgment in favor of what may be another interpretation of the laws of *kashrut*.

What does this mean for kosher food and the kosher-food consumer in America? In truth, it will mean very little. Even *Kashrus Magazine*, with its annual inventory of the many certifying agencies, warns its readers at the top of every page: "This listing includes certifications of various standards. Consult your rabbi for guidance upon which symbols to rely."[33]

One lawsuit stands out among all the rest of the kosher cases heard by the civil courts in the United States. It did not challenge the constitutionality of any state kosher enforcement scheme and its outcome announced no sweeping change in policy. To the contrary, as legal precedent, it is virtually insignificant. But the mere fact the lawsuit was ever filed speaks volumes about the difficulties of the kosher enforcement statutes.

The plaintiff was Hebrew National (now part of the giant corporate ConAgra empire), known for years as one of the leading producers of kosher products. Its advertising campaign ("we answer to a higher authority") is legendary in the field of food advertising. The defendant was Rabbi Schulem Rubin, director of New York's Kosher Law Enforcement Division. Following are the facts as alleged by Hebrew National.

On 19 June 1985, two inspectors from the Kosher Enforcement Division performed a routine inspection at a Hebrew National facility in Queens. The written report was unremarkable in that it found that Hebrew National was in full compliance with all the laws and regulations.

One year later, Hebrew National closed its Queens plant and moved its operations to Indianapolis, Indiana. Two New York labor unions responded with litigation, a boycott, and newspaper ads against Hebrew National. Then the unexpected came. On 15 May 1987, Hebrew National received a letter from Rabbi Rubin's Division of Kosher Enforcement demanding payment of $39,800 for violations of the kosher laws. According to the letter, the inspectors found one hundred pieces of meat in a nonkosher condition.

Hebrew National had ten days to pay the fine or evidence of the violation would be turned over to the New York State Attorney General. On 5 June 1987, Rabbi Rubin issued a press release announcing the fine against Hebrew National and announcing referral of the matter to the attorney general. A few days later, Hebrew National learned that the June 1985 inspection reports was altered; Hebrew National had never seen the altered report.

In December 1987, the New York State Attorney General announced that it would not bring any legal action against Hebrew National because the Kosher Law Enforcement Division had failed to conduct even a rudimentary investigation and because the circumstances of the case suggested impropriety and misconduct on the part of Rabbi Rubin.

The Department of Kosher Enforcement was not done. It tried to subpoena thousands of records from Hebrew National in an effort to find violations of the law. Hebrew National then took the extraordinary step of suing Rabbi Rubin in federal court for violation of Hebrew National's civil rights and violation of Hebrew National's constitutional rights.

The federal district court threw out the lawsuit because Hebrew National had not stated claims that could be addressed in federal court. It made no factual findings and made no legal determinations on the merits of Hebrew National's complaint. The damage, though, had been done, as the mere filing of papers had tarnished the entire program of state enforcement of kosher laws. Even though Hebrew National "lost" in federal court, no one can say that Rabbi Rubin or New York's Kosher Enforcement Division came out on top.[34]

There is a certain irony to this inevitable path away from the all-encompassing kosher food laws that established more-definite standards for kosher foods. To be sure, there were controversies within the Jewish communities over enforcement of the old kosher food laws. But not so long ago, Jewish merchants found themselves at the mercy of the old "Blue Laws," which restricted their ability to earn a living and keep their Saturday Sabbath as well.

Consider the case of Hyman Finkelstein, convicted of violating New York's Sabbath Law (since repealed). On 4 November 1962, shopkeeper Finkelstein offended the peace and dignity of the State of New York when he sold two quarts of milk, a loaf of bread, and some canned food to one customer, and then peddled milk, bread, corn flakes, and crackers to another. But he sold these items of food on a Sunday!

The Criminal Court of the City of New York found Finkelstein guilty as charged, although the three judges of the court were not without sympathy for Hyman's plight.[35] Observant Jew Hyman Finkelstein, running his one-man grocery on Atkins Avenue in Brooklyn, was protected in his faith by the kosher food laws of New York but oppressed by the same state's laws when he tried to sell a few simple foods on Sunday. The Blue Laws are gone and the kosher food laws are going, too.

Kosher food will survive. Kosher consumers will do what they have been doing all along: they will trust their rabbis and friends more than they will trust the state. The watchword will be: "Let the *nosher* beware!" (A nosher is someone who snacks, a Jewish grazer.) That's nothing new. The truth is that the nosher has always been wary of government intervention.

13

CRUEL AND UNUSUAL CONDIMENTS

Food in Prison

My compliments to the chef!
—*Texas death row inmate Doyle Skillern*
(executed 16 January 1985),
following his last meal of steak,
baked potato, peas, roll, coffee,
and banana pudding

When the federal government discovered that its long-standing budget deficit would soon become a surplus, politicians clamored to propose how to spend the newly found money. "Give it back to the taxpayers," said some. "Rescue social security," implored others. "Improve education," harked another group. I do not recall any politicians recommending that any part of the surplus—not even a penny's worth—be used to improve the quality of food in the federal prison system. What a surprise!

No discussion of food and the law is complete without at least a brief look at how we feed our prisoners. Do we feed them too well? Not well enough? Just right?

One view would ask: "Must Our Prisons Be Resorts?" That was the title of the lead article of the November 1994 issue of *Reader's Digest* and, among other examples of the prison system gone awry, it cited the case of a catered prime-rib dinner served to convicted killers and guests in a Massachusetts prison. That is one perspective on food in prison.

Another view of the fare served to some inmates is the

"special management diet," sometimes also called "nutraloaf," a meat-loaf-like blend of grated vegetables, flour, and, with luck, a small amount of meat. Nutraloaf was developed as a nutritionally adequate (barely) one-dish meal for unruly prisoners. As one can imagine from just reading the recipe from the Arizona Department of Corrections version of this culinary treat, it is not what most people would want to eat meal after meal:

Special Management Diet

Milk, dry or non-fat—2 oz
Flour, wheat, whole wheat—1 oz
Beef, ground raw—4 oz
Egg, whole—1
Potato, raw grated—3^1/2 oz.
Carrot, raw, chopped fine—3^1/2 oz.
Cabbage, raw, chopped fine—3^1/2 oz.
Celery, chopped fine—3^1/2 oz
Beans, navy, red or white, cooked and drained—5 oz
Tomato puree—1 oz. or 2 tbsp.
Oil, salad or shortening—2 oz. or 4 tbsp.

No substitution is permitted. Mix lightly, shape and place in meat loaf pan, bake at 350 degrees for 45 minutes. Cool under refrigeration, wrap in plastic or aluminum foil, and freeze. To serve, thaw, slice, and heat. Serve at 140 degrees or higher.

Two times the recipe will provide 2,750 calories. The loaves should be divided equally to provide for three meals. The breakfast meal would be served with four ounces of orange juice. The noon and evening meals would be served with water.[1]

A note to the recipe recommends one loaf per person per day. A loaf is to be cut into thirds; one third to be served with each meal. That works out to 1,375 calories daily (or 458.33 calories per meal). The morning meal would contain added calories from the four ounces of orange juice.

I have tried this dish. It is indeed a meal fit for a ... prisoner!

As you can imagine, the special management diet was never well received. Prisoners have sued over this and other variations of the loaf throughout the country but the courts have routinely upheld the legality of this bland and unappetizing fare.[2] Steven Carl Adams, an inmate at the Washington State Penitentiary in Walla Walla alleged that the way he was served nutraloaf violated his constitutional rights. As a result of some rather naughty behavior (throwing a styrofoam cup containing liquid at another inmate), prison officials put inmate Adams on a diet of nutraloaf for five straight days.

"I can't eat this stuff," complained inmate Adams, and so he went without food for the five days. Not surprisingly, he suffered hunger pains. Judge McNichols did not have a lot of case law to guide him in his decision. He was aware of a case in which the federal government unsuccessfully challenged the use of a similar loaf by Michigan's corrections authority. But in that case,[3] the Michigan food loaf offered a little more variety than the Washington nutraloaf did, being made from different raw ingredients every day. In that case, the federal court found that the Michigan food loaf was nutritionally adequate and therefore did not violate the constitution.

Washington State first tried to argue that its use of nutraloaf was not a form of punishment. As Judge McNichols so eloquently put it: "Nutra-loaf is punishment whichever way you look at it (or smell it)." What about the lack of variety? At least the Michigan loaf varied from day to day. Judge McNichols found that it was "highly questionable" whether Michigan's loaf was tastier or more appetizing than its Washington cousin. Besides, held the judge, in a fit of culinary sensitivity, if Adams found the nutraloaf so revolting, he should have refrained from eating it. "A healthy inmate can probably manage five days without food as long as he receives sufficient liquids (i.e. water)."[4] Of course, that was exactly what inmate Adams did. One has the impression that Judge McNichols and inmate Adams were not members of the same gourmet eating society.

Courts have been consistent in holding that there is no constitutional right to tasty and appetizing food. So long as it is nutritionally adequate, the constitution is satisfied. Even if meals are nutritionally deficient for a short time, courts are hesitant to find constitutional violations. In one case, two cold sandwiches and water three times a day for a limited period of time did not offend the constitution.[5]

Just as society's standards of what constitutes good food have evolved over the years, so have the standards and practices of food in prison changed. The infamous federal prison at Leavenworth, Kansas, provides us with a stark example of dining in the "big house" in the early days of the twentieth century.[6] Prison regulations required total silence during the meal. Yet, prisoners could request additional food by using these strictly defined signals:

> Should you desire additional food, make your wants known to the waiters in the following manner:
>
>> If you want bread, hold up your right hand.
>> Coffee or water, hold up your cup.
>> Meat, hold up your fork.
>> Soup, hold up your spoon.
>> Vegetables, hold up your knife.
>> If you desire to speak to an officer about food or service in the dining hall hold up your left hand.

Curiously, there was no signal for how to get more Dijon mustard. Perhaps the inmates were allowed to stand and ask, "Pardon me, do you have any..."

Wasting food was a serious offense:

> Wasting food in any form will not be tolerated. You must not ask for or allow the waiter to place more food on your plate than you can eat. When through with meal leave pieces of bread on left side of plate. Crusts and small pieces of bread must not be left on your plate.[7]

If that seems confusing, it was. Yet, as rigid as the 1904 Leavenworth regulations were, at least the inmates were allowed to "speak to an officer about food." It is not likely that federal prisoners complained a lot about their food. Regulations at other federal prisons were soon enacted to make complaining about food risky business:

> Do not make frivolous and groundless complaints about the food and the service. Every effort is made to get the best quality of food that can be purchased, to cook and serve it in the best possible way, and to have plenty for all, and the warden will promptly punish any convict who makes frivolous or groundless complaints for the apparent purpose of creating dissatisfaction among the convicts.
>
> Any complaint made by any convict about either the quality or quantity of the food, or the manner of serving it, will be fully inves-

tigated by the warden; if the complaint is justified, the matter will be remedied at once; if the complaint is groundless, the convict making it will be punished.[8]

Corrections officials must walk a fine line in fashioning a food program for prisoners. On the one hand, wardens realize that bad food can incite riots; for example, the poor quality of the food was one of the stated reasons for the deadly riots at Attica, New York, in 1971. On the other hand, if prison food is too good, it is perceived as coddling criminals. Prison is supposed to be punishment; what kind of punishment is it when the food is better on the inside than out on the streets?

Prisoner lawsuits over food are usually viewed with suspicion and scorn. Prisoner litigation has become a burden on state and federal courts. It is true that most prisoner lawsuits that challenge conditions of confinement are dismissed as frivolous and patently without legal merit. Many of these suits allege that the food served in prison either violates the prisoner's civil rights or is a violation of the Eighth Amendment to the U.S. Constitution. That amendment protects prisoners from cruel and unusual punishment.

A handful of cases have found food to be a violation of a prisoner's rights. These cases, along with the current philosophy of prison administration, have shaped the way prisoners and the public view food in prison.

The constitutional standard of cruel and unusual punishment under the Eighth Amendment is not necessarily easy to define. The U.S. Supreme Court has stated that a prisoner must show "the wanton and unnecessary infliction of pain" and the "unquestioned and serious deprivations of basic human needs."[9] Of course, very few prison food cases make it to the U.S. Supreme Court, so it has been left to the federal district courts to interpret the high court's articulation of a standard. When these cases do get into federal court, judges tend to view them with suspicion and even scorn.

Most prisoner lawsuits challenging conditions of confinement are brought *pro se,* meaning that the prisoners do not have lawyers representing them. It should not come as a surprise that most of these are quickly and summarily dismissed by the courts. Consider these actual cases: one inmate sued because he missed eight meals over a seven-month period;[10] another prisoner sued because he did not get a food tray for one meal.[11]

From these admittedly trivial cases, it would be easy to assume that all prisoner complaints about food are likely to be frivolous. Yet, there have been successful challenges to the food served in our prison system. Today, the most serious prison-food issue that is likely to find its way into the federal court system is the issue of religious freedom in prison. What must the prison authorities do to accommodate the dietary needs of prisoners whose religious beliefs take them out of the mainstream of prison food service?

Nathaniel Jackson, an African American, was an inmate in the New York State prison system since 1986. When he entered prison he identified himself as "Jewish" and participated in the prison's alternative kosher diet program at various facilities until he was transferred to Shawangunk in 1995. That's where the Jewish chaplain, after interviewing Jackson and reviewing his file, decided he wasn't really Jewish.

According to Rabbi Goodman (the chaplain), you are Jewish either by birth or by conversion. According to Jackson, he was Jewish because he read the Torah and ate kosher food. He also claimed he was born Jewish. Whose view controls?

The court held that it was improper to relegate the decision to the chaplain because the test is only whether Jackson's beliefs are "sincerely held" not whether he is Jewish under Judaic law. If Jackson is sincere in his beliefs, the prison system must allow him to participate in any alternative kosher food program it offers, as it would to any more commonly accepted Jewish inmate.[12]

Inmates of a Georgia county jail brought a civil rights action in connection with the conditions of confinement. The primary legal issue was the extent of racial segregation still existing in the jail but the quality of the food was also an issue. Judge Alexander Lawrence put the matter to rest:

> Incarceration in the Chatham County jail falls far short of amounting to cruel and unusual punishment. I recently inspected it. I have eaten the food served to prisoners at noon. While the jail will hardly make *Gourmet's* recommended list of restaurants, the fare is substantial and nutritious. In 1969 the Committee on Law Enforcement

of a grand jury reported that the jail was clean and sanitary and stated that "the prisoners are fed a well-balanced meal three times per day and that the menu is changed every day." Epicures will probably disagree with that opinion. Mr. Bobby L. Hill who has had an opportunity for first-hand evaluation of the menu testified that the food at the jail was "fair to bad." All I can say is, De gustibus non est disputandum.[13]

(That last Latin phrase means, "you can't argue over taste.")

We sometimes hear of inmates being placed on diets of stale bread and water. Although these diets may have happened in the past, you will not find them in today's prisons. A Wyoming statute required unruly inmates to be placed in solitary confinement and given only bread and water for up to five days. In 1983, a federal court struck it down as a violation of the Eighth Amendment: "A diet of bread and water is inconsistent with standards of decency required by the Constitution...."[14]

No chapter about food in prison would be complete without a discussion of "last meals." I hesitate to include this section because some might find it morbid and even tasteless. But the last meals selected by condemned prisoners speak volumes about the relationship between food and law, at least at the most desperate level of society.

Ask yourself a question: if you had only one more meal left on this good earth, what would you choose? Now compare your menu selections with what the prisoners on death row in Texas picked for their final suppers. I have chosen Texas for two reasons. First, Texas leads the nation in number of executions since the death penalty was reinstated back in the 1980s.[15] It is a dubious distinction but gives rise to the second reason. Texas has kept the best statistics on its executed criminals, including detailed menu selections.[16]

If you want to know my bias on this topic, here it is: I am totally opposed to the death penalty. There are a lot of reasons for my staunch opposition to capital punishment but my position was not weakened by what I discovered on this topic.

Not every condemned prisoner wants a last meal. Of the 212 Texas inmates executed since 1982, forty decided to forego the traditional last meal. That leaves 182 last meals to consider. The most popular

*"When they said 'bread and water,' I thought
they meant sourdough baguettes and Perrier."*

(Cartoon by Dennis Schmidt)

item was french fries, selected by 73 of the 182 dining inmates. Next came hamburgers (54), steak (39), and salad (30). Chicken (18) and eggs (18) were also popular items. Iced tea was a favored choice for the last beverage but 49 elected some sort of soft drink, including one who specified that it be a diet soda (he must have preferred the taste of diet drinks).

Only one inmate wanted wine with his dinner but prison officials would not serve any alcohol due to strict prison regulations. Post-meal smokes were also against prison rules.

No one asked for caviar or lobster or foie gras. The most exotic request was wild game. Prison officials refused to get it for the inmate and substituted a hamburger instead; the inmate declined the mundane burger and passed on his last meal.

As you might imagine, some inmates went all out. Here are a few examples:

Charles Tuttle (1 July 1993)—Four fried eggs sunny side up, four sausage patties, one chicken-fried steak patty, one bowl of white country gravy, five pieces of white toast, five tacos with meat and cheese only, four Dr. Peppers with ice on the side and five mint sticks.

William Little (1 June 1999)—Fifteen slices of cheese, three fried eggs, three buttered pieces of toast, two hamburger patties with cheese, two sliced tomatoes, one sliced onion, french fries with salad dressing, two pounds of crispy fried bacon, one quart of chocolate milk and one pint of fresh strawberries.

David Castillo (23 August 1998)—Twenty-four soft shell tacos, six enchiladas, six tostados, two whole onions, five jalapenos, two cheeseburgers, one chocolate shake, one quart of milk and one package of Marlboro cigarettes (prohibited by TDCJ policy).

Vernon Sattiewhite (15 August 1995) Six scrambled eggs with cheese, seven pieces of buttered white toast, fifteen pieces of bacon, three servings of hash browns, a bowl of grits with butter, jelly, and orange juice.

Richard Beavers (14 April 1994)—Six pieces of french toast with syrup, jelly, butter, six barbecued spare ribs, six pieces of well-burned bacon, four scrambled eggs, five well-cooked sausage patties, french fries with catsup, three slices of cheese, two pieces of yellow cake with chocolate fudge icing, and four cartons of milk.

Robert Streetman (7 January 1988)—two dozen scrambled eggs, flour tortillas, french fries and catsup.

Lest you think that all inmates gorged themselves at the final bell, Jeffrey Bass (16 April 1986) wanted only a plain cheese sandwich; James Smith (26 June 1990) wanted only yogurt; James Russell (19 September 1991) wanted only an apple.

Karla Faye Tucker captured the nation's attention when she became the first woman to be executed (3 February 1998). Her last meal was a banana, peach, and garden salad with ranch dressing.

Clifton Russell (31 January 1995) didn't care and took whatever was on the regular menu, which happened to be chili dogs, baked beans, corn, and peanut butter.

Robert Madden (28 May 1997) asked that his final meal be given to a homeless person; the record is silent as to whether prison officials honored his request.

John Thompson (8 July 1987) wanted only freshly squeezed orange juice.

If anyone wants to know, only three inmates specifically asked for mustard, a sad commentary indeed. (I had to put that in.)

I wanted to see for myself how good or how bad the food was in our prison system. I suppose I could have robbed a bank and discovered the realities of prison dining on a long-term basis. Although this may have given me a more reliable universe of meals on which to pass judgment, I chickened out and arranged for visits to the big house that did not require overnight stays.

My first visit was to the federal prison camp at Oxford, Wisconsin.[17] Former congressman Dan Rostenkowski did his stint at Oxford, so I expected the food to be more suited to the country-club set. This minimum-security camp has no walls, so prisoners could walk away if they were so inclined. Where they would go is another matter, because the prison camp is in a remote area in central Wisconsin. There is also a medium-security federal prison on the grounds and meals are supposedly the same at both institutions. Given the relatively small population of the camp (180 inmates) and the fact that it was probably filled with white-collar criminals and drug offenders (hence the low-security status), I expected some good eating.

I arrived at 9:30 A.M. and took a brief tour of the camp. The men sleep in tiny rooms without doors, four to a room. Privacy does not exist. The kitchen was busy getting ready for the first lunch line, to start at 10:30 A.M. Meals are served early in prison. The dinner meal is done by 5:00 P.M.

I got in line with the inmates and took exactly what they were eating. Baked chicken was the main course and everyone got two small pieces. A heaping side of rice came with a chunky tomato sauce and a side of green beans. A few slices of bread and a pat of margarine was next, followed by an all-you-can-eat salad bar, consisting of a mountain of iceberg lettuce and several cold vegetable salads. Inmates could take one dessert, which was either one piece of fruit or a giant peanut butter cookie; I opted for the cookie because I figured I would learn very little about prison food by eating an apple. Iced tea was the beverage of choice, although I saw many inmates with cans of soda. (I later learned that inmates were allowed to buy soda at the canteen, keep it in their rooms, and bring it to meals.)

The chicken was bland, somewhat overcooked, but acceptable. The rice with "chunky" tomato sauce turned out to be a major disappointment. Not only was the tomato sauce virtually tasteless, the "chunks" turned out to be potatoes. Talk about a starch overload! The green beans were canned and not unexpectedly mushy and salty. The highlight was the bread, made from scratch that morning. It was a dense, heavy white bread with a hint of sweetness that easily beats out all the supermarket white breads. It was bread my grandmother would have liked.

Perhaps the biggest surprise was the salad bar, a regular feature at the federal prison camp and one that most of the prisoners enjoyed. A choice of dressings meant no one would go hungry. The peanut butter cookie was like a rock and stayed with me for days.

I sat down with five of the prisoners and they were unanimous in praising the food. "It's the best of the worst," said one, referring to the fact that prison is a terrible place to be but if you have to be in a prison, this federal prison is not so terrible.

The favorite dishes for these five gentlemen were the hamburgers (generally, once a week), almost all the breakfasts (especially the made-from-scratch pancakes and french toast), and the chicken wings. Fish got high marks. Steve, with five more months to go on his sentence for wire fraud, was impressed with the daily salad bar and the recent Passover meal for the ten or so Jewish prisoners. He even got to eat gefilte fish. Unfortunately, grape juice stood in for the wine. Thomas, who had already been there for seventeen months, thought the food "pretty good" except for the turkey dogs. Gregory liked the turkey dogs but thought there was too much pork being served. Mike liked the pork. Robert, who served the prisoners, was not expecting the food to be so good. Several had been in county facilities where the food was much worse.

The canteen provided prisoners with those extras that made life bearable. On nights when the main course was not very popular, inmates would somehow concoct pizzas out of ingredients they had purchased during the week.

Holiday meals were special treats. Christmas dinner (11:00 A.M.) was a buffet provided to the inmates and their families that chose to visit: roast beef, roast chicken, turkey ham, mashed potatoes, natural gravy, bread dressing, seasoned broccoli, strawberry shortcake, fresh dinner rolls, cranberry sauce, fruit salad, soup and salad bar, chilled fresh milk, Kool-Aid, and hot coffee.

The canteen stocks a few special items during the holiday season at the federal prison. If you had the money, you could get these goodies: crabmeat, clams, oysters, kippered snacks, salmon, shrimp, del sol bacalao, guava paste, holiday cookies, caramel corn, candy canes, Hershey Kisses, chocolate-covered cherries, thin mints, peanut brittle, string cheese, and cappucino.

As good as these yummies may sound, one thing the federal prisoners could not get was a night out at their favorite restaurant back home. They could dream about that all they wanted.

Corrections staff were proud of the food served at Oxford and proud of the fact that they could feed these inmates for about $1.88 per day, per person. There were some inmates who requested special meals, mostly for religious reasons. These inmates cost the prison more than five dollars a day; kosher food, served not just to Jewish prisoners but also (mostly) to Muslim prisoners, is expensive. If the whole inmate population converted to Orthodox Judaism, they could break the bank.

Final verdict on lunch at Oxford: bland, healthful, and I wish I had grabbed a few loaves of that bread on the way out. I asked about nutraloaf—it's not in the repertoire. "We have other ways of dealing with unruly inmates," said an assistant to the warden, "and that usually means starting with a transfer."

I figured that the feds would easily outperform anything any state prison could offer. Living in Wisconsin meant a visit to a Wisconsin prison was a must. I went to the medium-security prison at Oshkosh—population 1,845 (that fluctuates daily). This is a serious prison and lunch here required removing my belt and shoes to satisfy the ultra-sensitive metal detector (there was no metal detector or even a search at the federal prison camp).

Wisconsin houses a little more than twenty thousand offenders in institutions running from the fenceless minimum security prisons and camps to the new "SuperMax" prison at Boscobel. Oshkosh is modern but unmistakably a prison. Secure walls with guard towers punctuate the landscape of the Fox Valley. It is also the largest prison in Wisconsin, built to house 1,494 inmates but is, as is typical in so many states, well over its stated capacity.

My visit to Oshkosh was filled with surprises, starting with a delicious cheese-filled blintz. Yes, it was a blintz! The light and airy cheese filling was flecked with cinnamon and warm spices and the crepe was elegant and refined. The presentation was first rate. Had I taken a wrong turn, veering through hyperspace and landing in some upscale New York restaurant? No, I had just missed the high school equivalency diploma banquet, prepared by a select group of inmates studying culinary arts under the caring and passionate eye of instructor Tom Lehorn, from the nearby Fox Valley Technical Institute.

Tom's sixteen culinary arts students were learning about a world of food they never even imagined was out there. Tom knew that it was unlikely that his students would end up in the kitchens of America's finest restaurants. Even if they found work (when they got out) as short-order cooks, they would know a little bit more about food than the next short-order cook. And they would care a little bit more.

The blintz was only the tip of the iceberg. That is an apt analogy because one of the students turned out to be master ice carver; he had prepared several dazzling ice sculptures (my favorite was the swan) and several delicate butter sculptures as well. I hesitate to write of Tom's program for fear that some politician will misinterpret it and try to shut it down. Tom's students knew that they had a good thing going—they got to eat their own food five days a week. But they worked hard at their training. I saw them studying menus, discussing portioning and recipes, with an intense and genuine seriousness.

Tom's training of these inmates was no different from the way he trains other students except for one little detail: knives. You can't be a skilled chef without knowing how to use a good knife. But prison authorities have a problem with inmates and knives. As a result, Tom trains each prisoner in the use of professional chef cutlery and then every knife is signed out to individual inmates and must stay in the physical possession of that inmate until it is returned. Tom knows that his "students" have histories, and all of them were not model citizens. They got to Oshkosh the old-fashioned way; they earned their sentences. But Tom has never had a bad incident with a knife.

If you are a state or federal prisoner reading this chapter and want to enroll in this kind of program, good luck. Whatever you do, do not run into federal court claiming that you have a constitutional right to attend a cooking class. The courts have already decided that issue and it is not in your favor.[18]

Tom's sixteen students do not cook for the general inmate population. Instead, a modern 26,000-square-foot kitchen turns out the meals for the 1,800 prisoners (and for another 500 inmates at a different nearby prison). The kitchen is staffed by inmates who make nearly everything from scratch. They bake 800–1,000 loaves of bread each day—although I found the bread lighter and less flavorful than the bread at the federal prison.

Lunch at Oskosh that day was pasta (mostaccioli) with meat sauce and a tossed salad with bread, and chocolate cake for dessert. The pasta was not made from scratch but the meat sauce was prepared in large kettles. As I toured the kitchen, I sensed the aroma of beef roast; it was USDA Choice top inside sirloin being roasted for a later meal. It turns out that USDA Choice gives a more economical yield for these particular cuts.

Freezers were all locked to prevent theft. Who would steal frozen fruit juice? As it turns out, inmates had been taking cans of the stuff, mixing it with bread yeast to produce a kind of "hooch." The bread yeast was also kept under lock and key, with the necessary amounts doled out by staff when needed to make the dough. Knives here are also signed out to individual inmates. Whenever a knife is missing, the central kitchen goes into lockdown until the knife is found. They are dead serious about these things.

The kitchen crew was working hard to get the food out to the living units in time for the lunchtime deadline. It went in bulk to units like the one we visited, a brick building, housing about 150 inmates. There the kitchen would receive the food, plate the portions, and feed the prisoners quickly and efficiently. The central kitchen made up about fifty meals in styrofoam containers for inmates in segregation. Bad boys! Although Wisconsin does serve its version of nutraloaf, it is considered a last resort and no one at Oshkosh that day was getting the loaf. Wisconsin has two different loaves: a breakfast loaf and a different one for lunch and dinner. The breakfast loaf has presented a unique problem for Wisconsin corrections officials: inmates were liking it so much they began to request it even after being excused from segregation. Here's the recipe:

Wisconsin Department of Corrections Breakfast Loaf

1.5 oz Product 19 Cereal or Total Cereal (Dry)
1.5 oz Instant Nonfat Dry Milk
2 tsp. Hard Margarine Stick—melted
2 oz Seedless Raisins
4 oz Dry bread crumbs
8 fluid ounces Orange Juice, prepared from concentrate
4 oz Egg White (fresh or frozen), beaten

Combine cereal, bread crumbs and nonfat dry milk. Add orange juice, margarine, egg whites and raisins to dry mixture. Mix thoroughly and place in greased bread pan. Bake until loaf reaches an internal temperature of 165 degrees F (approx. 1 hour and 325 degrees F). Yield 1 loaf (22 oz. raw weight).

Fully cooked Breakfast Loaves should be refrigerated at 40 degrees F (or less) for up to two days. May be served warm or cold.[19]

Lunch was adequate. Although the pasta was way beyond the al dente stage, the sauce was flavorful, with enough beef and onions to make for a credible sauce. It could have used some pepper and oregano but it was certainly decent. This menu item is normally served with grated parmesan cheese but for some reason they could not get the parmesan that day. The peas were frozen, not canned, and tasted fine. The salad was simple but the dressing, an Italian-style dressing made from scratch, was excellent. The chocolate cake had a rich dark cocoa flavor and scored high marks with this eater.

The bread, as noted before, was disappointing, especially because the loaves smelled so good as they were coming out of the oven. There were garlic rolls that day, which I did not try but which several around me said were good. The bread and the rolls came with butter, not margarine. That is a matter of state law. So, too, is the requirement that the inmates be given the opportunity to drink four glasses of milk every day. Wisconsin taxpayers could save themselves about $150,000 a year if these requirements were repealed. The milk is 1% milk (fat content) and the milk at the Oshkosh prison comes from the Department of Corrections own dairy herd at Waupun, about thirty miles away.

There are complaints about the food at Oshkosh. Over the past year, inmates filed forty-four formal complaints about food and food service but all were resolved. That represents fewer than 2 percent of the total complaints filed. One complaint was that the kitchen started reducing the size of the pancakes. The inmate's perception was accurate, but he got nowhere; the now smaller pancakes were still larger than what was called for in "the manual." Welcome to the bureaucracy.

I sat down with five inmates and we talked about food and life in Oshkosh. Kevin was there on a parole revocation stemming from a second-degree sexual assault conviction. He had been around the block, having done time for burglary, too. He has been in eight different institutions. Kevin was a big fan of the burgers the kitchen sometimes served and he hated the turkey pastrami. Kevin was also a good customer of the canteen and conceded he was a "junk food junkie." The canteen and the prison food had led to Kevin bulking up; he admitted to gaining weight at Oshkosh although he seemed in great shape to me. When asked what he would eat the day he got out, Kevin did not hesitate: "I'm going right to Damon's for a big porterhouse."

John, twenty-seven, came from the projects in South Boston and he was doing time at Oshkosh for incest. John's Boston accent was as distinctive as his matter-of-fact bravado that showed through as he listed all the jails and prisons he had frequented over the years. From Walpole (Massachusetts) to Whiteville (Tennessee), John had made the rounds. The food at Oshkosh was the best and the food in Tennessee was the worst. John's favorite was the lasagna. When John hits the streets, it will be "surf 'n turf" (steak and lobster) and a plate of scallops. We reminisced about the 1986 World Series; I remember being so depressed when the Red Sox blew game six, and John remembers smashing two television sets. I made his day when I told him that the Sox were a game ahead of the Yankees. (When the Yankees overtook the Red Sox and again took the World Series, I came close to smashing two television sets myself.)

Eddie, thirty-eight, had been revoked for violating parole (drugs and sexual assault) and he, too, had been around the block. Eddie grew up in Chicago and soul food was his heritage and that was what he wanted. "Why can't we get ham hocks and black-eyed peas and greens? Make 'em right and that's the best." The menu at Oshkosh was too boring, too routine, for Eddie. Eddie was tired of the lasagna. If I had had a smoked ham hock with me, I'd have given it to him without hesitation. Good luck, Eddie. You know what he wants for his first meal on the outside.

Tom, forty-five years old, was in for parole revocation (the underlying conviction was not made clear), and he had just had all of his teeth removed. "It's not because of the food," he laughed. Tom wanted to talk about Tennessee; it was a popular topic among the inmates because Wisconsin had sent a lot of prisoners to Tennessee due to lack of room. The inmates hated the food in Tennessee. Tom lost thirty pounds in fifteen months there. To be fair, I should go to Tennessee and try their prison food but that will have to wait until the second edition of *Habeas Codfish*. Tom liked the lasagna and did not care much for the cold cuts. When he gets out, he's going to a grocery store where he will buy a great big steak. He'll take that bad baby home and grill it the way he likes it. By then he'll have new teeth.

Then there was Jessie, thirty-two years old, doing time for sexual assault, but the proud recipient that day of his high school equivalency diploma. He spoke softly but with an eloquence that captured the room. Jessie was raised in a home where Mexican food was served every day. "I grew tired of it but now I appreciate it and I miss it," said Jessie. When the prison serves burritos, Jessie is happy (though they are not like Mama makes) and he does not like the turkey pastrami. He's fond of the ice cream that they get a few times a month. "When I get out, I will go home and ask Mama to make her homemade tortillas, rice, *fidelo*, and *calavasco*." Congratulations, Jessie, and don't give up.

It was nearly 12:25 P.M. and I had to leave the unit so the guards could do their count, one of four done each day at the prison. It was no longer time to dream of steak and smoked ham hocks and Mama's *fidelo.*

The staff shared with me the prison menu from 1879 (note that the noon meal is "dinner" and the evening meal is "supper"). Please don't ever lecture me about "the good old days."

> *Sunday:* Breakfast: hash of meat, potatoes, and onion; coffee; Dinner and Supper (one meal): roast beef, potatoes, bread, and tea.
>
> *Monday:* Breakfast: boiled beef, warmed over with potatoes, bread, and coffee; Dinner: bean soup and bread; Supper: bread, syrup, and tea.
>
> *Tuesday:* Breakfast: same as Monday; Dinner: pork shanks, potatoes and bread; Supper: bread, butter, and tea.
>
> *Wednesday:* Breakfast: bread, hash, and coffee; Dinner: pork, beans, and bread; Supper: bread, syrup, and tea.
>
> *Thursday:* Breakfast: same as Monday; Dinner: vegetable soup and bread; Supper: bread, butter, and tea.
>
> *Friday:* Breakfast: hash, bread, and coffee; Dinner: pork shanks, potatoes, and bread; Supper: bread, syrup, and tea.
>
> *Saturday:* Breakfast: same as Monday; Dinner: bean soup and tea; Supper: bread, butter, and tea.

I do not believe for a minute that the food I ate at the minimum-security federal prison camp at Oxford and the medium-security state prison at Oshkosh is typical of the food served to the 1.3 million state and federal prisoners in the United States today. I suspect it was substantially better than what most inmates are getting. Yet one thing is common to the meals served all prisoners in our jails and prisons: choice, or rather the lack of it. When I come home after a day of work, I sometimes find it frustrating to decide what to eat for dinner. Should we go out? Fire up the grill? Find something in the freezer? Cook up a storm?

I sometimes say to myself: "I wish someone would decide for me and make the food appear for me." I don't think I would like that on a permanent basis. Freedom of choice in what we eat is a precious thing. When you are a prisoner, you have no say in what you eat for breakfast, lunch, or dinner. You can be confident that your food will be nutritionally adequate. After that, all bets are off.

14

JUST DESSERTS

*... common experience suggests that prepared food
such as a cake might contain a piece of hair and ...
people should be alert to the possibility that a piece
of hair might be found in prepared food.*
*—The Louisiana Court of Appeals,
explaining in* Cain v. Winn-Dixie Louisiana
*why people who become ill after finding a hair
in a cake cannot recover damages
for any illness resulting from the incident*

Habeas Codfish opened with an array of appetizers to stimulate our taste buds for this banquet of inquiry into food and the law. I suspect we have room for a few more bites. The dessert table is ready, so try these morsels of juicy jurisprudence. They are again marked as exhibits because we never know what evidence we will need for our day in court.

Exhibit A—Seattle, Washington. Lawson D. Butler was on the FBI's "Ten Most Wanted List" for escaping from the Oregon State Penitentiary where he was doing hard time for armed robbery. His nickname was "Two-Quart" because of his passion for ice cream. When he was on the lam in Seattle, a crowd gathered around a soda fountain to watch Butler consume his famous two quarts of ice cream in one sitting. He barely escaped after the FBI learned of his whereabouts but was later captured in Los Angeles. Lawson "Two-Quart" Butler would have made a fine poster child for the Milk Marketing Board, even back in 1952. Seattle can be proud of its connection between food and the law.[1]

Exhibit B—Montgomery, Alabama. Consider the plight of Omar Taylor. On 2 December 1978, Omar robbed Moseley's Grocery Store of about $600. He got thirty years for his efforts. The police "encouraged" Mr. Taylor to confess, partly on the strength of the fingerprint evidence they had secured from the scene of the crime. The suspect had taken a package of hot dogs to the checkout counter where he robbed Mr. Moseley of the money from the register. But what good is money when you have no hot dogs? Mr. Taylor took the money but foolishly left behind the hot dogs, loaded with his incriminating prints. Don't feel too bad for Mr. Taylor—the Alabama Court of Appeals overturned his conviction because the Montgomery police botched the arrest and violated Taylor's Fourth Amendment rights.[2]

Exhibit C—Baltimore, Maryland. Three officers of U.S. Caviar and Caviar, Limited, were sentenced to prison terms for engaging in a massive scheme of fraud and deception in importing and selling caviar. The company also agreed to pay a $10.4 million fine for violating virtually every import law involving caviar.[3] They were known to occasionally substitute tiny black eggs from American paddlefish and shovelnose sturgeon and pack it into tins labeled as genuine (and more expensive) Russian caviar. This is not a problem at the bars I frequent, but I am sure I would not take kindly to discovering that I was eating paddlefish caviar with my beer.

Exhibit D—Oregon. The federal District Court for the State of Oregon had little trouble ruling in favor of the government that two hundred cases of tomato "catsup" (the legal distinction between "catsup" and "ketchup" remains unclear to this day) were adulterated because samples of the wretched condiment contained very large quantities of bacteria, yeast, and mold. The name of this 1914 case says it all: *United States v. Two Hundred Cases of Adulterated Tomato Catsup.* You can look it up.[4] (My exhaustive computer research uncovered not a single case of adulterated mustard.)

Exhibit E—Brazil. Brazil? Not really. But this case is just *nuts.* Yes, that's what this lawsuit was all about, a libel charge involving nuts. The plaintiff, a California nut company, imported and sold Brazil nuts known as "natural" nuts. That meant that they were cured, dried, and processed after being imported. The defendant, a Midwest rival, sold Brazil nuts that were cured, dried, and processed before being imported. The defendant sent out a letter to its brokers telling them that "natural" Brazil nuts were "green" and likely to shrink or get moldy. The letter warned that Food and Drug inspectors might be very unhappy with these "green nuts." A jury awarded the plaintiff more than $400,000 for libeling its nuts. The judge was amused but threw out the jury's award with a curt "Nuts to you!"[5]

Exhibit F—Mansfield, Louisiana. On 18 July 1998, Mrs. N. E. Hairston went to the cupboard to fetch herself something to eat. Finding that the cupboard was bare, she went to the local Burger King and bought a Whopper™ (i.e., a big hamburger—for those who just arrived on the planet). She took it home and ate half. Within thirty minutes she was sick and went to the hospital the next day where the diagnosis was gastroenteritis caused by food poisoning. She sued Burger King but the judge ruled in favor of the fast-food restaurant because Mrs. Hairston couldn't convince him that the food poisoning came from the Whopper. It could have come from the oatmeal she ate earlier in the week. Is that why we need tort reform?[6]

Mrs. Hairston was not the only burger eater to be bounced by the Louisiana Court of Appeal. Little Latrunda Latrice Fuggins (that's her name) lost her suit against Burger King when she came down with gastroenteritis after eating a Whopper. The trial court was satisfied that Latrunda had enough evidence to warrant going to trial, but the court of appeals stepped in and ruled in Burger King's favor.[7]

Exhibit G—San Diego, California. There is definitely something fishy about this case. The police charged Nicholas Vitalich with assault with a deadly weapon for whacking his girlfriend with a ten-pound tuna. It won't be long before we start doing background checks on anyone buying fish.[8]

Exhibit H—Somewhere else in California. What kind of criminal would rob a woman and then beat her with a salami? A very bad one! That describes Terry Hopkins, whose conviction for assault by means of force likely to produce great bodily injury was upheld by the California Appeals Court. The court struggled with some apparent inconsistencies in the transcript, as it was not clear whether the salami was sliced or not. No matter, the court found Hopkins guilty of "assault with an edible weapon," giving new meaning to my favorite item on the antipasto platter: hard salami.[9]

Exhibit I—Orleans Parish, Louisiana. Clifton Howard Jr. could well be the poster child for the abusive conditions in American prisons. In 1985, Mr. Howard purchased a package of Sunbeam cookies from the prison canteen. He claims that he damaged one of his teeth when he bit into a rock concealed in one of the cookies. He sued the cookie company in federal court, claiming that the incident violated his civil rights, not to mention his dental rights. Howard asked for $25,000 in damages and also wanted the court to order Sunbeam to send him a fresh package as "punitive damages."

I do not mean to disparage Mr. Howard's credibility as a litigant or his right to engage in the great American pastime of suing the pants off anyone who walks down the street, but his prior history does make me wonder. In 1984, Howard and two other inmates sought $75,000 in damages from WNOL-TV for not airing a television movie listed in a newspaper movie guide. That lawsuit claimed that the "excitement and happiness and joy" of the inmates was compromised when the station aired *Warlock Moon* instead of *The Split*. In case you've forgotten, *The Split* is about a prison breakout.[10]

Exhibit J—Annapolis, Maryland. When a local bakery began selling "anatomically correct" gingerbread men, a group of concerned citizens (a euphemism for busybodies with too much time on their hands) tried to get the local prosecutor to file charges under a state law prohibiting the sale of nude pictures to minors. The prosecutor had better things to do. Obscenity laws are controversial enough but when you add cookie dough to the mixture, the results can be, shall we say, "crumby?"[11]

Exhibit K—Belleville, Illinois. Sometimes just a little taste can bring on a lawsuit. In 1992, a Belleville woman sued Publishers Clearinghouse, the national sweepstakes conglomerate, because she suffered severe respiratory distress as a result of licking one of the sweepstakes prize stamps. Whether the glue on the back of a sweepstakes stamp is "food" is certainly a matter of some debate and national importance but I am sure we can all sympathize with this poor woman.[12]

Exhibit L—San Francisco, California. I know you've been wondering when I would finally get to this one, the famous "Twinkie Defense" case.

***The Fat Police arrest Chef Emeril for trafficking in seared
foie gras, conspiracy to serve a lobster with drawn butter,
and two counts of aggravated crème brûlée.***

(Cartoon by Dennis Schmidt)

Dan White was a former city supervisor who shot and killed Mayor George Moscone and Supervisor Harvey Milk. His defense was that of "diminished capacity," meaning that he did not possess the mental state that would allow him to form the intent to kill, a necessary element of the crime of first-degree homicide. In the absence of intent, White would be guilty of involuntary manslaughter, a much-less-serious crime.

The evidence of intent seemed overwhelming. White armed himself with a Smith and Wesson .38 revolver and ten hollow-point bullets. He entered city hall through a basement window in order to avoid the metal detector at the front door. He shot the mayor five times, two of the shots being inflicted to the head at very close range. He exited the mayor's office, reloaded his gun, and found his way to Supervisor Milk's office where he shot the supervisor five times, one at very close range.

The defense came to be known as the "Twinkie Defense." Contrary to popular belief, White's defense was not that his diet of large amounts of junk food, especially Twinkies, caused him to go on a murderous rampage. The defense was more along the lines of using his consumption of junk food as a symptom of his depression. Twinkies were not even a major part of his junk-food binges; he ate large amounts of potato chips, candy bars, cupcakes, McDonald's fare, and, to some degree, Twinkies and other snack foods. Journalistic license and the amusing sound of "Twinkie Defense" had more to do with the legacy of the case than the facts.

Dan White had a long history of eating junk foods, although he had never committed murder in the past. He even ordered ice cream and candy bars regularly during the trial. Whatever the connection between Dan White's diet and his mental state on the day of the shootings, the jury convicted him of the lesser crime of manslaughter. He was sentenced to seven years in prison.

We often say that "we are what we eat." Does that also mean "we *do* what we eat?" The medical establishment has started to address the connection between junk food consumption and aggressive behavior.[13]

While we're in San Francisco, consider the case of short-order cook Hasheim Zayed, charged with murdering his restaurant manager after she berated him for making a customer a poached egg. What prompted the manager to criticize Zayed? Apparently poached eggs were not on the menu. Maybe Zayed was eating too many Twinkies on the side.[14]

Exhibit M—Madison, Wisconsin. I may be prejudiced in show-casing my own home town in this chapter, but this incident shows how ketchup can lead to lawlessness and depravity. The headline in the *Wisconsin State Journal* read: "Ketchup Misunderstanding Lands Man in Jail." A Michigan man thought he would have some fun at the expense of Madison's citizenry by smearing ketchup all over his body, pretending that it was blood. I am sure many readers got quite the chuckle from the article but I wrote this letter to the newspaper:

> To the editor:
>
> The police report in the December 31 [1998] edition struck a nerve with its headline: "Ketchup Misunderstanding Lands Man in Jail." The story told of how a Michigan man caused a major commotion on State Street when he scared many people by being covered with ketchup. According to the police he was also intoxicated at the time.
>
> Once again we see the mischief that ketchup and the lesser condiments can cause in our society. On the other hand, mustard is rarely the cause of unrest, civil disruptions, and unseemly behavior. To the contrary, mustard usage is frequently associated with manners, decency, civility, and good breeding.
>
> I hope that your readers learn from the tragic story of the ketchup-spattered drunkard and see that our civilization will flourish only when we make mustard an integral part of our daily lives.[15]

They published the letter, proving that when newspapers are hard up for copy, they will print just about anything. Of course, it also goes to show the utter depravity of some criminals among us.

Exhibit N—Jackson, Michigan. Those Michiganders can be a criminal lot when it comes to food. One Eli Bradley Jr. did what a lot of us often do when shopping for grapes: we taste a few before buying. According to the police, Mr. Bradley tasted more than a few when he visited Polly's Food Store. Security guards, standing ever vigilant by the grapes, allegedly saw Mr. Bradley pop two pounds of the little fruity morsels into his mouth. The district attorney decided that shoplifting would not deliver a stern-enough message and charged Bradley with felony larceny.[16]

Exhibit O—Grant County, Washington. Are you a fan of Baby Ruth candy bars? So am I. This American classic first appeared in 1920 and was named, not for the New York Yankee baseball hero, but for the daughter of President Cleveland. Millions have been sold but only one merits inclusion in this book. In 1980, Edward L. Gates bought the historic Baby Ruth, bit into it, and found something "gristly" or "spongy." He claimed to have fallen ill and . . . I will spare the details. Fortunately, there were no serious or permanent injuries. Nevertheless, he sued Standard Brands, manufacturer of the candy bar.

What was the offending object? According to the company's expert witness, the item alleged to have been in the Baby Ruth was a snake vertebra. It was not even a fresh snake vertebra; according to the expert, an archaeologist at Central Washington University, it was at least several hundred years old and maybe even several thousand years old. Nothing like a well-aged snake vertebra to liven up a chocolate bar! Mr. Gates lost in the trial court but the Washington Court of Appeals reversed and gave him a new trial. I wonder where that piece of evidence is today.[17]

Exhibit P—Boston, Massachusetts. As a native New Englander, I must bring this matter to your attention. In 1986, the Massachusetts House of Representatives voted to make the corn muffin the state's official muffin. The Senate, though, threatened to block the measure by introducing its own bill to make the cranberry muffin the official state muffin.

I remember a rotund friend of mine who liked to say, "You can't have too many muffins." On the other hand, you can have too many silly laws.[18]

Exhibit Q—Chicago, Illinois. If you have ever dined out with a group of friends, you may have noticed a little warning on the menu: "15 percent gratuity added to parties of six or more." How can they get away with that? How can a restaurant make a *gratuity* mandatory?

That was the point Michael Smolyansky tried to make in 1997 when he alleged consumer fraud on the part of the Signature Room atop the John Hancock Building. Smolyansky's lawyer claimed that his client was not notified in advance of the mandatory gratuity. When the bill came (nearly $300, including the tip), Smolyansky was outraged but paid the bill so as not to embarrass his guests. He later sued in

Cook County Circuit Court but ultimately dropped the suit. We need lawsuits like these, don't we?[19]

Exhibit R—Jersey City, New Jersey. This is a case that will surely live in culinary infamy. Judge William Clark had before him a case that challenged the power of Jersey City to restrict certain activities of a labor group. How, then, does food enter the controversy? It does not, except that Judge Clark decided to visit some faraway planet as he was writing the court's opinion: "The effect of mustard, let us say, upon the human body lies in the field of physiology, an exact science, and is certain. Mustard is not protected by the Constitution."[20]

Mustard is not protected by the Constitution? Why not? And what did this rash generalization have to do with the issue before Judge Clark? Nothing. Absolutely nothing. Although the U.S. Supreme Court ultimately modified Judge Clark's decision,[21] it never bothered to undo the harm that the lower court did to mustard's reputation and legal standing.

It is time for some right-thinking jurist to overturn Judge Clark's random attack on mustard.

Exhibit S—Oakland, California. This one may not take the cake but it certainly takes the cookie. Juan Aldarando was charged with stealing a ginger pecan cookie from the Critics Corner Cafe. Interesting tidbit? Not really. But what happened to Juan after his arrest will surely arouse your passions. According to Mr. Aldarando, he endured "the most degrading" punishment imaginable: he was handcuffed and made to listen to a police officer sing the famous Rupert Holmes hit, "Escape (The Pina Colada Song)."

Cruel? Maybe. Unusual? Without a doubt.[22]

Exhibit T—Kinsman, Ohio. This Ohio town is the birthplace of Clarence Darrow, America's most famous defense lawyer. He represented radical labor organizer Eugene Debs in the famous Pullman case and later represented John Scopes in the "Monkey Trial" at Dayton, Tennessee, where the theory of evolution came under attack by the powers of popular religion. What does Clarence Darrow have to do with food? He was involved in no famous food lawsuits but is remembered by food lovers everywhere for these words of wisdom: "I don't like spinach, and I'm glad I don't, because if I liked it I'd eat it, and I'd just hate it."[23]

That's the kind of logic that makes defense lawyers so feared and so formidable.

Exhibit U—Washington, D.C. It's frightening how often Washington, D.C., comes up in this investigation of food and the law. Most often, it is in the context of some federal law or lawsuit. This case, arising out of a lawsuit filed by an FBI agent against the District of Columbia, grabbed my attention for an entirely different reason.

On a warm day in May 1942, the plaintiff ate lunch at defendant's lunch counter in the District of Columbia. He ate a hot dog (described by the court as a "frankfurter-on-roll sandwich") a slice of Boston cream pie, and a glass of tea. A few hours later he became violently ill and was hospitalized for four days. Another FBI worker (an attorney, no less), had the same meal at the same time, except that he drank milk instead of tea, and suffered substantially the same symptoms.

The plaintiff successfully sued the restaurant for personal injuries resulting from food poisoning. On appeal, the restaurant claimed that in the absence of scientific laboratory results, any finding of food poisoning was conjecture. The appellate court was willing to accept the jury's verdict and excused the lack of scientific proof in graphic terms:

> Only the most litigious plaintiff would have had the presence of mind, in the throes of intermittent attacks of vomiting and diarrhea to arrange for laboratory tests and chemical analyses of his vomitus and excreta to be brought into court to prove his case. A man can hardly be expected to prepare a lawsuit while writhing on an ambulance stretcher or a hospital bed.[24]

Why not? This is America, where lawsuits are sport and NFL stands for "national fever over litigation." But what caught my attention was the curious testimony of the restaurant manager who told the jury that on the day in question he had cut the Boston cream pie into *seven* slices and even ate one of the slices himself, with no ill effects. Seven slices? No one cuts a pie into seven slices! The jury obviously disbelieved him with that tall tale and was willing to award the plaintiff whatever damages he wanted. Seven slices indeed!

Exhibit V—Pottstown, Pennsylvania. While we are on the subject of pies, we must consider the home town of Mrs. Smith's Pie Company. Despite the down-home name, Mrs. Smith's was the largest producer of frozen dessert pies, at least back in 1972. When Mrs. Smith tried to buy the Lloyd J. Harris Pie Company, the Department of Justice stepped in and tried to stop the sale because it thought Mrs. Smith would gain a monopoly foothold in the frozen dessert market, in violation of the Clayton Antitrust Act. Sure enough, said the court, the deal would give Mrs. Smith much too big a slice of the pie.[25]

Exhibit W—Chicago, Illinois. We return to Chicago because that is the corporate headquarters of Jay's Foods, a major snack manufacturer. The case in point goes back more than sixty years, when the Kraft-Phenix Cheese Company, owner of the registered trademark "O-Ke-Doke" tried to prevent Consolidated Beverages from registering the mark "O-Kee-Dokee."

This will take some concentration. O-Ke-Doke was the mark used for a cheese-flavored popcorn snack. O-Kee-Dokee was the mark that Consolidated wanted to use for soft drinks. Okeedokee? The trademark office ruled that the two items were so different (did "not belong to the same general class of merchandise") that there would be no likelihood of confusion in allowing both O-Ke-Doke cheese-flavored popcorn and O-Kee-Dokee soft drinks to coexist. The U.S. Court of Customs and Patent Appeals agreed with the difference:

> It is commonly known that soft drinks have for their main purpose the quenching of thirsts and, even though they may be flavored, ordinarily are never considered as a food. Popcorn is derived from corn and is certainly a food. Cheese is made from milk and likewise is a nutritious food product.[26]

Put the two together and you have an O-Ke-Doke, O-Kee-Dokee gourmet feast. What does Chicago have to do with this? I found a bag of O-Ke-Doke cheese-flavored popcorn at the local convenience store, more than sixty years after its appeal. I've not found any trace of O-Kee-Dokee soft drinks on the market today but maybe I don't shop in the right circles. Still, I am amazed that O-Ke-Doke cheese-flavored popcorn has withstood the test of time. The Chicago connection? O-Ke-Doke is now part of the Jay's snack-food empire. I don't know when this happened or whether the government considered any possible antitrust implications or national security concerns to the deal.

Okee-dokee?

Exhibit X—Oklahoma. I promised I would get back to this case, the 1924 decision of the Oklahoma Supreme Court in which civilization as we know it was saved from the jacketless barbarians. It was the case that started me on this journey and I cannot write *Habeas Codfish* without sharing with you the wisdom of *Fred Harvey et al. v. Corporation Commission of Oklahoma.*[27]

It was the golden era of rail travel in America. At many of the railway stations in Oklahoma, hungry passengers could satisfy their appetites at a Fred Harvey Restaurant. Most of us too young to remember the Fred Harvey railway restaurants may still remember the Fred Harvey restaurants along the turnpikes of the 1950s and 1960s; it was the same operation.

At the various railway stations, Fred Harvey would operate both a dining room and a lunch counter. To eat in the dining room, men had to wear coats. There the service was "table d'hôte," presumably more elegant and refined than at the lunch counter. Curiously, the lunch-counter service, although less formal in terms of attire, was generally more expensive because everything was "à la carte."

This dual system of eating—dining room with a dress code and lunch counter without—offended the chairman of the Oklahoma Corporation Commission, the agency that regulated rail service in the state of Oklahoma. Thus, the chairman decided to charge both the Atchison, Topeka and Santa Fe Railroads as well as the Fred Harvey Company with unlawful discrimination. When the commission issued its cease and desist order, the railroad and Fred Harvey appealed to the courts.

The Oklahoma Supreme Court was doubtful that the commission had the power to regulate anything that Fred Harvey did but went along with the assumption that it was acting as an agent of the railway. There was also the thorny question of passengers traveling in interstate commerce, over which the commission probably had no jurisdiction. Nevertheless, the court took on the discrimination issue directly and forcefully.

First, the court pointed out that gentlemen who happened to show up at the dining room without a coat would be furnished one, without charge, by the good people of Fred Harvey. "The obstinate patron who, by refusing to wear a coat, pays at the lunch counter a higher price for a meal than he would pay in the dining room, must charge his loss to his own stubbornness and bear his self-inflicted injury without complaint of discrimination."

The corporation commission found the rule unreasonable for another reason: the mandatory wearing of a coat in hot weather made travelers uncomfortable. Justice Lydick, known for preciously little else in the annals of American jurisprudence, penned this eloquent defense of the rule, not in terms of cold legal precedent but rather in terms of table manners and civilized behavior:

> Society in America has for years assumed jurisdiction to a great extent to dictate certain regulations of dress in first-class dining rooms, and these conventions of society cannot be entirely ignored, without disastrous results to those who serve a metropolitan public in such capacity. Civilized society has developed the masculine attire from the breech-clout to the coat and trousers. Always a part of the masculine garb, and often a major portion of feminine dress, is worn as an adornment to satisfy the conventions of society rather than for bodily comfort and protection. Unlike the lower animals, we all demand the maintenance of some style and fashion in the dinning-room, but where to draw the line between the breech-clout and the full-dress suit, tailored in Paris or New York, presents a question often affording great difference of opinion, and that is the trouble here.
>
> Just laws are not originally created by the legislature. They are first made by the people (society) and are merely discovered and announced by those whom we call lawmakers. Miss Edith Johnson, long a student and writer of note on subjects akin to the one under consideration, testified in this case and said: "The enforcement of certain social conventions has a tendency to maintain and elevate the tone of society ... in its general sense." She says the rule is "to maintain the morale and aesthetic tone of the Harvey eating service," and is a reasonable one. Mrs. J. H. Miley, also well experienced as a student and writer, on the witness stand approved the rule, saying that in such places as the first-class dining room, "the custom of the people requires men to go well groomed, because it makes them respect themselves more and it makes others with them respect them more."
>
> To abrogate this rule and require the dining room manager to draw the line of dress at mere cleanliness would lead quickly to personal disputes over differences of opinion. To permit the coatless to enter would bring in those with sleeveless shirts, and even the shirt-

less garb that we frequently see where no formality is required. Man's coat is usually the cleanest of his garments, and the fact that he is required to wear a coat serves notice that decorum is expected and creates a wholesome psychological effect.

Fred Harvey equips these dining rooms with most luxurious furnishings, pleasing to the trained and appreciative eye, satisfying to the aesthetic taste, and places the patrons amidst surroundings best calculated to stimulate the appetite. Food seldom elsewhere excelled is served by well-garbed and efficient attendants. Certainly it is not amiss to require the gentlemen who there would dine to wear a coat for 20 minutes, as he sits in front of the cooling electric fans always there afforded. Our nation's Chief Executive has recently well said that "a true citizen of a real republic cannot exist as a segregated, unattached fragment of selfishness, but must live as a constituent part of the whole society, in which he can secure his own welfare only as he secures the welfare of his fellow men." Complaints against such rule, by those unwilling to momentarily endure a slight discomfort, out of regard for the feelings, tastes, and desires of others, are few compared with the storm of protests the abrogation of the rule would ultimately produce. The order requires the abrogation of the rule even in pleasant weather, and we are quite sure that the order itself is more unreasonable and arbitrary than the rule is even charged to be. The expert witnesses agree that the rule is almost universally adopted at railway dining rooms, in dining cars, and first-class hotels, in deference to the conventions of human society generally.

It must be remembered that while much power is by law given to the Corporation Commission in the regulation of public utilities, yet the utility is not the property of the commission or the state, but belongs to the company and its stockholders, and the officers and directors by them selected must, under proper regulation, be permitted to manage the property in such proper way as to earn and pay, if they lawfully can, just dividends to the stockholders. Regulation must not be so far extended as to constitute management or operation.

It was not intended by the writers of our organic law that the funds of our state, raised by the taxation of our people, should be expended by the Corporation Commission in the conduct of extensive and expensive hearings upon just what rules of style and fashion should be followed by a great public utility. Lawmakers must not completely destroy personal liberty. It would be unwise to leave matters like this to the discretion of inexperienced public officers, selected by a vote of the people, and whose policies and rules would likely change at every election. It is well, ordinarily at least, that we be slow to abrogate rules in such regard, made by those whose successful life's experience well qualify them to formulate such internal policies. The rule is not unreasonable.

And that, dear friend, is how the Oklahoma Supreme Court saved elegant dining from the coatless barbarians.

Exhibit Y—Oklahoma. Convicted murderer Thomas Grasso asked for a double cheeseburger, mussels, a strawberry milk shake, pumpkin pie, a lemon, a mango, and a can of his favorite cold spaghetti. It was his last meal and prison authorities were not too careful about selecting the right cold spaghetti product. His final (or almost final) words were, "I did not get my SpaghettiOs." This may seem trivial to some, but when the law takes the life of a man, his last meal is no trivial matter to him. No lawsuit was ever filed in the matter.[28]

Exhibit Z—Bucks County, Pennsylvania. Only in America can we find a case of a serial bread squeezer. Samuel Feldman terrorized the area grocery stores by squeezing bagels and loaves of bread. He also pressed his thumb into various cookies. Why would he do this? He apparently had an unpleasant experience purchasing a stale loaf of bread and decided he would be especially careful in evaluating bakery goods for possible purchase. According to the criminal complaint, his squeezing and pressing caused more than $7,000 in damage to the items over a three-year period. Prosecutors said that Mr. Feldman left handprints and finger marks on 175 bags of bagels, 227 bags of potato dinner rolls, and 3,087 loaves of bread. In September 2000, he was convicted of malicious mischief and disorderly conduct.

Do you remember Victor Hugo's Jean Valjean, literature's most famous food thief (he stole a loaf of bread)? I don't think Sam Feldman will ever be the sympathetic hero of the remake of *Les Misérables*.[29]

What a fine meal that was! We have tasted everything from soup to nuts (a *lot* of nuts). The only thing left is to chew on it and digest it well. We need just a final verdict and the chef may go home.

15

THE FINAL VERDICT

*An orange floating in an open sewer
does not change it into a fruit salad.*
—*Concurring opinion of Justice Robert Hansen
in* Court v. State *(an obscenity case),
proving that some jurists will go to any
lengths to bring food into the courtroom*

The law has a way of changing itself, refining itself, sometimes even reversing itself. The dissenting opinion of today may well be the majority opinion of some future generation.

No matter what political persuasion you espouse, the law is organic. It moves, it throbs, and it breathes. Sometimes it comforts the power elite, sometimes it heralds the winds of change. When it comes to food, the law is no different. Nothing that you have read is cast in stone. That is what made writing *Habeas Codfish* such a challenge. For example, I discovered and wrote about the Pizza Hut/Papa John's case when the lower court had ruled in Pizza Hut's favor—and then revised everything I had written when the appeals court threw out the verdict.

I suspect that some of what you have just read will have been rendered obsolete or downright wrong by subsequent court decisions or legislative action. That is the nature of law. (That is also why authors write second editions.)

It is time to take stock of all of these topics and decide if the law aids in the delivery of safe food, honest food, nutritious food, and tasty food. It is time to reflect.

I subscribe to *Gourmet News,* the leading trade periodical of the gourmet food industry. One would think that this newspaper would be chock full of news about new and exciting gourmet foods. One would expect to read about the latest infused olive oils, goats' milk cheeses, mustards (of course), confections, and exotic sauces. *Gourmet News* covers that kind of news but its pages are increasingly filled with stories about who is suing whom and what new federal regulations affect the industry.

No one in the food business is exempt from the implications of the law. If you want to make jams from the berries in the backyard and sell them at the local growers market, you'd better become familiar with the hundreds of rules and regulations that affect you. Chances are that you will not be allowed to make these delicious jams in your home kitchen. You will probably need a license and will have to make the jams in a separate inspected kitchen, free of porous surfaces and loaded with expensive stainless steel. Your label will probably have to conform to state standards. You need to know the law.

When the government decided to mandate nutritional labeling, the gourmet food industry lobbied for an exemption for small manufacturers. The theory behind such an exemption was that the costs of the nutritional analyses and the resulting new labels would be too burdensome on small businesses, possibly driving them from the marketplace. On the other hand, why should the size of a manufacturer defeat a consumer's right to know? The result was that the National Association for the Specialty Food Trade successfully convinced Congress to carve out an exemption for small businesses.

If the small business exemption diminishes the consumer's arsenal of nutritional information, so be it. On the plus side, cottage industries that have the potential to make high-quality artisan foods can at least survive a little longer. Food law involves power; powerful interests shape the laws that affect how we eat and what we eat more than the less-powerful interests. That is hardly a new or startling revelation.

Food law invariably involves the regulation of human conduct. In the United States, we allow dozens of agencies and bureaucracies to govern what we eat and how we eat. It is tempting to suggest that one unified Department of Food and Beverage would be a more logical approach to food safety, honesty, and nutrition. After all, there is a

Department of Transportation, a Department of Defense, a Department of Education. These federal agencies recognize a single function and address it in a single agency.

We have seen the conflicts that inevitably arise from separate and often competing jurisdictions that regulate food. The FDA, the FTC, the EPA, the USDA, and the various states and municipalities create anything but a single coherent system of food law. Not to mention the various courts that hear all kinds of civil cases relating to food. It makes sense to bring it all under one roof.

It makes sense but it may not work for one simple and indisputable reason: the new super Department of Food and Beverages (or whatever you want to call it) would be so big and unwieldy that it might be impossible to control. Food is such a major part of our lives that no single agency can possibly get a handle on it. The current system, balkanized as it is through years of turf fighting and tradition, will probably continue unchanged for many more years.

There is one unifying force that can still make sense out of the hodgepodge system of federal regulation: the courts. If there are inconsistencies and irregularities that come about as a result of so many agencies being involved in food regulation, a unified judiciary may be the best hope for bringing it all together.

The judicial system of dispute resolution is awkward, at best, but it has its place. Although it is very easy to point our fingers at the thousands of lawsuits that clog our courtrooms, few of us would willingly give up our rights to sue when we have been harmed by the wrongful conduct of others.

The "tort reform" bandwagon assumes that juries are too-easily swayed. It draws our attention to the high-profile but nonrepresentative cases. The McDonald's hot coffee case was the exception, not the rule. No one writes about the many lawsuits that never make it to the courthouse for lack of adequate representation or simply an unwillingness to go through the tortured process of the system.

Lawsuits can play a key role in food safety and food honesty. It is a matter of economics. Suppose, for example, that you are the manufacturer of a particular food product and you know that one hundred people every year, of the five million who buy it, will get sick from it. You could cut that number in half by investing $10 million in a certain new technology. Do you spend the money?

The answer is not obvious. What are the costs of *not* buying the new technology? If you can reasonably expect only twenty of the injured eaters to come forward and demand compensation amounting to, let us say, $500,000 each year, you may decide that it is a better economic choice to forego the new technology and just pay out the money. If, however, the cost of litigation is substantially higher than $500,000, you may be tempted to invest in a technology that reduces the risk of harm to your consumers.

Lawsuits—or rather the threat of lawsuits—can change the behavior of powerful companies. If we think that "runaway" jury awards are indeed a problem, the solution may be to create products and encourage corporate behavior that do not induce such verdicts.

Most of modern food law is not resolved in the courtroom. It is shaped in broad form by legislative bodies and then fine-tuned by administrative agencies. The rules and regulations at all levels of government are massive and illustrate how important it is for those who want to shape food policy in the coming years to become not just familiar but proficient at rule-making procedures. You cannot wait to join the battle in litigation; it may be too late to do anything useful.

Before we clear the table and store away the leftovers, I want to mention briefly a few hot topics that never made it onto tonight's menu. The subject of organic food labeling could well have been a chapter unto itself. What is "organic"? Who decides? Can food that is otherwise organic but is also irradiated be deemed organic? What are the penalties for passing off food that is not organically grown as organic?

Although thousands of farmers, consumers, and businesses are involved in the struggle over a sensible organic food labeling law, the issue is basically one of definition and classification. A particular food grown in a particular way with or without the addition of particular substances (as in chemicals) will be classified as organic if the government says it is organic. Really, it is that simple, and it demonstrates the undeniable principle in law that the power to define is the power to rule.

The whole organic labeling issue reminds me of the story of the man who asked, "If we call a cow's tail a leg, how many legs does a cow have?" His listener replied, "Five." "No, it's still four. Calling a tail a leg does not make it a leg. It's still a tail." (I have no idea who first told that story.)

In the world of food law, the man was wrong—the cow indeed has five legs! The government decree that a tail is a leg is tantamount to that United States Supreme Court ruling that a tomato (botanically a fruit) is a vegetable.[1]

Another of today's most controversial issues is that of genetically modified foods. Again, the definition of a genetically modified food is crucial to resolution of the controversy, but there are other complex matters to consider. The first is safety. Are genetically modified foods hazardous to human health? If the government opines that they are safe, does that mean that they are really safe?

The cow's tail analogy does not seem to work well here. When it comes to health, I'm not sure I am willing to trust the government edict that a genetically modified food is safe. Involved here is more than a definition or classification, it is life and death.

Then we have the issue of labeling genetically modified foods. Do consumers have the right to know if a food or food ingredient is genetically altered? Most of the food industry opposes mandatory labeling because it might alarm consumers needlessly.[2]

The issues surrounding genetically modified foods demonstrate that good science[3] and good law do not necessarily go hand in hand. To further complicate this issue, it is not clear who has jurisdiction over the matter. The EPA, FDA, and USDA are (or should be) involved in these questions.

A third matter of grave concern is mad cow disease. After an initial scare that landed Oprah Winfrey in court (chapter 10), fear of this potentially deadly disease on American soil all but vanished. In early 2001, when threats of mad cow disease once again spread through Europe, U.S. concerns reappeared. Is this really a legal issue?

How we decide to stop the possible spread of mad cow disease is a question of science and public health policy. How we implement those policies is a matter of law. One approach is to require a system of tracking cows that find their way to the market place. Under this system, a bar-coded ear tag can trace any at-risk animal back to the home herd. (It is even possible to trace a package of contaminated meat back to the original herd.) Canada imposed a mandatory tracing scheme on 1 January 2001.[4]

Will the United States adopt a similar regime of mandatory tracing? At a meeting of the National Cattlemen's Beef Association, the consensus was for animal identification on a voluntary basis only. One rancher said, "If it's something that would make me more money or give me better access to foreign trade, I might consider it. But I don't think there needs to be another government bureaucracy forced down our throats."[5]

The threats of mad cow disease and mad corn disease remind us that we may buy locally (at our local supermarkets) but we eat globally. Our legal system needs to recognize this fact.

We demand much of the foods we eat and we somehow expect the law to be ultimate enforcer. Law, in all areas but especially in the field of food, can only do so much.

Someone asked me: "If I could study one food and become an expert in the field of food law, what would that food be?" I thought long and hard and arrived at an answer. "Study the oyster."

I used to love oysters—raw with a squirt of lemon juice and a dusting of freshly ground pepper. I won't eat raw oysters any more because I'm afraid of them. I used to crave them but this book has turned me against these magical delicacies. I learned that people have been injured by eating pearls hidden in oysters (they are not really hidden, they were just never detected by the oyster shucker and not removed). Sometimes people are injured by pieces of shell. Sometimes people get sick from naturally occurring bacteria in the oysters. Federal and state agencies are struggling with rules and regulations to cover all facets of the oyster industry in an effort to make oysters safer.

The truth is that the law cannot make food safe. It can encourage people to change their behavior but it can do very little to directly affect food. Oysters, for example, have a reputation for being delicious but not for being law-abiding citizens.

I don't think I will ever eat another raw oyster. Then again, I'm beginning to remember how great they tasted. Blue Points, Chincoteagues, Cotuits, Wellfleets, Olympias (oh so sweet!), Malpeques, and Belon. They were so delicious. But I might crack a tooth or get sick. Of course, I (or my estate) can always sue.

What will be the next attention-grabbing food law issue? Can anything top the McDonald's hot-coffee case or the litigation between Oprah and the cattle ranchers? If I were to guess, I would keep my eyes focused on another lawsuit involving the fast-food giant and its ubiquitous fries.

McDonald's fries are legendary; I never cared much for their thin overcooked burgers, but the fries were something else. Those thin, crispy wands of potato heaven were as good as fries got. Did I care that they were cooked in beef fat? Not I. They tasted great, and when that first McDonald's opened in my town of Worcester, Massachusetts (was it on Park Avenue?), I had never even heard of cholesterol (much less could have spelled it). But I have to give them credit: those were awesome fries.

In 1990, McDonald's announced that it was changing to pure vegetable oil for cooking its fries. Vegetarians and those who for one reason or another could or would not eat anything cooked in beef fat were delighted. The logic was impeccable: if you deep-fry a potato (a vegetable) in vegetable oil, the result is vegetarian. The problem was that at some time—and it is not clear when that time was—McDonald's started to add beef flavoring to the cut potatoes before they were flash frozen. (One ex-McDonald's franchisee told me it was only a few years after the switch to vegetable-oil frying.)

"So where's the beef?" Where's the litigation? In May 2001, a Seattle lawyer filed a class action lawsuit on behalf of Hindus and vegetarians. The suit alleges that McDonald's has misled millions into believing that McDonald's fries were suitable for vegetarians. McDonald's has countered with an explanation that it had never represented its fries to be vegetarian fare.

For a Hindu following a strict vegetarian regime, the revelation that the fries consumed over the last decade were laced with beef flavoring must be terrifying. But is it worth a lawsuit? Is it "actionable?" (That's lawyerspeak for "Will a jury award the plaintiff lots of money?")

As *Habeas Codfish* goes to press, the case is in its infancy and its future is uncertain. For us, it is an opportunity to conclude our investigation by applying our four expectations of food to a most unusual set of facts.

1. Food should taste good. The fries at McDonald's taste "better" because of the added beef flavoring. This judgment is, of course, a matter of opinion. If McDonald's were to leave out the beef flavoring, the taste would certainly be different, and you can bet your next Happy Meal that McDonald's has done plenty of research to justify the addition of beef flavoring to its fries. Curiously, McDonald's does not add

beef flavoring to the fries sold in countries, such as India, where the populace does not eat beef for religious or cultural reasons.

2. Food should be nutritious. Even this becomes a matter of opinion because some people look at nutrition in a rather broad sense; that is, food should nourish the soul as well as the body. For a strict vegetarian, and especially for a strict Hindu vegetarian, consumption of any beef violates principles of good nutrition, spiritual and physical.

3. Food should be honestly represented. This is the crux of the litigation. Did McDonald's mislead the public by claiming to have switched to 100 percent vegetable oil but then adding beef flavoring without telling people? McDonald's seems to argue, "We never said we wouldn't add beef flavoring and never told people the fries weren't flavored with a little beef." Is that acceptable?

4. Food must not harm us. Although the government is unlikely ever to regard the addition of natural beef flavoring as a harmful adulterant, any amount of beef ingested by a practicing Hindu is considered devastating and most injurious. One plaintiff, distraught over the realization of what he had been ingesting over the years, has planned a trip to India for the purpose of bathing in the Ganges River as an attempt to reduce his sin. But for him, great harm has already been done.[6] Will that harm—*should* that harm—be recognized in a court of law?

NOTES
WARNING AND DISCLAIMER
LEGAL CASES CITED

NOTES

Chapter 1. Assault with a Breadly Weapon

1. Giles MacDonogh, *A Palate in Revolution* (London: Robin Clark, 1987), p. 50.

2. Vernon Pizer, *Eat the Grapes Downward* (New York: Dodd, Mead, and Company, 1983), pp. 94–95.

3. Rebecca L Spang, *The Invention of the Restaurant* (Cambridge: Harvard University Press, 2000), p. 9.

4. James Trager, *The Food Chronology* (New York: Henry Holt and Company, 1995), p. 64.

5. *The Sunday Telegraph* (London), 14 March 1993; Joseph Wechsberg et al., *The Cooking of Vienna's Empire* (New York: Time-Life Books, 1968), pp. 178–79.

6. Alexis Soyer, *The Pantropheon; or, A History of Food and Its Preparation in Ancient Times* (1853; reprint, London: Paddington Press, 1977), p. 211.

7. Online; available: <http://www.dumblaws.com>.

8. Trager, *The Food Chronology*, p. 45.

9. Katie Holder and Jane Newdick, *A Dash of Mustard* (London: Chartwell Books, 1997), p. 18.

10. Trager, *The Food Chronology*, p. 158.

11. *Nix v. Hedden*, 149 U.S. 304 (1893).

12. Alexis Soyer, *The Pantropheon*, p. 211.

13. Court papers in *State of New Hampshire v. Michael Towne*, provided by attorney R. Peter Decato.

14. "News of the Truly Bizarre" wire service (originally reported in the *New York Times*), 11 September 1998.

15. *Wisconsin State Journal* (news service), 9 January 2001, p. A5.

16. Pizer, *Eat the Grapes Downward*, p. 15.

17. Carolyn Wyman, *Spam: A Biography* (San Diego: Harcourt Brace, 1999), p. 102.

18. *Hormel Foods Corp. v. Jim Henson Productions*, 95 Civ. 5473 (S.D.N.Y. 1995), affirmed at 73 F.3d. 497 (2d Cir. 1996).

19. *Lansing State Journal*, 17 March 1981.

20. *Casey v. State*, 266 So.2d 366 (Fla. App. 1972).

21. *Kroger Grocery and Baking Co. v. Dempsey*, 143 S.W.2d 564 (1940).

22. *Messner v. Red Owl Stores*, 57 N.W.2d 659 (Minn. 1953).

23. *National Law Journal*, 24 August 1987, p. 39.

24. *Treasure Island Catering v. State Bd. of Equalization*, 120 P.2d 1 (Cal. 1941).

25. *People v. Waldbaums*, 386 N.Y.S.2d 526 (1976).

26. *People v. Waldbaums*, 386 N.Y.S.2d 526 (1976), quoting from *In Matter of Cullinan*, 93 App. Div. 427 (1904).

27. *People v. Waldbaums*, quoting *People v. Friedman*, 157 App. Div. 437 (1913).

28. *Newberry v. Cohen's (Smoked Salmon), Ltd.*, 54 LGR 343 (1956).

29. Ibid.

30. Ibid.

31. H. E. Jacob, *Six Thousand of Bread* (New York: Lyons Press, 1944), p. 140.

32. I made that up! I'm checking to see if you read these endnotes. If you quote me on this, shame on both of us! Remember, I used to practice law, so everything I write must be taken with—a grain of salt? (I'm also seeing if my editor is awake.)

33. Jacob, *The Story of Bread*, p. 140.

34. James Trager, *The Food Chronology*, p. 204.

35. Ibid., p. 209.

36. Ibid., p. 261.

Chapter 2. Big Beef Supreme

1. James Trager, *The Food Chronology* (New York: Henry Holt and Company, 1995), p. 48.

2. Ibid., p. 50.

3. Ibid., p. 91.

4. Ibid., p. 609.

5. Ibid., p. 655.

6. Ibid., p. 708.

7. Upton Sinclair, *The Jungle* (1906; reprint, New York: Barnes & Noble, 1995), pp. 142–45.

8. William L. Prosser, "The Assualt upon the Citadel (Strict Liability to the Consumer)," 69 *Yale Law Journal* 1099 (1960), p. 1105, n. 40.

9. James Trager, *The Food Chronology*, p. 314.

10. 60 Fed.Reg. 6,774 (1995) (codified at 9 C.F.R. secs. 308, 310, 320, 325, 326, 327, 381).

11. For a critical view of HACCP, see Sharlene W. Lassiter, "From Hoof to Hamburger: The Fiction of a Safe Meat Supply," 33 *Willamette Law Review* 411 (1997).

12. *Supreme Beef Processors v. U.S. Dept. of Agriculture*, 113 F.Supp.2d 1048 (N.D. Tex. 2000).

13. 21 U.S.C. sec. 610(c).

14. *Supreme Beef Processors v. U.S. Dept. of Agriculture*, 113 F.3d at 1053, n.3 (N.D. Tex. 2000).

15. *Supreme Beef Processors v. U.S. Dept. of Agriculture*, 113 F.Supp.2d 1048 (N.D. Tex. 2000).

16. Supreme Beef appealed this action to the court that had ruled in its favor on the main legal issue, but the court held that the government was free to enforce its rights as a purchaser of meat totally separate from whatever it was doing illegally as a regulator. *Memorandum Order*, 11 July 2000.

17. *American Federation of Government Employees v. Glickman*, 215 F.3d 7 (C.A.D.C. 2000).

18. Marian Burros, "The 'Yuck Factor:' How Clean Are Salad Bars?" *New York Times*, 25 August 1999, p. B1.

19. Vince Straten, *Can You Trust a Tomato in January?* (New York: Simon & Schuster, 1993), p. 10.

Chapter 3. Nutrition Facts, Nutrition Fictions

1. See, generally, the excellent law review article by Jean Lyons and Martha Rumore, "Food Labeling—Then and Now," 2 *Journal of Pharmacy and Law* 171 (1993).

2. *United States v. Coca Cola*, 241 U.S. 265 (1916). The government alleged that Coca-Cola was adulterated by virtue of the addition of caffeine and misbranded because it had no coca and little cola.

3. *United States v. Ten Cases, More or Less, Bred Spred, et al.*, 49 F.2d 87 (8th Cir. 1931).

4. Ibid., quoting *United States v. Lexington Mill Co.*, 232 U.S. 399, 409 (1915).

5. *U.S. v. 30 Cases, More or Less, Leader Brand Strawberry Fruit Spread*, 93 F.Supp. 764 (S.D. Iowa 1950).

6. *United States v. 651 Cases, More or Less, of Chocolate Chil-Zert,* 114 F. Supp. 430 (N.D.N.Y. 1953).

7. Ibid.

8. James Trager, *The Food Chronology* (New York: Henry Holt and Company, 1995), p. 496.

9. Letter from Gary M. Wells, 16 May 1995.

10. 21 Code of Federal Regulations (C.F.R.) sec. 133.173(a)(5).

11. *Kraft, Inc. v. F.T.C.,* 970 F.2d 311 (7th Cir. 1992).

12. Vince Straten, *Can You Trust a Tomato in January?* (New York: Simon & Schuster, 1993), p. 188.

13. 21 C.F.R. sec. 155.194 Catsup.

14. *Libby, McNeill & Libby v. U.S.,* 148 F.2d 71 (2d Cir. 1945).

15. Ibid.

16. *United States v. An Article of Food … Manischewitz … Diet Thins,* 377 F.Supp. 746 (E.D.N.Y. 1974).

17. Ibid.

18. 21 C.F.R. sec. 164.150 Peanut butter.

19. *RELCO Inc. v. Consumer Product Safety Commission,* 391 F.Supp. 841, 849 n.10 (S.D. Tex. 1975).

20. Straten, *Can You Trust a Tomato in January?* p. 131.

21. *Arent v. Shalala,* 70 F.3d 610 (C.A.D.C. 1995).

22. *Public Citizen et al. v. Shalala,* 932 F.Supp. 13 (D.D.C. 1996).

23. *State v. Goldberg,* 166 P.2d 664, 665 (Kan. 1946).

24. *State v. Shoaf,* 102 S.E. 705 (N.C. 1920).

25. *Community Nutrition Institute, et al. v. Block,* 749 F.2d 50 (C.A.D.C. 1984).

26. Ibid.

27. 9 C.F.R. sec. 319.180(b).

28. See 9 C.F.R. sec. 319.182(b).

Chapter 4. Food Fight

1. "Pizza Facts," online; available: <http://www.pizzaware.com>.

2. Daniel Roth, "This Ain't No Pizza Party," *Fortune,* 9 November 1998.

3. Marcella Hazan, *More Classic Italian Cooking* (New York: Alfred A. Knopf, 1978), pp. 60–63.

4. *Pizza Hut, Inc. v. Papa John's International, Inc.,* 80 F. Supp. 2d 600 (N.D. Tex. 2000).

5. 15 U.S.C. sec. 1125. (a)(1)(B).

6. *Pizza Hut, Inc. v. Papa John's International, Inc.,* 80 F. Supp. 2d 600 (N.D. Tex. 2000).

7. *Pizza Hut, Inc. v. Papa John's International, Inc.,* 227 F.3d 489 (5th Cir. 2000).

8. Ibid.

9. Ibid.

10. *Tylka v. Gerber Products* (unpublished), Case No. 96C 1647, 29 June 1999 (N.D. Ill.).

11. Ibid.

Chapter 5. Java Jurisprudence

1. *Y.B.*, 9 Hen. VI, f 536 (1431).

2. *Nelson v. Armour Packing Company*, 90 S.W. 288, 76 Ark. 352 (1905).

3. *Connecticut Pie Co. v. Lynch*, 61 App.D.C. 81, 57 F.2d 447 (1932).

4. *Pillars v. R.J. Reynolds Tobacco Co*, 117 Miss. 490, 78 So. 365 (1918).

5. *Bagre v. Daggett Chocolate Co.*, 126 Conn. 659, 13 A.2d 757 (1940).

6. *Klein v. Duchess Sandwich Co.*, 14 Cal.2d 272, 93 P.2d 799 (1939).

7. *Finocchiaro v. Ward Baking Company*, 104 R.I. 5, 241 A.2d 619 (1968).

8. *Scanlon v. Food Crafts*, 193 A.2d 610 (Conn. Cir. Ct. 1963).

9. Ibid.

10. *Holloway v. Bob Evans Farm*, 695 N.E.2d 991 (Ind. App. 1998).

11. *Doyle v. Pillsbury Co.*, 476 So.2d 1271 (Fla. 1985).

12. *Gentry v. Stokely-Van Camp*, Tennessee Court of Appeals (unpublished), 12 March 1982, reported at CCH, Product Liability Reporter, par. 9259 (1982).

13. *Wallace v. Coca-Cola Bottling Plants*, 269 A.2d 117 (Me. 1970).

14. *Martel v. Duffy-Mott Corp.*, 166 N.W. 2d 541 (Mi. App. 1968).

15. *Torba v. J.M. Smucker Company*, 888 F.Supp. 851 (N.D. Ohio 1995).

16. *Green v. Boddie-Noell Enterprises, Inc.*, 966 F.Supp. 416 (W.D. Va. 1997).

17. George Dicum and Nina Luttinger, *The Coffee Book: Anatomy of an Industry from Crop to the Last Drop* (New York: The New Press, 1999), p. 38. This estimate is based on 1996 consumption.

18. *McMahon v. Bunn-O-Matic Corp.*, 150 F.3d 651 (7th Cir. 1998).

19. Ibid.

20. Ibid.

21. Ibid.

22. Ibid.

Chapter 6. Bones of Contention

1. *Mix v. Ingersoll Candy Co.*, 6 Cal.2d 674, 59 P.2d 144 (1936).

2. *Bethia v. Cape Cod Corp.*, 103 N.W.2d 64 (Wis. 1960).

3. Ibid.

4. *Hochberg v. O'Donnell's Restaurant*, 272 A.2d 846 (D.C. Ct. App. 1971).

5. *Ex parte Morrison's Cafeteria of Montgomery v. Haddox*, 431 So.2d 975 (Ala. 1983).

6. *Yong Cha Hong v. Marriott Corporation and Gold Kist, Inc.*, 656 F.Supp. 445 (D.C. 1987).

7. *Jackson v. Nestlé-Beich,* 589 N.E.2d 547 (Ill. 1992).

8. *Mexicali Rose v. Superior Court (Clark),* 262 Cal. Rptr. 750, 754 (Cal. App. 1 Dist. 1989).

9. *Mexicali Rose v. Superior Court,* 822 P.2d 1292 (Cal. 1992).

10. *Webster v. Blue Ship Tea Room,* 198 N.E.2d 309 (Mass. 1964).

11. *Yong Cha Hong v. Marriott Corporation and Gold Kist, Inc.,* 656 F.Supp. 445 (D.C. 1987).

Chapter 7. The Legacy of Mr. Peanut

1. The term "trademark" is defined by federal law in 15 U.S.C. sec. 1127.

2. 15 U.S.C. secs. 1051–1127. The Lanham Act was passed in 1946 and has been amended several times since.

3. *Brown v. Board of Education,* 347 U.S. 483 (1954).

4. *Miranda v. Arizona,* 384 U.S. 436 (1966).

5. *Planters Nut and Chocolate Co. v. Crown Nut Co.,* 305 F.2d 916 (CCPA 1962).

6. James Trager, *The Food Chronology,* (New York: Henry Holt and Company, 1995), p. 387.

7. Excerpts from the *Modern Packaging* article are from the court decision in the Mr. Peanut case, cited above.

8. *Planters,* 305 F.2d, at 920.

9. Ibid.

10. Ibid.

11. Ibid., at 928.

12. Ibid.

13. *Mishewaka Mfg. Co, v. Kresge Co.,* 316 U.S. 203 (1942).

14. The story of the battle between Henri's and Kraft Foods is well told by Joseph P. Kahn, in "Whipped," *Inc.* (Magazine), February 1985.

15. *Henri's Food Products v. Kraft,* 717 F.2d 352 (7th Cir. 1983).

16. Press release of *SunWild Foods, Inc.,* 9 January 1995.

17. *Wisconsin State Journal,* 7 March 1983, p. 1.

18. *National Law Journal,* 7 June 1993.

19. *Stork Restaurant v. Sahati,* 166 F.2d 374 (9th Cir. 1948).

20. Ibid.

21. Ibid.

22. *James Burroughs Ltd. v. Sign of the Beefeater, Inc.,* 540 F.2d 266 (7th Cir. 1976).

23. *Weiss Noodle Co. v. Golden Cracknel and Specialty Co.,* 290 F.2d 845 (CCPA 1961).

24. Ibid.

25. *Orange Crush Co. v. California Crushed Fruit Co.,* 297 F. 892 (D.C.C.A. 1924).

26. *Lincoln Restaurant Corp. v. Wolfie's Rest. Inc.,* 291 F.2d 302 (2d Cir. 1961).

27. Ibid.

28. *Schieffelin and Co. v. Jack Co. of Boca, Inc.*, 850 F.Supp. 232 (S.D.N.Y. 1994).

29. *Campbell v. Acuff-Rose Music, Inc.*, 510 U.S. 569 (1994).

30. *Schieffelin and Co. v. Jack Co. of Boca, Inc.*, 850 F.Supp 232 (S.D.N.Y. 1994).

Chapter 8. McBully

1. *Taco Cabana International, Inc. v. Two Pesos, Inc.*, 932 F.2d 1113 (5th Cir. 1991), affirmed at 505 U.S. 763 (1992).

2. Ibid.

3. Cato the Elder, in *Plutarch's Lives* (sec. 9).

4. *Hutchison v. KFC*, 883 F.Supp. 517 (D. Nev. 1993).

5. *Buffets, Inc. v. Klinke*, 73 F.3d 965 (9th Cir. 1996).

6. *Henning v. Kitchen Art Foods*, 127 F.Supp. 699 (S.D. Ill. 1954).

7. Jean Anthelme Brillat-Savarin, "Aphorisms," in *The Physiology of Taste, or, Meditations on Transcendental Gastronomy* (New Haven, Conn.: Leete's Island Books, [1980?]), p. 3.

8. *Publications International, Ltd. v. Meredith Corp.*, 88 F.3d 473 (7th Cir. 1996).

9. Ibid.

10. Ibid.

11. Ibid.

12. Ibid.

13. Ibid.

14. *General Mills, Inc. v. Hunt-Wesson, Inc.*, 103 F.3d 978 (Cal. Fed. 1997).

15. Vince Straten, *Can You Trust a Tomato in January?* (Simon & Schuster, 1993), pp. 140–44.

16. *McDonald's Corp. v. McBagel's, Inc.*, 649 F.Supp. 1268 (S.D.N.Y. 1986).

17. Ibid.

18. *Quality Inns International, Inc. v. McDonald's Corporation*, 695 F. Supp. 198 (D.C. Md. 1988).

19. *McDonald's v. Druck and Gerner, DDS., d/b/a McDental*, 814 F. Supp. 1127 (N.D.N.Y. 1993).

20. *AP Worldstream*, 10 November 1995.

21. *Associated Press State and Local Wire*, 14 January 2000.

22. *Agence France Presse*, 4 December 1996.

23. *Baltic News Service*, 20 August 1996.

Chapter 9. Ladle and Slander

1. *Dooling v. Budget Publishing Company*, 144 Mass. 258, 10 N.E. 809 (1887).

2. *Mayfair Farms, Inc. v. Socony Mobil Oil Co., Inc.*, 68 N.J.Sup. 188, 172 A.2d 26 (1961).

3. *Miranda v. Arizona*, 384 U.S. 436 (1966).

4. *Mapp v. Ohio*, 367 U.S. 643 (1961).

5. The Warren Court free press jurisprudence covers a line of cases extending from *New York Times, Co. v. Sullivan*, 376 U.S. 254 (1964) through *Gertz v. Robert Welch, Inc.*, 418 U.S. 323 (1974).

6. *Steak Bit of Westbury, Inc. v. Newsday, Inc.*, 70 Misc.2d 437, 334 N.Y.S.2d 325 (Sup. Ct. Nassau County 1972).

7. Ibid.

8. *Havalunch v. Mazza*, 294 S.E.2d 70 (W.Va. 1981).

9. Ibid.

10. *Mashburn v. Collins*, 355 So.2d 879 (La. 1977).

11. Ibid.

12. *Mr. Chow of New York v. Ste. Azur S.A.*, 759 F.2d 219 (2d Cir. 1985).

13. Ibid.

14. Ibid.

15. Ibid.

16. *Greer v. Columbus Monthly Publishing Corp.*, 4 Ohio App.3d 235, 448 N.E.2d 157 (1982).

17. Ibid.

18. Ibid.

19. *Pritsker v. Brudnoy*, 389 Mass. 776, 452 N.E.2d 227 (1983).

20. Ibid.

21. The Café de la Gare case was heard in small-claims court and the court's decision is unpublished. The Café de la Gare is no longer in operation but Chef Maryann Terillo remains active on the food scene in New York. When we last checked, her catering business, The Two Divas, is flourishing.

22. *Restaurant Business*, June 1992.

23. *Ihle v. Florida Publishing Co.*, 5 Med.L.Rep. (BNA) 2005 (Fla. Cir. Ct. 1979).

24. *San Francisco Sunday Examiner and Chronicle*, 12 March 2000, Datebook section, pp. 40–41.

25. Interview with Michael Bauer, March 2000.

Chapter 10. From Bad Apples to Mad Cows

1. *Auvil v CBS "60 Minutes,"* 800 F.Supp. 941 (E.D. Wash. 1992).

2. Ibid.

3. *Auvil v. CBS "60 Minutes,"* 67 F.3d. 816 (9th Cir. 1995).

4. Ibid., footnote 8.

5. The spring/summer 1998 issue of the *DePaul Business Law Journal* contains a lengthy symposium on the constitutionality of the various agricultural disparagement laws, present and proposed. 10 *DePaul Bus. L.J.* (1998).

Professor David J. Bederman's exhaustive analysis, 10 *DePaul Bus. L.J.* 191, contains all of the specific statutory references.

6. *Engler v. Winfrey*, 201 F.3d 680 (5th Cir. 2000).

7. The jury's verdict was upheld on appeal. *Engler v. Winfrey*, 201 F.3d 680 (5th Cir. 2000).

8. *Food Lion v. Capital Cities/ABC, Inc.*, 194 F.3d 505 (4th Cir. 1999).

Chapter 11. It's Not Nice to Defraud Mother Nature!

1. Much of the historic information on margarine comes from S. F. Riepma, *The Story of Margarine* (Washington, D.C.: Public Affairs Press, 1970). The book is out of print and hard to find. I recognize its obvious bias, as Dr. Riepma was president of the National Association of Margarine Manufacturers when he wrote the book.

2. James Trager, *The Food Chronology* (New York: Henry Holt and Company, 1995), pp. 276–77.

3. *Collins v. New Hampshire*, 171 U.S. 20 (1898).

4. *Plumley v. Massachusetts*, 155 U.S. 461 (1894).

5. Act of 5 June 1877, ch. 415, 1877 N.Y. Laws 441.

6. Geoffrey P. Miller, "Public Choice at the Dawn of the Special Interest State: The Story of Butter and Margarine," 77 *California Law Review* 83 (1989), notes 123–34 and accompanying text. Miller's article is an excellent and detailed history of the early days of antimargarine legislation.

7. Ibid., note 141.

8. *People v. Marx*, 2 N.E. 29 (1885).

9. Ibid., notes 206–7.

10. Ibid., note 220.

11. Riepma, *The Story of Margarine*, p. 94, note 1.

12. 17 *Congressional Record* 5082 (1886).

13. This little tidbit does not appear in the published Supreme Court opinion but is noted in the dusty old brief filed by Welch's lawyer.

14. *State v. Welch*, 129 N.W. 656 (Wis. 1911).

15. Brief of defendant Welch.

16. *John F. Jelke Co. v. Emery*, 214 N.W. 369 (Wis. 1927).

17. Chapter 96, Laws of 1931 (Wisconsin).

18. *John F. Jelke Co. v. Hill et al.*, 242 N.W. 576 (Wis. 1932).

19. *A. Magnana Co. v. Hamilton*, 292 U.S. 40 (1934).

20. National Association of Margarine Manufacturers, "Average Per Capita Consumption of Margarine and Butter (1930–97)."

21. *Dairy Queen of Wisconsin v. McDowell*, 51 N.W.2d 34, (on motion for rehearing) 52 N.W.2d 791 (1952).

22. *Dairy Queen of Wisconsin v. McDowell*, 52 N.W.2d 791 (1952).

23. *Coffee-Rich, Inc. v. Department of Agriculture*, 234 N.W.2d 270 (Wis. 1975).

24. Wisconsin stats., sec. 97.18(3)(9b).

25. Wis. stats., sec. 97.18(4).

26. Wis. stats., sec. 97.18(5).

27. *Anderson, Calyton and Co. v. Washington State Dept. of Agriculture,* 402 F.Supp. 1263 (W.D. Wash. 1975).

28. *General Foods v. Priddle,* 569 F.Supp. 1378 (D.C. Kan. 1983).

29. Ibid.

30. 7 U.S.C. sec. 608 et seq. Sometimes this act is referred to as the Agricultural Adjustment Act; the two are coordinate plans of a single plan to raise and stabilize farm prices.

31. 7 U.S.C. sec. 608(b).

32. See, generally, *West Lynn Creamery v. Healy,* 512, U.S. 186 (1994).

33. 7 U.S.C. sec. 608(6).

34. *West Lynn Creamery v. Healy,* 512 U.S. 186 (1994).

35. 7 U.S.C. secs. 4501 et seq.

36. 7 U.S.C. sec. 4501.

37. 7 U.S.C. sec. 4502(e).

38. 7 U.S.C. sec. 4501(d).

39. 7 U.S.C. sec. 3401.

40. 7 U.S.C. sec. 4601.

41. 7 U.S.C. sec. 4801.

42. 7 U.S.C. sec. 2901.

43. 7 U.S.C. sec. 4901.

44. 7 U.S.C. sec. 2701.

45. 7 U.S.C. 608(c)(6)(I).

46. *Glickman v. Wileman Bros. and Elliott,* 521 U.S. 457 (1997).

47. A group of Michigan dairy producers tried to challenge the required dairy assessments in federal court and lost. *Nature's Dairy et al. v. Glickman,* Docket No. 98-1073. The Sixth Circuit affirmed the decision in an unpublished decision. 173 F.3d 429 (1999). Unpublished decisions are not supposed to be cited as legal precedent but there is no rule that says books like this one cannot refer to them.

48. *Fancy Food and Culinary Products Magazine,* April 2000, p. 14.

49. This story was reported by John Stossel on the ABC News program, *20/20,* on 24 March 2000. Mr. Stossel's opinion was that the dairy industry should not be allowed to claim a monopoly on the word "milk." online; available: <http:/www.abcnews.go.com/onair/GiveMeABreak/stossell_000324 _gmb_feature.html>.

50. Wis. stats., sec. 118.01(2)(d)2b.

51. *Queensboro Farm Products v. Wickard,* 137 F.2d 969 (2d Cir. 1943).

Chapter 12. Not So Strictly Kosher

1. There are hundreds of sources for this basic material on the laws of *kashrut.* Several Internet resources are particularly useful. The web site

<www.kashrut.com> contains a wealth of information, both current and historical. For example, Rabbi Mordechai Becher's article, "Soul Food: The Jewish Dietary Laws," is both precise and thoughtful; online, available: <http://kashrut.com/articles/soul_food/>. Another compact and practical guide to the laws of *kashrut* can be found in "Kashrut: Jewish Dietary Laws," online, available: <http://www.jewfaq.org/kashrut .htm>. Joan Nathan's *Jewish Cooking in America* (New York: A. Knopf, 1994) is not only one of the best Jewish cookbooks available, it is also a valuable source of information on *kashrut* and its development. See also Eli W. Schlossberg's *The World of Orthodox Judaism* (Northvale, N.J.: Jason Aronson, 1996).

2. Leviticus 11:3; Deuteronomy 14:6.

3. Leviticus 11:9; Deuteronomy 14:9.

4. Joan Nathan, *Jewish Cooking in America*, p. 6.

5. "This method is painless, causes unconsciousness within two seconds, and is widely recognized as the most humane method of slaughter possible." From "Kashrut: Jewish Dietary Laws" (see note 1 above).

6. Leviticus 7:26–27; Deuteronomy 17:10–14.

7. The *shochet* examines the lungs with particular care. Lungs that are very smooth indicate a highly desirable animal. The Hebrew word for smooth is *glatt,* the origin of the phrase *glatt kosher,* which is regarded as the highest degree of kosher.

8. Exodus 23:19; Exodus 34:26; Deuteronomy 14:21.

9. Arlene Mathes-Scharf, "Is Your 'Kosher' Yogurt Kosher?" online, available: <http://www.kashrut.com/articles/Yogurt/>.

10. John Cooper, *Eat and Be Satisfied: A Social History of Jewish Food* (Northvale, N.J.: Jason Aronson, 1993). Chapter 2, "The Dietary Laws," is especially insightful on the origins of the laws of *kashrut.*

11. See, generally, Marvin Harris, *Good to Eat: Riddles of Food and Culture* (New York: Simon & Schuster, 1985).

12. Orthodox Union Department of Public Relations web site at www.ou.org /oupr/2001/ouko01.htm.

13. Orthodox Union information brochure: "A Guide to the Kosher Food Market," sent to the author by Rabbi Howard Katzenstein, head of trademark compliance for the Orthodox Union, February 2000.

14. *Kashrus Magazine,* September 1999 issue.

15. *Levy v. Kosher Overseers Assoc. of America,* 104 F.3d 38 (2d Cir. 1997).

16. *Kashrus Magazine,* December 1999, p. 11.

17. See "Kashrut: Jewish Dietary Laws," online, available: <http:/www .jewfaq.org/kashrut.htm>.

18. Mark A. Berman, "Kosher Fraud Statutes and the Establishment Clause: Are They Kosher?" 26 *Columbia Journal of Law and Social Problems* 1 (1992), see footnote 57 and accompanying text.

19. N.Y. Agric. and Mkts., Law Sec. 201(a) (McKinney 1991).

20. 266 U.S. 497 (1925).

21. The case of *Cantwell v. Connecticut*, 310 U.S. 296 (1940) held that the protections of the Free Exercise Clause of the First Amendment applied to the states through the Fourteenth Amendment. The court first applied the Establishment Clause to the states in *Everson v. Board of Education*, 330 U.S. 1 (1947).

22. *Zorach v. Clauson*, 343 U.S. 306 (1952).

23. *Larkin v. Grendel's Den*, 459 U.S. 116 (1982). The court held that the practice violated the First Amendment.

24. *Sossin Systems, Inc. v. City of Miami Beach*, 262 So. 2d 28 (Fla. App. 1972).

25. *Ran-Dav's County Kosher v. State*, 579 A.2d 316 (N.J. App. 1990).

26. *Ran Dav's County Kosher, Inc. v. State*, 608 A.2d 1353 (N.J. 1992).

27. *Lemon v. Kurtzman*, 403 U.S. 602 (1971).

28. Ibid.

29. Mark A. Berman, "Kosher Fraud Statutes and the Establishment Clause: Are They Kosher?" 26 *Columbia Journal of Law and Social Problems* 1 (1992) (arguing against the constitutionality of kosher food laws); Catherine Beth Sullivan, "Are Kosher Food Laws Constitutionally Kosher?" 21 *Boston College Environmental Affairs Law Review* 201 (1993) (arguing in support of their constitutionality).

30. *Barghout v. Bureau of Kosher Meat and Food Control*, 66 F.3d 1337 (4th Cir. 1995).

31. *Commack Self-Service Kosher Meats v. Rubin*, 106 F.Supp.2d 445 (E.D.N.Y. 2000).

32. N.J.A.C. sec. 13:45A-21.1 to 21.8 (2000).

33. *Kashrus Magazine*, September 1999, pp. 41–72.

34. *National Foods, Inc. v. Rubin*, 727 F.Supp. 104 (S.D.N.Y. 1989).

35. *People v. Finkelstein*, 38 Misc. 2d 791, 239 N.Y.S.2d 835 (1963).

Chapter 13. Cruel and Unusual Condiments

1. Recipe provided by John Turner, public information officer for the Arizona Department of Corrections, 1984.

2. *United States v. State of Michigan*, 680 F.Supp. 270 (W.D. Mich. 1988); *Smith v. Oregon Dept. of Corrections*, 792 P.2d 109 (Or. 1990).

3. *United States v. State of Michigan*, 680 F.Supp. 270 (W.D. Mich 1988).

4. *Adams v. Kincheloe*, 743 F.Supp. 1385 (E.D. Wash. 1990).

5. *Rust v. Grammer*, 858 F.2d 411 (8th Cir. 1988).

6. U.S. Attorney General, *Rules and Regulations for the Government and Discipline of the United States Penitentiary, McNeil Island, Washington*, secs. 70 and 71 (1911); U.S. Attorney General, *Rules and Regulations for the Government and Discipline of the United States Penitentiary at Atlanta, Georgia*, secs. 375 and 376 (1910).

7. Ibid.

8. Ibid.

9. *Rhodes v. Chapman,* 452 U.S. 337 (1981).

10. *Berry v. Brady,* 192 F.3d 504 (5th Cir. 1999).

11. *Wilkins v. Roper,* 843 F.Supp. 1327 (E.D. Mo. 1994).

12. *Jackson v. Mann,* 196 F.3d 316 (2d Cir. 1999).

13. *Stroman v. Griffin,* 331 226 F.Supp. 226 (S.D. Ga. 1971).

14. *Jenkins v. Werger,* 564 F.Supp. 806 (D. Wyoming 1983).

15. In 1972, the U.S. Supreme Court ruled that the death penalty, as then administered in the United States, was unconstitutional (*Furman v. Georgia,* 408 U.S. 238 [1972]). This case resulted in a brief moratorium in executions until states recast their laws and the Supreme Court, in a series of cases, cleared the way for the death penalty to once again be a constitutionally permissible punishment when handed down under certain conditions.

16. Texas Department of Criminal Justice statistics as shown on its official web site, http://www.tdcj.tx.us/stat/finalmeals.htm. I have based my research on executions and last meals through 4 May 2000; you can find data on dozens more since that date.

17. Visit to Federal Prison Camp at Oxford, Wisconsin, 19 May 2000.

18. It is hard to believe but there is no constitutional right to attend a cooking class. See *Murdock v. Washington,* 193 F.3d 510 (7th Cir. 1999).

19. State of Wisconsin, Department of Corrections, Doc. 306, S.I.M.P. no. 42 (effective 1 Oct. 1997).

Chapter 14. Just Desserts

1. Paul Dickson, *The Great American Ice Cream Book* (New York: Atheneum, 1972), pp. 56–57.

2. *Taylor v. State,* 399 So.2d 875 (Ala. App. 1980).

3. *Baltimore Sun,* 22 July 2000.

4. *United States v. Two Hundred Cases of Adulterated Tomato Catsup,* 211 F. 780 (D. Ore. 1914).

5. *Continental Nut Co. v. Robert L. Berner Co.,* 393 F.2d 283 (7th Cir. 1968).

6. *Hairston v. Burger King Corp.,* Eleventh Judicial District Court for the Parish of DeSoto, Louisiana, affirmed at 764 So.2d 176 (La. App. 2000).

7. *Fuggins v. Burger King,* 760 So.2d 605 (La. App. 2000).

8. *Wisconsin State Journal,* 17 June 1999, p. 10A.

9. *People v. Hopkins,* 44 Cal.App.3d 669 (1975).

10. *The Times-Picayune,* 22 March 1985, p. A26.

11. Rodney R. Jones and Gerlad F. Uelmen, *Supreme Folly* (New York: Norton, 1990), p. 55.

12. *National Law Journal,* 11 January 1993, p. 47.

13. See Sandy Rover, "What You Eat, What You Are: Sugar and Violent Behavior: Doctors, Nutritionists Spar on the Effect of Diet," *Washington Post,* 5 December 1984; Carl Luty, "Junk Food Junkies: Are You Sure You Can Spot

Them?" *NEA Today,* December 1995. The facts of the Dan White incident are described in greater detail in several sources, more prominently: Mike Weiss, *Double Play, The San Francisco City Hall Killings* (Reading, Mass.: Addison-Wesely Publishing Co., 1984); Randy Shilts, *The Mayor of Castro Street: The Life and Times of Harvey Milk* (New York: St. Martin's Press, 1982).

14. *News of the Truly Bizarre* (wire service), 27 November 1998.

15. Letter to the editor, *Wisconsin State Journal,* 21 January 1999.

16. *National Law Journal,* 16 May 1988, p. 47.

17. *Gates v. Standard Brands,* 719 P.2d 130 (Wash. App. 1986).

18. *New York Times,* 6 April 1986.

19. *Chicago Sun-Times,* 16 May 1997, p. 3.

20. *Committee for Industrial Org. v. Hague,* 25 F.Supp. 127 (D.C.N.J. 1938).

21. *Hague v. Industrial Org.,* 307 U.S. 496 (1939).

22. *News of the Truly Bizarre* (wire service), 7 April 1998 (attributed to the *Nando Times*).

23. *Gourmet,* November 1958, p. 31.

24. *Lohse v. Coffey,* 32 A.2d 258 (D.C.C.A. 1943).

25. *United States v. Mrs. Smith's Pie Co.,* 440 F.Supp. 220 (E.D. Pa. 1976).

26. *Kraft-Phenix Cheese Corp. v. Consolidated Beverages, Ltd.,* 107 F.2d 1004 (CCPA 1939).

27. *Fred Harvey et al. v. Corporation Commission of Oklahoma,* 229 P. 428 (Okla. 1924).

28. *Newsweek,* 3 April 1995, p. 19.

29. *New York Times,* 24 September 2000, sec. 3, p. 4.

Chapter 15. The Final Verdict

1. See chapter 2, note 11.

2. "Modified Foods Put Companies in a Quandary," *New York Times,* 4 June 2000, p. 1.

3. Jeff Wheelwright, "Don't Eat Again until You Read This," *Discover,* March 2001, p. 36.

4. Barry Shlachter, *Fort Worth Star-Telegram,* reprinted in the *Wisconsin State Journal,* 20 February 2001. p. C6.

5. Ibid.

6. *New York Times,* 20 May 2001, reported at http://www.nytimes.com /2001 /05/20/national/20HIND.html.

WARNING AND DISCLAIMER

In our litigation-wild culture, warnings and disclaimers are everywhere. The notice on the cup of coffee from McDonald's that its contents are hot is an attempt not only to put the consumer on notice of the obvious but also to create a defense to the inevitable lawsuit that will ensue after the hot beverage burns someone. Whether this is effective in preventing successful lawsuits is uncertain at best. This book would not be complete without a few warnings and disclaimers of its own.

Here's one that should be apparent, but I guess you never know in today's world: FOR EXTERNAL USE ONLY. So don't eat the book, okay?

If that isn't enough, try this one: DO NOT OPERATE HEAVY MACHINERY WHILE READING THIS BOOK.

I suppose I could advise you to refrigerate after opening but I doubt you would want to store this book next to the butter or whatever you spread on your toast. Should I tell you to shake well before using?

There is one serious and for-real disclaimer that I must insert here: READERS SHOULD NOT CONSTRUE THE CONTENTS OF THIS BOOK AS LEGAL ADVICE FOR ANY PARTICULAR SITUATION. In plain English that means I am not your lawyer. If you publish a book of recipes lifted from your favorite cookbooks, you might get sued. I know, back in chapter 8 I wrote that you would probably be on firm legal grounds in publishing such a book. That does not mean a few of the original cookbook authors won't haul you in to court and make your life miserable. Before you embark on any food-related venture, hire your own lawyer and do not think for a minute that this book is a substitute for a real lawyer.

I will make this as clear as aspic on a galantine of turkey: I am your entertaining author this week, not your attorney. Just as you would not think of
suing Dave Barry or Stephen King for something you picked up in one of their
books, so too would you not even dream of suing me for what turned out to
be bad legal advice (which I never gave you). And please do not think about
suing the publisher either.

Let me illustrate with a case. Wilhelm Winter and Cynthia Zheng were
mushroom lovers. I use the past tense because I suspect they are no longer
big fans of the fungus for reasons that will be soon obvious. In 1988, Willy and
Cindy went mushroom hunting, armed only with their recently purchased
Encyclopedia of Mushrooms. This fine reference book was written by two
English mushroom "experts" and was originally published in England. An
American publishing house, GP Putnam's Sons, recognized a demand for the
book in the States and began selling the text.

Relying on the pictures and descriptions of various mushrooms in the
book, Willy and Cindy harvested a bunch of mushrooms and took them home.
They cooked them and got very sick. They sued the publisher under the banner of products liability, alleging breach of warranty, negligence, negligent
misrepresentation, and false representation. They lost.

The Ninth Circuit Court of Appeals in *Winter v. GP Putnam's Sons* (938 F.2d
1033 [9th Cir. 1991]) refused to extend the principles of "product" liability to
the information contained in books. The court also refused to extend to publishers any duty to investigate the contents of the texts they publish.

The moral of this story is simple: Let the reader beware!

There is another reason for not relying on anything in this fine book. The
law changes, and food law changes more than most. Like a delicate soufflé,
today's binding legal precedent may rise gracefully in one moment, only to
fall into an inedible lump the next.

How about this one: MAY BE HABIT FORMING.

I can only hope. Thanks for reading.

LEGAL CASES CITED

For those who must know the citations of all the cases referred to in this book, here they are. I can understand why law students, lawyers, and judges may want to use this, but if you do not fall into one of these categories and still find this listing useful, I suggest that you get out more often.

Adams v. Kincheloe, 743 F.Supp. 1385 (E.D. Wash. 1990)

A. Magnana Co. v. Hamilton, 292 U.S. 40 (1934)

American Federation of Government Employees v. Glickman, 215 F.3d 7 (C.A.D.C. 2000)

Anderson, Calyton and Co. v. Washington State Dept. of Agriculture, 402 F.Supp. 1263 (W.D. Wash. 1975)

Arent v. Shalala, 70 F.3d 610 (C.A.D.C. 1995)

Auvil v. CBS "60 Minutes," 800 F.Supp. 941 (E.D. Wash. 1992)

Auvil v. CBS "60 Minutes," 67 F.3d. 816 (9th Cir. 1995)

Bagre v. Daggett Chocolate Co., 13 A.2d 757 (Conn. 1940)

Barghout v. Bureau of Kosher Meat and Food Control, 66 F.3d 1337 (4th Cir. 1995)

Berry v. Brady, 192 F.3d 504 (5th Cir. 1999)

Bethia v. Cape Cod Corp., 103 N.W.2d 64 (Wis. 1960)

Brown v. Board of Education, 347 U.S. 483 (1954)

Buffets, Inc. v. Klinke, 73 F.3d 965 (9th Cir. 1996)

Cain v. Winn-Dixie Louisiana, 757 So.2d 712 (La. App. 1999)

Campbell v. Acuff-Rose Music, Inc., 510 U.S. 569 (1994)

Hutchison v. KFC, 883 F.Supp. 517 (D. Nev. 1993)

Hygrade Provision Co. v. Sherman, 266 U.S. 497 (1925)

Ihle v. Florida Publishing Co., 5 Med.L.Rep. (BNA) 2005 (Fla. Cir. Ct. 1979)

In Matter of Cullinan, 93 App. Div. 427 (1904)

Jackson v. Mann, 196 F.3d 316 (2d Cir. 1999)

Jackson v. Nestlé-Beich, 589 N.E.2d 547 (Ill. 1992)

James Burroughs Limited v. Sign of the Beefeater, Inc., 540 F.2d 266 (7th Cir. 1976)

Jenkins v. Werger, 564 F.Supp. 806 (D. Wyoming 1983)

John F. Jelke Co. v. Emery, 214 N.W. 369 (Wis. 1927)

John F. Jelke Co. v. Hill et al., 242 N.W. 576 (Wis. 1932)

Kentucky Fried Chicken v. Diversified Packaging, 549 F.2d 368 (5th Cir. 1977)

Klein v. Duchess Sandwich Co., 93 P.2d 799 (Cal. 1939)

Kraft, Inc. v. F.T.C., 970 F.2d 311 (7th Cir. 1992)

Kraft-Phenix Cheese Corp. v. Consolidated Beverages, Ltd., 107 F.2d 1004 (CCPA 1939)

Kroger Grocery and Baking Co. v. Dempsey, 143 S.W.2d 564 (Ark. 1940)

Larkin v. Grendel's Den, 459 U.S. 116 (1982)

Lemon v. Kurtzman, 403 U.S. 602 (1971)

Levy v. Kosher Overseers Assoc. of America, 104 F.3d 38 (2d Cir. 1997)

Libby, McNeill & Libby v. U.S., 148 F.2d 71 (2d Cir. 1945)

Lincoln Restaurant Corp. v. Wolfie's Rest. Inc., 291 F.2d 302 (2d Cir. 1961)

Lohse v. Coffey, 32 A.2d 258 (D.C.C.A. 1943)

Mapp v. Ohio, 367 U.S. 643 (1961)

Mashburn v. Collins, 355 So.2d 879 (La. 1977)

Mayfair Farms, Inc. v. Socony Mobil Oil Co., Inc., 172 A.2d 26 (N.J. Sup. 1961)

McDonald's v. Druck and Gerner, DDS., d/b/a McDental, 814 F. Supp. 1127 (N.D.N.Y. 1993)

McDonald's Corp. v. McBagel's, Inc., 649 F.Supp. 1268 (S.D.N.Y. 1986)

McMahon v. Bunn-O-Matic Corp., 150 F.3d 651 (7th Cir. 1998)

Messner v. Red Owl Stores, 57 N.W.2d 659 (Minn. 1953)

Mexicali Rose v. Superior Court, 822 P.2d 1292 (Cal. 1992)

Mexicali Rose v. Superior Court (Clark), 262 Cal. Rptr. 750, 754 (Cal. App. 1 Dist. 1989)

Miranda v. Arizona, 384 U.S. 436 (1966)

Mishewaka Mfg. Co, v. Kresge Co., 316 U.S. 203 (1942)

Mix v. Ingersoll Candy Co., 59 P.2d 144 (Cal. 1936)

Mr. Chow of New York v. Ste. Azur S.A., 759 F.2d 219 (2d Cir. 1985)

Murdock v. Washington, 193 F.3d 510 (7th Cir. 1999)

National Foods, Inc. v. Rubin, 727 F.Supp. 104 (S.D.N.Y. 1989)

Nature's Dairy et al. v. Glickman, Docket No. 98-1073, aff'd at 173 F.3d 429 (6th Cir. 1999) (unpublished decision)

Nelson v. Armour Packing Company, 90 S.W. 288 (Ark. 1905)

Newberry v. Cohen's (Smoked Salmon) Ltd., 54 LGR 343 (1956)

New York Times Co. v. Sullivan, 376 U.S. 254 (1964)

Nix v. Hedden, 149 U.S. 304 (1893)

Orange Crush Co. v. California Crushed Fruit Co., 297 F. 892 (D.C.C.A. 1924)

People v. Finkelstein, 239 N.Y.S.2d 835 (1963)

People v. Friedman, 157 App. Div. 437 (1913)

People v. Hopkins, 44 Cal.App.3d 669 (1975)

People v. Marx, 2 N.E. 29 (N.Y. 1885)

People v. Waldbaums, 386 N.Y.S.2d 526 (1976)

Pillars v. R.J. Reynolds Tobacco Co., 78 So. 365 (Miss. 1918)

Pizza Hut, Inc. v. Papa John's International, 227 F.3d 489 (5th Cir. 2000)

Pizza Hut Inc. v. Papa John's International, Inc., 80 F. Supp. 2d 600 (N.D. Tex. 2000)

Planters Nut and Chocolate Co. v. Crown Nut Co., 305 F.2d 916 (CCPA 1962)

Plumley v. Massachusetts, 155 U.S. 461 (1894)

Pritsker v. Brudnoy, 452 N.E.2d 227 (Mass. 1983)

Publications International, Ltd. v. Meredith Corp., 88 F.3d 473 (7th Cir. 1996)

Public Citizen et al. v. Shalala, 932 F.Supp. 13 (D.D.C. 1996)

Ran-Dav's County Kosher v. State, 579 A.2d 316 (N.J. App. 1990)

Ran Dav's County Kosher, Inc. v. State, 608 A.2d 1353 (N.J. 1992)

Quality Inns International, Inc. v. McDonald's Corporation, 695 F. Supp. 198 (D.C. Md. 1988)

Queensboro Farm Products v. Wickard, 137 F.2d 969 (2d Cir. 1943)

RELCO Inc. v. Consumer Product Safety Commission, 391 F.Supp. 841 (S.D. Tex. 1975)

Rhodes v. Chapman, 452 U.S. 337 (1981)

Rust v. Grammer, 858 F.2d 411 (8th Cir. 1988)

Scanlon v. Food Crafts, 193 A.2d 610 (Conn. Cir. Ct. 1963)

Schieffeln and Co. v. Jack Co. of Boca, Inc. 850 F.Supp. 232 (S.D.N.Y. 1994)

Smith v. Oregon Dept. of Corrections, 792 P.2d 109 (Or. 1990)

Sossin Systems, Inc. v. City of Miami Beach, 262 So. 2d 28 (Fla. App. 1972)

State v. Goldberg, 166 P.2d 664, 665 (Kan. 1946)

State v. Shoaf, 102 S.E. 705 (N.C. 1920)

State v. Welch, 129 N.W. 656 (Wis. 1911)

Steak Bit of Westbury, Inc. v. Newsday, Inc., 334 N.Y.S.2d 325 (Sup.Ct. Nassau County 1972)

Stork Restaurant v. Sahati, 166 F.2d 374 (9th Cir. 1948)

Stroman v. Griffin, 331 F.Supp. 226 (S.D. Ga. 1971)

Supreme Beef Processors v. U.S. Dept. of Agriculture, 113 F.Supp.2d 1048 (N.D. Tex. 2000)

Taco Cabana International, Inc. v. Two Pesos, Inc., 932 F.2d 1113 (5th Cir. 1991), affirmed at 505 U.S. 763 (1992)

Taylor v. State, 399 So.2d 875 (Ala. App. 1980)

Treasure Island Catering v. State Bd. of Equalization, 120 P.2d 1 (Cal. 1941)

Tylka v. Gerber Products (unpublished), Case No. 96 C 1647, 29 June 1999 (N.D. Ill.)

United States v. An Article of Food . . . Manischewitz . . . Diet Thins, 377 F.Supp. 746 (E.D.N.Y. 1974)

United States v. Coca Cola, 241 U.S. 265 (1916)

United States v. Lexington Mill Co., 232 U.S. 399, 409 (1915)

United States v. Mrs. Smith's Pie Co., 440 F.Supp. 220 (E.D. Pa. 1976)

United States v. 651 Cases, More or Less, of Chocolate Chil-Zert, 114 F. Supp. 430 (N.D.N.Y. 1953)

United States v. State of Michigan, 680 F.Supp 270 (W.D. Mich. 1988)

United States v. Ten Cases, More or Less, Bred Spred, et al., 49 F.2d 87 (8th Cir. 1931)

United States v. Two Hundred Cases of Adulterated Tomato Catsup, 211 F. 780 (D. Ore. 1914)

U.S. v. 30 Cases, More or Less, Leader Brand Strawberry Fruit Spread, 93 F.Supp. 764 (S.D. Iowa 1950)

Webster v. Blue Ship Tea Room, 198 N.E.2d 309 (Mass. 1964)

Weiss Noodle Co. v. Golden Cracknel and Specialty Co., 290 F.2d 845 (CCPA 1961)

West Lynn Creamery v. Healy, 512 U.S. 186 (1994)

Wilkins v. Roper, 843 F.Supp. 1327 (E.D. Mo. 1994)

Winter v. GP Putnam's Son, 938 F.2d. 1033 (9th Cir. 1991)

Y.B. 9 Hen. VI, f 536 (1431)

Yong Cha Hong v. Marriott Corporation and Gold Kist, Inc., 656 F.Supp. 445 (D.C. 1987)

Zorach v. Clauson, 343 U.S. 306 (1952)